ما لابد من معرفته عن الإسلام

WHAT MUST BE
KNOWN ABOUT
ISLAM

2nd Edition: June 2003

© Maktaba Dar-us-Salam, 2002
King Fahd National Library Cataloging-in-Publication Data
Al-Arfaj, Muhammad bin Ali
What must be known about Islam-Riyadh.
311p., 14x21 cm.
ISBN 9960-892-06-9
I-Islam, General Principles   II- Title
210 dc.   1423/4715

Legal Deposit no. 1423/4715
ISBN 9960-892-06-9

ما لابد من معرفته عن الإسلام

WHAT MUST BE KNOWN ABOUT ISLAM

Compiled by
Muhammad bin 'Ali Al-Arfaj

Translated by
Darussalam

DARUSSALAM

DARUSSALAM
GLOBAL LEADER IN ISLAMIC BOOKS
Riyadh • Jeddah • Al-Khobar • Sharjah
Lahore • London • Houston • Newyork

Second Edition: June 2003

Supervised by: **Abdul Malik Mujahid**

HEADOFFICE:

P.O. Box: 22743, Riyadh 11416 K.S.A.Tel: 00966-01-4033962/4043432 Fax: 4021659
E-mail: darussalam@awalnet.net.sa Website: www.dar-us-salam.com

K.S.A. Darussalam Showrooms:
Riyadh
Olaya branch:Tel 00966-1-4614483 Fax: 4644945
Malaz branch: Tel 4735220 Fax: 4735221
- **Jeddah**
  Tel: 00966-2-6879254 Fax: 6336270
- **Al-Khobar**
  Tel: 00966-3-8692900 Fax: 00966-3-8691551

U.A.E
- Darussalam, Sharjah U.A.E
  Tel: 00971-6-5632623 Fax: 5632624

PAKISTAN
- Darussalam, 36 B Lower Mall, Lahore
  Tel: 0092-42-724 0024 Fax: 7354072
- Rahman Market, Ghazni Street
  Urdu Bazar Lahore
  Tel: 0092-42-7120054 Fax: 7320703

U.S.A
- Darussalam, Houston
  P.O Box: 79194 Tx 772779
  Tel: 001-713-722 0419 Fax: 001-713-722 0431
  E-mail: sales@dar-us-salam.com
- Darussalam, New York
  572 Atlantic Ave, Brooklyn
  New York-11217, Tel: 001-718-625 5925

U.K
- Darussalam International Publications Ltd.
  226 High Street, Walthamstow,
  London E17 7JH, Tel: 0044-208 520 2666
  Mobile: 0044-794 730 6706 Fax: 0044-208 521 7645
- Darussalam International Publications Limited
  Regent Park Mosque, 146 Park Road,
  London NW8 7RG Tel: 0044-207 724 3363
- Darussalam
  398-400 Coventry Road, Small Heath
  Birmingham, B10 0UF
  Tel: 0121 77204792 Fax: 0121 772 4345
  E-mail: info@darussalamuk.com
  Web: www.darussalamuk.com

FRANCE
- Editions & Librairie Essalam
  135, Bd de Ménilmontant- 75011 Paris
  Tél: 0033-01- 43 38 19 56/ 44 83
  Fax: 0033-01- 43 57 44 31
  E-mail: essalam@essalam.com

AUSTRALIA
- ICIS: Ground Floor 165-171, Haldon St.
  Lakemba NSW 2195, Australia
  Tel: 00612 9758 4040 Fax: 9758 4030

MALAYSIA
- E&D Books SDN. BHD.-321 B 3rd Floor,
  Suria Klcc
  Kuala Lumpur City Center 50088
  Tel: 00603-21663433 Fax: 459 72032

SINGAPORE
- Muslim Converts Association of Singapore
  32 Onan Road The Galaxy Singapore- 424484
  Tel: 0065-440 6924, 348 8344 Fax: 440 6724

SRI LANKA
- Darul Kitab 6, Nimal Road, Colombo-4
  Tel: 0094-1-589 038 Fax: 0094-74 722433

KUWAIT
- Islam Presentation Committee
  Enlightment Book Shop
  P.O. Box: 1613, Safat 13017 Kuwait
  Tel: 00965-244 7526, Fax: 240 0057

INDIA
- Islamic Dimensions
  56/58 Tandel Street (North)
  Dongri, Mumbai 4000 009,India
  Tel: 0091-22-3736875, Fax: 3730689
  E-mail:sales@IRF.net

SOUTH AFRICA
- Islamic Da'wah Movement (IDM)
  48009 Qualbert 4078 Durban,South Africa
  Tel: 0027-31-304-6883
  Fax: 0027-31-305-1292
  E-mail: idm@ion.co.za

Contents

Marriage: Its Fruits And Benefits For The Short And Long Term

In The Name Of Allâh, The Most Beneficent, The Most Merciful

Introduction

Indeed, all praise is for Allâh: we praise Him, repent to Him, and seek His forgiveness and help. We seek refuge in Allâh from the evil of our selves and of our wicked deeds. Whomsoever Allâh guides, none can lead astray; and whomsoever Allâh leaves astray, none can guide. And I bear witness that none has the right to be worshipped except Allâh alone, and He has no partner; and I bear witness that our Prophet Muhammad is His servant and Messenger. O Allâh, send many blessings and salutations upon him, his family, and his Companions until the Day of Judgement.

﴿يَٰٓأَيُّهَا ٱلَّذِينَ ءَامَنُوا۟ ٱتَّقُوا۟ ٱللَّهَ حَقَّ تُقَاتِهِۦ وَلَا تَمُوتُنَّ إِلَّا وَأَنتُم مُّسْلِمُونَ﴾

O you who believe! Fear Allâh as He should be feared, and die not except as Muslims.[1]

﴿يَٰٓأَيُّهَا ٱلنَّاسُ ٱتَّقُوا۟ رَبَّكُمُ ٱلَّذِى خَلَقَكُم مِّن نَّفْسٍ وَٰحِدَةٍ وَخَلَقَ مِنْهَا زَوْجَهَا وَبَثَّ مِنْهُمَا رِجَالًا كَثِيرًا وَنِسَآءً وَٱتَّقُوا۟ ٱللَّهَ ٱلَّذِى تَسَآءَلُونَ بِهِۦ وَٱلْأَرْحَامَ إِنَّ ٱللَّهَ كَانَ عَلَيْكُمْ رَقِيبًا﴾

O mankind be dutiful to your Lord, Who created you from a single person, and from him He created his wife, and from them both He created many men and women; and fear Allâh through Whom you demand your mutual (rights), and (do not cut the relations of) the wombs (kinship). Surely, Allâh is Ever and All-Watcher over you.[2]

﴿يَٰٓأَيُّهَا ٱلَّذِينَ ءَامَنُوا۟ ٱتَّقُوا۟ ٱللَّهَ وَقُولُوا۟ قَوْلًا سَدِيدًا ۝ يُصْلِحْ لَكُمْ أَعْمَٰلَكُمْ وَيَغْفِرْ لَكُمْ ذُنُوبَكُمْ وَمَن يُطِعِ ٱللَّهَ وَرَسُولَهُ فَقَدْ فَازَ فَوْزًا عَظِيمًا﴾

O you who believe! Keep your duty to Allâh and fear Him, and speak (always) the truth. He will direct you to do righteous good deeds and will forgive you your sins. And whosoever

---

[1] (*Aal 'Imran* 3: 102)

[2] (*An-Nisa'* 4:1)

obeys Allâh and His Messenger, he has indeed achieved a great achievement.[1]

In these times, there is an urgent need to educate people regarding the affairs of their religion in simple and clear language, so that they can worship Allâh sincerely, in accordance to what Allâh legislated in His Book and to what the Prophet ﷺ pronounced with his tongue. This need is especially felt among the common man and those who are new adherents to the religion of Islam. Islam must be presented in an easy and plain manner so that people can enter into Islam in flocks, and so that we can all be blessed with those words that the Prophet ﷺ said to 'Ali, may Allâh be pleased with him:

«لَأَنْ يَهْدِيَ اللهُ بِكَ رَجُلًا وَاحِدًا خَيْرٌ لَكَ مِنْ حُمْرِ النَّعَمِ»

"For Allâh to guide one man through you is better for you than red camels."[2]

And he ﷺ also said:

«خَيْرُ النَّاسِ أَنْفَعُهُمْ لِلنَّاسِ»

"The best of people is the one who benefits people most."[3]

Beneficial knowledge and righteous deeds; indeed these are the keys of success and the basis for safety in this life as well as in the next. When Allâh guides a person to both beneficial knowledge and righteous deeds, then that person has achieved happiness in both abodes. And then, if he completes those blessings by spreading knowledge, disseminating it among the people, then the meanings of righteousness and piety are complete in him, and he becomes like good rain: wherever it falls, it benefits. This was the way that the

---

[1] (*Al-Ahzab* 33:70, 71)

[2] Prime possessions at the time. It is an agreed upon narration; recorded by Al-Bukhari and Muslim.

[3] Al-Qudha'i in *Musnad Ash-Shihab* (2:23), and it was to him that As-Suyuti ascribed it in *Al-Jami' As-Saghir* (2:9) and As-Suyuti put an abbreviation indicating it to be *Hasan*. It is also recorded by At-Tabarani in *Al-Awsat* (6:368).

It is also in *Majma' Al-Bahrain* (1:131,132) and Al-Qudha'i related it in *Musnad Ash-Shihab* (1:108). Al-Albani mentioned the *Hadith* in *As-Sahihah* and said, "Indeed the *Hadith* is *Hasan*." Refer to *As-Sahihah* no. 426

righteous scholars of every era and region lived.

A group of students of knowledge — may Allâh Almighty reward them well — have resolved to put together this book, which contains that which a Muslim must know, presented in clear and plain words; it consists of a summary of many topics, such as *'Aqeedah* (beliefs), acts of worship, and manners. By perusing this book, the reader can gain a clear, yet basic, picture of Islam; for a Muslim reader, it may serve as a first source of reference for Islamic rulings, laws, prohibitions, and manners. It is hoped that this book will reach those who call to Islam in different lands, who can translate it into all languages — so that through it, those whom Allâh Almighty wills may be guided to the truth; and so that the proof will be established upon those who reject this message after it reaches them. It is hoped that this book will serve as a key to goodness, and as guidance to people in different lands; and it is further hoped that those who participated in putting this book together will achieve reward and success.

And in conclusion to this introduction, it does not escape me to thank all those who helped or contributed to the release of this book — eminent scholars and students of knowledge alike, for they spared no effort until, in the end, this book has now — and all praise is for Allâh — entered the realm of existence.

May Allâh Almighty grant success to all of His believing worshippers in the different lands, and we ask Him to grant us understanding in the religion and steadfastness upon it, as well as sincerity in speech and deed. Indeed He is able to answer our prayers. And our last request is: all the praise is due to Allâh, the Lord of all that exists. O Allâh, send blessings and salutations upon our Prophet Muhammad, his family, and all of his Companions.

Written by one who is in dire need of his Lord's forgiveness,

Muhammad bin 'Ali Al-'Arfaj

May Allâh Almighty forgive him, his parents, and all Muslims

The Completeness Of The *Shari‘ah*

1) It is clear that Allâh Almighty sent His Prophet Muhammad ﷺ to mankind as a mercy from Him and as a favor — to take them out of the levels of darkness and to bring them into the light — by His permission — and to guide them to the straight path.

2) Before the advent of the Prophet ﷺ, the Arabs were in a state of ignorance and misery, for they worshipped idols, buried young girls alive, shed blood for the most trifling reasons, and often times, for no reason at all. Their lives were constrained and limited; they sought judgement in their affairs with fortune-tellers and false deities.

3) Then Allâh Almighty sent our noble Prophet ﷺ, and through him, Allâh removed them from the layers of darkness and brought them into the light — removed them from the darkness of disbelief and polytheism and brought them into the light of faith and *Tawhid*, from the darkness of ignorance and thought-lessness to the light of knowledge and forbearance, from the darkness of oppression and injustice to the light of justice and benefaction, from the darkness of disunity and discord to the light of harmony and agreement, from the darkness of selfishness and despotism to the light of humbleness and mutual counsel, and from the darkness of poverty and tension to the light of richness and well being. Indeed, Allâh Almighty removed them from the darkness of death – for they were nothing more than the walking dead – to the light of a happy life:

﴿أَوَ مَن كَانَ مَيْتًا فَأَحْيَيْنَٰهُ وَجَعَلْنَا لَهُۥ نُورًا يَمْشِى بِهِۦ فِى ٱلنَّاسِ كَمَن مَّثَلُهُۥ فِى ٱلظُّلُمَٰتِ لَيْسَ بِخَارِجٍ مِّنْهَا كَذَٰلِكَ زُيِّنَ لِلْكَٰفِرِينَ مَا كَانُوا۟ يَعْمَلُونَ﴾

Is he who was dead (without faith by ignorance and disbelief) and We gave him life (by knowledge and faith) and set for him a light (of belief) whereby he can walk among men, like him who is in the darkness (of disbelief, polytheism and hypocrisy) from which he can never come out? Thus it is made fair seeming to the disbelievers that which they used to do.[1]

Through the Prophet ﷺ, Allâh Almighty completed the religion and completed all good and lofty manners in man. The Prophet ﷺ ordered the people to worship none but Allâh alone, without associating partners with Him, and he ﷺ ordered them to be dutiful to their parents, to join ties with relations, and to show generosity to the poor and needy. The Prophet ﷺ said:

«إِنَّ اللهَ كَتَبَ الْإِحْسَانَ عَلَى كُلِّ شَيْءٍ»

Indeed Allâh has written *Ihsan* (doing good deeds and doing them in a good way) upon all things.[2]

Regarding matters that they disagreed about, the Prophet ﷺ ordered them to seek judgement with Allâh Almighty and His Messenger ﷺ.

The more knowledge one gains about Islam, the more will he honor and revere it, which is why the Companions — who had a more complete knowledge of the religion — adhered better to its teachings, from its major aspects to its more minor of details. It is most strange today to find that the majority of people have turned away from the teachings of Islam (which is complete), opting to replace them with man-made laws, laws that are clearly contradictory, laws that not only allow injustice, but legislate it as well. And that is why those laws are constantly changing: each new person that comes thinks that his view of justice and order is better than the views of those who preceded him; and so the process continues as long as laws are derived from the weakness and foolishness of weak minds.

The Islamic *Shari'ah*, on the other hand, is applicable and suitable for all times and places: fourteen hundred years have passed, yet because of its completeness, Islam establishes rights for all areas and levels in society. Anyone who is just — even if he is from the opponents of Islam — must see that Islam provides a peaceful, safe, and comfortable life for its adherents in this life, with laws that are applicable and suitable to individuals, societies, and governments.

Much have we heard and read that attests to this, for some of the Orientalists who write to establish the truth and not to pursue

---

[1] (*Al-An'am* 6:122)

[2] Muslim (2:1548), in a *Hadith* related by Shaddad bin Aws.

political objectives admit that the development of modern Europe stemmed from the light of Islam in Spain and from the books that they stole from Muslims during their wars with them in the East and West.

Taylor, a priest, said, "Indeed Islam spread throughout Africa and wherever it spread, virtues spread with it. Generosity, virtue, and mutual support are from its influences while bravery and courage are from its results."

Kuntainz said, "Muslims are distinguished from others by the noble characteristics and lofty manners that the admonitions of the Qur'ân have stamped onto their souls and onto the souls of their parents; others, on the other hand, are bereft of all of that." He also said, "From the greatest of qualities that a Muslim is distinguished by is his self-dignity; in times of hardship and of ease, he sees that honor and dignity are only for Allâh, His Messenger, and for himself."

Hanotaux, the Foreign Minister of France in his time, said, "This religion of Islam stands on strong pillars and supports; it is the only religion that allows for throngs and flocks of people to enter it. The strong inclination of people to adhere to the religion of Islam is stronger than other such inclinations in any other religion. Indeed Islam has crossed the threshold of every populated region and has spread throughout the lands."

This is what some of the Orientalists have to say about Muslims:

As soon as Muslims turned away from the teachings of their religion, becoming ignorant of its rulings, and choosing, instead, contradictory laws made by men, corruption spread among their ranks; prevarication, hypocrisy, mutual hatred toward one another became rampant. They lost their unity and became ignorant about their present and future situation. They became heedless of what benefits them and what harms them, and they became satisfied with the life of merely eating, drinking, and sleeping. And so now, they do not compete with others in the pursuit of virtue and superiority. Yet when one of them is able to harm his brother, he is not negligent in inflicting that harm.

Many Orientalists have spoken much to this effect: that Islam is all-embracing and comprehensive in providing benefits for its adherents and in warding off evil, and that were the Muslims to truly adhere to their religion, they would be the most advanced nation with the happiest adherents; however, because they wasted, they have become lost, and they are satisfied with merely having Muslim names.

We do not, however — and all praise is for Allâh — need their testimony to establish the greatness of Islam. We merely mention their testimonies because the adherents of Islam are weak in their understanding and application of their religion, and because some of the enemies of Islam have grasped that which the Muslims do not perceive. While some of those enemies extol the completeness of Islam, Muslims have turned to systems and laws that are contradictory in their very nature. Without a doubt the true religion that guarantees to provide for the needs of all of mankind is Islam: the religion of true loftiness, of true justice, of civilization and freedom in its truest sense, of action, of mutual love and cooperation, of knowledge, and of encouragement to all noble professions and trades. Islam is not limited to rulings about worship and dealings; it embraces all aspects of life, all matters that can benefit mankind, and it is suitable for every place and time until the Day of Judgement.

It is sad to note that Muslims are ignorant of the truth they have with them; many Muslims, unfortunately, have turned against their own religion, attacking it at every turn, and many have come to prefer the people of the west to Muslims. Such people think that it is religion that has caused them to fall behind — how wrong they are! They have caused themselves to fall behind only by neglecting the teachings of their religion. Satisfied with laziness and ignorance, they live in a state of confusion.

From the greatest ways of deviation is to claim that the laws of Islam do not provide for the needs of all, and that people need laws derived from other sources to govern their daily problems; how can a Muslim make such a claim! And does not such a claim suggest disbelief in this verse:

﴿ ٱلۡیَوۡمَ أَكۡمَلۡتُ لَكُمۡ دِینَكُمۡ وَأَتۡمَمۡتُ عَلَیۡكُمۡ نِعۡمَتِی وَرَضِیتُ لَكُمُ ٱلۡإِسۡلَـٰمَ دِینࣰا ﴾

This day, I have perfected your religion for you, completed My favor upon you, and have chosen for you Islam as your religion.[1]

Indeed, Islam is most complete! Whoever reflects on its completeness will find no word that is suitable to describe its perfection and completion: for they are realities that man's words cannot put shape to. If mankind, including the most genius of men, were to gather and work together, they could not come up with a system even close to the perfect system of Islam. Enough for a genius is to recognize and acknowledge the perfection and greatness of Islam. Indeed, Islam is the greatest favor that Allâh Almighty blessed His worshippers with, for can there be a greater favor than guiding someone to Islam and making him from among its adherents. That is why Allâh Almighty reminded us of that favor, saying:

﴿لَقَدْ مَنَّ ٱللَّهُ عَلَى ٱلْمُؤْمِنِينَ إِذْ بَعَثَ فِيهِمْ رَسُولًا مِّنْ أَنفُسِهِمْ يَتْلُواْ عَلَيْهِمْ ءَايَٰتِهِۦ وَيُزَكِّيهِمْ وَيُعَلِّمُهُمُ ٱلْكِتَٰبَ وَٱلْحِكْمَةَ وَإِن كَانُواْ مِن قَبْلُ لَفِى ضَلَٰلٍ مُّبِينٍ﴾

Indeed Allâh conferred a great favor on the believers when He sent among them a Messenger from among themselves, reciting to them His verses (the Qur'ân), and purifying them, and instructing them (in) the Book (the Qur'ân) and *Al-Hikmah* (the wisdom and the Sunnah), while before that they had been in manifest error.[2]

Reminding His creatures of His great favor upon them, and of their responsibility of being thankful for that favor, Allâh Almighty says:

﴿ٱلْيَوْمَ أَكْمَلْتُ لَكُمْ دِينَكُمْ وَأَتْمَمْتُ عَلَيْكُمْ نِعْمَتِى وَرَضِيتُ لَكُمُ ٱلْإِسْلَٰمَ دِينًا﴾

This day, I have perfected your religion for you, completed My favor upon you, and have chosen for you Islam as your religion.[3]

Some of our pious predecessors used to say, "What a great religion it is indeed; all it needs are men that adhere to it."[4]

---

[1] (*Al-Ma'idah* 5:3)

[2] (*Aal 'Imran* 3:164)

[3] (*Al-Ma'idah* 5:3)

[4] This section was taken with minor editing from *Risalah Kamalush-Shari'ah* by Shaikh 'Abdullah bin Humaid.

The Four Issues[1]

Know, may Allâh (سبحانه وتعالى) have mercy on you, that it is incumbent upon us to learn four issues:

1) Knowledge: Knowledge of Allâh Almighty, His Prophet ﷺ, and the religion of Islam, through revealed sources.
2) Action that is based on that knowledge.
3) Calling others to that knowledge and to its application.
4) Patience when treading that path — i.e., the path of knowledge, of action, and of calling others to both.

The proof for these issues is found in this Chapter of the Qur'ân:

بِسْمِ ٱللَّهِ ٱلرَّحْمَٰنِ ٱلرَّحِيمِ

﴿وَٱلْعَصْرِ ۝ إِنَّ ٱلْإِنسَٰنَ لَفِى خُسْرٍ ۝ إِلَّا ٱلَّذِينَ ءَامَنُوا۟ وَعَمِلُوا۟ ٱلصَّٰلِحَٰتِ وَتَوَاصَوْا۟ بِٱلْحَقِّ وَتَوَاصَوْا۟ بِٱلصَّبْرِ﴾

By *Al-'Asr* (the time). Verily! Man is in loss, except those who believe and do righteous good deeds, and recommend one another to the truth, and recommend one another to patience.[2]

Ash-Shafi'i — may Allâh have mercy on him — said, "Had Allâh revealed this *Surah* alone as a proof upon His creation, it would be enough for them."

Al-Bukhari — may Allâh have mercy upon him — gave this heading to one of the chapters of his compilation: Knowledge before speech and action.[3] The proof for that is in this verse:

﴿فَٱعْلَمْ أَنَّهُ لَآ إِلَٰهَ إِلَّا ٱللَّهُ وَٱسْتَغْفِرْ لِذَنۢبِكَ﴾

So know that *Laa Ilaha Illallâh* (none has the right to be worshipped but Allâh), and ask forgiveness for your sin.[4]

---

[1] See *Thalathah Al-Usul* by Shaikh Muhammad bin 'Abdul-Wahhab, may Allâh have mercy upon him.
[2] (*Al-'Asr* 103:1-3)
[3] *Sahih Al-Bukhari* (1:22) in the Book Of Knowledge.
[4] (*Muhammad* 47:19)

In this verse, Allâh Almighty refers to knowledge before speech and deed.

Know (may Allâh Almighty have mercy on you) that there are three issues that all Muslims, both male and female, must learn and apply:

1) Allâh Almighty created us and provided for us, and He did not leave us to wander aimlessly. He sent us a Messenger ﷺ: whoever follows and obeys him enters Paradise, and whoever disobeys him enters the Hellfire, for Allâh Almighty says:

﴿إِنَّآ أَرْسَلْنَآ إِلَيْكُمْ رَسُولًا شَٰهِدًا عَلَيْكُمْ كَمَآ أَرْسَلْنَآ إِلَىٰ فِرْعَوْنَ رَسُولًا ۝ فَعَصَىٰ فِرْعَوْنُ ٱلرَّسُولَ فَأَخَذْنَٰهُ أَخْذًا وَبِيلًا﴾

Verily, We have sent to you (O men) a Messenger to be a witness over you, as We did send a Messenger to Fir'awn. But Fir'awn disobeyed the Messenger, so We seized him with a severe punishment.[1]

2) Allâh Almighty is not pleased when others besides Him are worshipped or when others are associated with Him in worship – regardless of whether it is a high-ranking angel or a sent Prophet. Allâh Almighty says:

﴿وَأَنَّ ٱلْمَسَٰجِدَ لِلَّهِ فَلَا تَدْعُوا۟ مَعَ ٱللَّهِ أَحَدًا﴾

And the *Masjids* are for Allâh, so invoke not anyone along with Allâh.[2]

3) Whoever obeys the Messenger of Allâh ﷺ and believes and applies *Tawhid*, he is forbidden from taking the enemies of Allâh Almighty and His Messenger ﷺ as friends, guardians, or protectors, even if they are the closest of relatives. Allâh Almighty says:

﴿لَّا تَجِدُ قَوْمًا يُؤْمِنُونَ بِٱللَّهِ وَٱلْيَوْمِ ٱلْأَخِرِ يُوَآدُّونَ مَنْ حَآدَّ ٱللَّهَ وَرَسُولَهُۥ وَلَوْ كَانُوٓا۟ ءَابَآءَهُمْ أَوْ أَبْنَآءَهُمْ أَوْ إِخْوَٰنَهُمْ أَوْ عَشِيرَتَهُمْ أُو۟لَٰٓئِكَ كَتَبَ فِى قُلُوبِهِمُ ٱلْإِيمَٰنَ وَأَيَّدَهُم بِرُوحٍ مِّنْهُ وَيُدْخِلُهُمْ جَنَّٰتٍ تَجْرِى مِن تَحْتِهَا ٱلْأَنْهَٰرُ خَٰلِدِينَ فِيهَا رَضِىَ ٱللَّهُ عَنْهُمْ وَرَضُوا۟ عَنْهُ أُو۟لَٰٓئِكَ حِزْبُ ٱللَّهِ

---

[1] (*Al-Muzzammil* 73:15,16)
[2] (*Al-Jinn* 72:18)

أَلَا إِنَّ حِزْبَ ٱللَّهِ هُمُ ٱلْمُفْلِحُونَ ﴾

You will not find any people who believe in Allâh and the Last Day, making friendship with those who oppose Allâh and His Messenger, even though they were their fathers, or their sons, or their brothers, or their kindred (people). For such He has written faith in their hearts, and strengthened them with *Ruh* (proofs, light and true guidance) from Himself. And We will admit them to Gardens (Paradise) under which rivers flow, to dwell therein (forever). Allâh is pleased with them, and they with Him. They are the party of Allâh. Verily, it is the party of Allâh that will be the successful.[1]

---

[1] (*Al-Mujadilah* 58:22)

The Three Foundations
A Muslim Must Know And Apply

1) Knowledge of his Lord: And He is Allâh Almighty, Who created His worshipper from nothing, and bestowed upon him all kinds of blessings. Allâh Almighty is the Creator of the heavens and earth, of night and day, of the sun and moon. It is He Who sends down rain and causes vegetation to grow and provides for His creatures. And it is He alone Who deserves to be worshipped.

2) Knowledge of His religion, which is Islam: Allâh Almighty says:

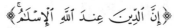

Truly, the religion with Allâh is Islam.[1]

3) Knowledge of His Prophet, Muhammad ﷺ: He is Muhammad bin (the son of) 'Abdullah bin 'Abdul-Muttallib bin Hashim. Hashim was from the Quraish and the Quraish are from the Arabs. And Muhammad ﷺ was the final and best Prophet.

The Different Levels In The Religion Of Islam: Islam, *Iman* and *Ihsan*

Islam

Islam means to surrender to Allâh with *Tawhid*, to submit to Him with obedience and purity from *Shirk* (associating partners with Allâh) and from its adherents. For one to be Muslim, one must have the following three:

1) He believes that Allâh is the One, and that He has no partner and that none has the right to be worshipped except Him.

2) He submits to Allâh Almighty with obedience to Him; he executes those orders that the Messenger of Allâh, Muhammad ﷺ, came with, meaning that he believes him in what he says, obeys him in what he commands, and stays away from that which he forbids — as Allâh Almighty says:

---

[1] (*Aal 'Imran* 3:19)

﴿وَمَآ ءَاتَىٰكُمُ ٱلرَّسُولُ فَخُذُوهُ وَمَا نَهَىٰكُمْ عَنْهُ﴾

And whatsoever the Messenger gives you, take it, and whatsoever he forbids you, abstain (from it).[1]

3) He purifies his heart from all forms and kinds of *Shirk*. One becomes a Muslim when he utters the two testimonies of faith, and when he applies the rest of the pillars of Islam.

The Pillars Of Islam Are Five

1) To bear witness that none has the right to be worshipped except Allâh and that Muhammad is the Messenger of Allâh.

2) To establish the prayer (*Salat*).

3) To give *Zakat* (the obligatory charity).

4) To fast the month of Ramadhan.

5) To make pilgrimage (*Hajj*) to the Sacred House (Ka'bah), for whoever is able to do so.

The First Pillar: The Two Testimonies

The Meaning Of The Two Testimonies

1) *Laa Ilaha Illallâh*: "None has the right to be worshipped" negates all that is worshipped other than Allâh, and "except Allâh" establishes that worship is for Allâh alone and that He has no partner in worship, just as He has no partner in His dominion. Hence there is none that deserves to be worshipped except Allâh - and how perfect is He!

2) "And that Muhammad is the Messenger of Allâh": i.e., I believe that he ﷺ is the Messenger of Allâh, and so I obey him in what he commands, believe him in what he informs, and abstain from that which he prohibits or warns against; and I worship Allâh only according to the way that he ﷺ legislated.

Iman (Faith)

Iman, upon which success in this world and the next depends, is composed of the following three elements:

---

[1] (*Al-Hashr* 59:7)

1) Acknowledgement with one's tongue.

2) Faith in one's heart.

3) And action with one's limbs.

Iman increases with obedience, decreases with disobedience. One must have in him the preceding three elements for him to be a believer (*Mu'min*). But what do those elements mean?

Acknowledgement With One's Tongue

This means that one acknowledges with his tongue and bears witness to the fact that none has the right to be worshipped except Allâh and that Muhammad is the Messenger of Allâh ﷺ.

Faith In One's Heart

This means that one believes with his heart in that which he uttered with his tongue, so that he is saved from being among the hypocrites, about whom Allâh Almighty says:

﴿وَمِنَ ٱلنَّاسِ مَن يَقُولُ ءَامَنَّا بِٱللَّهِ وَبِٱلۡيَوۡمِ ٱلۡأٓخِرِ وَمَا هُم بِمُؤۡمِنِينَ﴾

And of mankind, there are some who say: "We believe in Allâh and the Last Day" while in fact they believe not.[1]

Action With One's Limbs

This means to apply the pillars of Islam and its obligatory duties — prayer, *Zakat*, fasting Ramadhan, *Hajj* to Allâh's Sacred House (i.e., Ka'bah), for whoever is able to do so. From the completeness of action is for one to be dutiful to his parents, to join ties with relations, to be kind and generous to the creation, for all of these are proofs that establish the veracity of the *Iman* in his heart.

Iman, then, is not merely a word that is uttered by the tongue; moreover, the heart must believe it and then action must follow. It has been related that Al-Hasan Al-Basri said, "*Iman* does not come with adornment or wishful thinking, but it is something that settles in the heart and is witnessed by action."

---

[1] (*Al-Baqarah* 2:8)

The Pillars Of *Iman* Are Six

1) Belief in Allâh.

2) Belief in the angels.

3) Belief in the Divine Books that Allâh revealed to His Messengers

4) Belief in all of the Messengers.

5) Belief in the Last Day, when Allâh will resurrect all of creation from their graves and then judge them for their deeds. Allâh Almighty says:

$$﴿فَمَن يَعْمَلْ مِثْقَالَ ذَرَّةٍ خَيْرًا يَرَهُ ۝ وَمَن يَعْمَلْ مِثْقَالَ ذَرَّةٍ شَرًّا يَرَهُ﴾$$

So, whosoever does good equal to the weight of an atom (or a small ant), shall see it. And whosoever does evil equal to the weight of an atom (or a small ant), shall see it.[1]

6) Belief in *Al-Qadar* (Divine Preordainment) — both the good and bad of it, the sweet and bitter of it. This means that the Muslim believes that, before Allâh created the creation, He had knowledge of all that was to occur; he believes that whatever Allâh wills happens and that Allâh has complete power; and he believes that only that which Allâh wills takes place in the universe: what He wills happens, what He doesn't will, doesn't happen. When one of Allâh's worshippers has *Iman* in *Al-Qadar*, he is greatly influenced in many ways — for example, the following:

i)   He has patience when faced with hardship:

$$﴿مَا أَصَابَ مِن مُّصِيبَةٍ فِي ٱلْأَرْضِ وَلَا فِي أَنفُسِكُمْ إِلَّا فِي كِتَٰبٍ مِّن قَبْلِ أَن نَّبْرَأَهَآ إِنَّ ذَٰلِكَ عَلَى ٱللَّهِ يَسِيرٌ﴾$$

No calamity befalls on the earth or in yourselves but is inscribed in the Book of Decrees (*Al-Lawh Al-Mahfuz*), before We bring it into existence. Verily, that is easy for Allâh.[2]

ii) He is satisfied and calm because he knows that Allâh decreed his provision, his life span, and all of the matters that he

---

[1] (*Az-Zalzalah* 99:7, 8)
[2] (*Al-Hadid* 57:22)

wants and achieves. The Prophet ﷺ said:

«ثُمَّ يُرْسِلُ الْمَلَكَ فَيَنْفُخُ فِيهِ الرُّوحَ وَيُؤْمَرُ بِأَرْبَعِ كَلِمَاتٍ: بِكَتْبِ رِزْقِهِ وَأَجَلِهِ وَعَمَلِهِ...»

Then He sends the angel who blows into him the *Ruh* (spirit). And He orders him (the angel) to write four matters: his provision, his (time of) death, his deeds...[1]

And the proof for the six pillars is this verse:

﴿لَّيْسَ ٱلْبِرَّ أَن تُوَلُّواْ وُجُوهَكُمْ قِبَلَ ٱلْمَشْرِقِ وَٱلْمَغْرِبِ وَلَٰكِنَّ ٱلْبِرَّ مَنْ ءَامَنَ بِٱللَّهِ وَٱلْيَوْمِ ٱلْءَاخِرِ وَٱلْمَلَٰئِكَةِ وَٱلْكِتَٰبِ وَٱلنَّبِيِّۦنَ﴾

It is not *Al-Birr* (piety, righteousness) that you turn your faces towards the east and (or) the west (in prayers); but *Al-Birr* is (the quality of) the one who believes in Allâh, the Last Day, the Angels, the Book, the Prophets...[2]

And the proof for *Al-Qadar* is the following verse:

﴿إِنَّا كُلَّ شَيْءٍ خَلَقْنَٰهُ بِقَدَرٍ﴾

Verily, We have created all things with *Qadar* (Divine Preordainments of all things before their creation, as written in the Book of Decrees (*Al-Lawh Al-Mahfuz*).[3]

In the famous *Hadith* of Jibril, 'Umar, may Allâh be pleased with him, said, "One day, as we were sitting with the Messenger of Allâh ﷺ, a man appeared before us: he had on a garment that was pure white and his hair was pure black; though no sign of travel was upon him, not one of us knew him. He sat directly in front of the Prophet ﷺ, making his knees touch those of the Prophet ﷺ, and placing his hands on the Prophet's thighs. He said, 'O Muhammad! Inform me about Islam.' The Messenger of Allâh ﷺ said,

«الإِسْلَامُ أَنْ تَشْهَدَ أَنْ لَا إِلَهَ إِلَّا اللهُ وَأَنَّ مُحَمَّدًا رَسُولُ اللهِ، وَأَنْ تُقِيمَ الصَّلَاةَ، وَتُؤْتِيَ الزَّكَاةَ، وَتَصُومَ رَمَضَانَ، وَتَحُجَّ الْبَيْتَ إِنِ

---

[1] Recorded by Al-Bukhari (6:303).
[2] (*Al-Baqarah* 2:177)
[3] (*Al-Qamar* 54:49)

اسْتَطَعْتَ إِلَيْهِ سَبِيلًا»

'Islam is to bear witness that none has the right to be worshipped but Allâh and that Muhammad is the Messenger of Allâh; to establish the prayer; to give *Zakat*; to fast Ramadhan; to make pilgrimage to the House (Ka'bah), for whoever is able to do so.' (Recorded by Muslim)[1]

The man said, 'You have spoken the truth.'" 'Umar, may Allâh be pleased with him, said, "We were amazed at him because he first asked a question and then affirmed the veracity of the answer. He then said, 'Inform me about *Iman*.' The Prophet ﷺ said,

«الْإِيمَانُ أَنْ تُؤْمِنَ بِالله وَمَلَائِكَتِهِ وَكُتُبِهِ وَرُسُلِهِ وَبِالْيَوْمِ الآخِرِ وَتُؤْمِنَ بِالْقَدَرِ خَيْرِهِ وَشَرِّهِ»

'To believe in Allâh, His Angels, His Books, His Messengers, the Last Day, and to believe in Divine Preordainment, the good of it and the bad of it.'"

One cannot reach the level of *Iman* unless he is first a Muslim.

Al-Ihsan

Literally, it means doing something proficiently and with sincerity; what it means in the *Shari'ah* is for you to worship Allâh Almighty as if you see Him, though you don't see him, He certainly sees you. The following verse is a proof for *Ihsan*:

﴿إِنَّ ٱللَّهَ مَعَ ٱلَّذِينَ ٱتَّقَوا۟ وَّٱلَّذِينَ هُم مُّحْسِنُونَ﴾

Truly, Allâh is with those who fear Him (keep their duty unto Him), and those who are *Muhsinun* (good-doers).[2]

One cannot reach the level of *Ihsan* unless he is first a Muslim and a believer (*Mu'min*).

Worship ('Ibadah)

Its definition: It is a comprehensive term for all that Allâh loves and is pleased with from sayings and deeds, both outer and inner.

---

[1] *Sahih Muslim* (1:139)
[2] (*An-Nahl* 16:128)

There are many kinds of worship: Prayer, supplication, love, fear, sacrifice, making vows, etc. All forms of worship must be dedicated purely for Allâh Almighty, Who says:

$$﴿وَمَآ أُمِرُوٓاْ إِلَّا لِيَعۡبُدُواْ ٱللَّهَ مُخۡلِصِينَ لَهُ ٱلدِّينَ حُنَفَآءَ﴾$$

And they were commanded not, but that they should worship Allâh, and worship none but Him Alone.[1]

Whoever dedicates any kind of worship to other than Allâh, then he has committed major *Shirk*, and his recompense is an eternal life in the Hellfire. Allâh Almighty says:

$$﴿قُلۡ إِنَّمَآ أَدۡعُواْ رَبِّي وَلَآ أُشۡرِكُ بِهِۦٓ أَحَدًا﴾$$

Say: "I invoke only my Lord, and I associate none as partners along with Him."[2]

And Allâh Almighty says:

$$﴿إِنَّهُۥ مَن يُشۡرِكۡ بِٱللَّهِ فَقَدۡ حَرَّمَ ٱللَّهُ عَلَيۡهِ ٱلۡجَنَّةَ وَمَأۡوَىٰهُ ٱلنَّارُۖ وَمَا لِلظَّٰلِمِينَ مِنۡ أَنصَـارٖ﴾$$

Verily, whosoever sets up partners in worship with Allâh, then Allâh has forbidden Paradise for him, and the Fire will be his abode. And for the wrongdoers there are no helpers.[3]

The Existence Of Allâh

That Allâh Almighty exists, is a reality about which there is no doubt; the following attests to that reality:

1) The sending of Messengers and the revelation of Books.

2) The natural disposition of man, which Allâh created him upon.

3) The sound and reasoning mind.

First, The Natural Disposition Of Man

This is often seen when man is afflicted with a disaster or calamity, or when all helpers and friends abandon him: his natural disposition impels him to ask Allâh and to invoke Him to remove the calamity.

---

[1] (*Bayyinah* 98:5)

[2] (*Al-Jinn* 72:20)

[3] (*Al-Ma'idah* 5:72)

The Noble Qur'ân confirms this, saying that man turns to Allâh to remove any calamity that afflicts him:

$$\text{﴿وَإِذَا مَسَّ ٱلْإِنسَٰنَ ضُرٌّ دَعَا رَبَّهُۥ مُنِيبًا إِلَيْهِ﴾}$$

And when some hurt touches man, he cries to his Lord, turning to Him in repentance.[1]

The Qur'ân even gives a clear example of this, the example of a man who is on a boat. As the boat is sailing in clear skies, the ocean suddenly becomes violent and the boat rocks violently. The imminence of death puts him in a state of extreme fear, and it is at this point that he returns to his natural disposition and to his own self by turning to his Lord, hoping to be saved by Him, and supplicating sincerely to Him, without associating partners with Him. Allâh Almighty says:

$$\text{﴿هُوَ ٱلَّذِى يُسَيِّرُكُمْ فِى ٱلْبَرِّ وَٱلْبَحْرِ حَتَّىٰ إِذَا كُنتُمْ فِى ٱلْفُلْكِ وَجَرَيْنَ بِهِم بِرِيحٍ طَيِّبَةٍ وَفَرِحُوا۟ بِهَا جَآءَتْهَا رِيحٌ عَاصِفٌ وَجَآءَهُمُ ٱلْمَوْجُ مِن كُلِّ مَكَانٍ وَظَنُّوٓا۟ أَنَّهُمْ أُحِيطَ بِهِمْ دَعَوُا۟ ٱللَّهَ مُخْلِصِينَ لَهُ ٱلدِّينَ لَئِنْ أَنجَيْتَنَا مِنْ هَٰذِهِۦ لَنَكُونَنَّ مِنَ ٱلشَّٰكِرِينَ﴾}$$

He it is Who enables you to travel through land and sea, till when you are in the ships and they sail with them with a favorable wind, and they are glad therein, then comes a stormy wind and the waves come to them from all sides, and they think that they are encircled therein, they invoke Allâh, making their faith pure for Him Alone, saying: "If You deliver us from this, we shall truly be of the grateful."[2]

Thus we find the innate belief of man in Allâh's generosity, and no one will deny that except one who is intransigent in the face of the truth.

Second, The Sound And Reasoning Mind

The human mind, if fair and sincere, has no choice but to acknowledge Allâh's existence, especially when considering this rule: "Nothingness cannot create something." Allâh Almighty says:

---

[1] (*Az-Zumar* 39:8)
[2] (*Yunus* 10:22)

﴿أَمْ خُلِقُوا مِنْ غَيْرِ شَيْءٍ أَمْ هُمُ ٱلْخَٰلِقُونَ ۝ أَمْ خَلَقُوا ٱلسَّمَٰوَٰتِ وَٱلْأَرْضَ بَل لَّا يُوقِنُونَ﴾

Were they created by nothing, or were they themselves the creators? Or did they create the heavens and the earth? Nay, but they have no firm belief.[1]

The conclusion of this verse is based on the following premises. "Did nothing create something?" The answer is that "nothing" doesn't create anything at all. Then comes the next premise: "Did you create yourselves?" The answer is no, we didn't create ourselves. And then follows the third premise, "If you weren't created by 'nothing' and you didn't create yourselves, did you create the universe and its intricate system?" The answer: the one who cannot create himself cannot create anything else and the one who cannot benefit himself cannot benefit others. The conclusion then is this: if we were not created by "nothingness", if we didn't create ourselves, and if we didn't create the universe, then there must be a creator, and He is Allâh Almighty, the Creator of all that exists — as He Almighty says:

﴿ٱللَّهُ خَٰلِقُ كُلِّ شَيْءٍ﴾

Allâh is the Creator of all things.[2]

By merely observing and contemplating the creation, one is shown that there is a creator, and that is why Allâh ordered us to ponder, study, and contemplate His creation, for the creation indicates the Supreme and Perfect Creator. Allâh Almighty says:

﴿إِنَّ فِي خَلْقِ ٱلسَّمَٰوَٰتِ وَٱلْأَرْضِ وَٱخْتِلَٰفِ ٱلَّيْلِ وَٱلنَّهَارِ وَٱلْفُلْكِ ٱلَّتِي تَجْرِي فِي ٱلْبَحْرِ بِمَا يَنفَعُ ٱلنَّاسَ وَمَآ أَنزَلَ ٱللَّهُ مِنَ ٱلسَّمَآءِ مِن مَّآءٍ فَأَحْيَا بِهِ ٱلْأَرْضَ بَعْدَ مَوْتِهَا وَبَثَّ فِيهَا مِن كُلِّ دَآبَّةٍ وَتَصْرِيفِ ٱلرِّيَٰحِ وَٱلسَّحَابِ ٱلْمُسَخَّرِ بَيْنَ ٱلسَّمَآءِ وَٱلْأَرْضِ لَءَايَٰتٍ لِّقَوْمٍ يَعْقِلُونَ﴾

Verily! In the creation of the heavens and the earth, and in the alternation of night and day, and the ships which sail through

---

[1] (*At-Tur* 52:35,36)
[2] (*Az-Zumar* 39:62)

the sea with that which is of use to mankind, and the water (rain) which Allâh sends down from the sky and makes the earth alive therewith after its death, and the moving (living) creatures of all kinds that He has scattered therein, and in the veering of winds and clouds which are held between the sky and the earth, are indeed *Ayat* (proofs, evidences, signs, etc.) for people of understanding.[1]

---

[1] (*Al-Baqarah* 2:164)

Tawhid And Its Categories

The Definition Of *Tawhid*:

To single out Allâh with worship, love, fear, obedience, submission, hope; and with seeking protection and help. To believe that He is One in His Self and in His Attributes, that He is One in His Sovereignty and in His actions. Indeed, He is One in His Self, in His Names, and in His Attributes; there is none that is equal, comparable, or similar to Him.

$$﴿لَيْسَ كَمِثْلِهِ شَيْءٌ وَهُوَ السَّمِيعُ البَصِيرُ﴾$$

There is nothing like Him, and He is the All-Hearer, the All-Seer.[1]

He is One in His Sovereignty and actions; as Creator, Planner, and Sustainer of all that exists, He has no partner:

$$﴿قُلِ اللَّهُمَّ مَالِكَ المُلْكِ تُؤْتِي المُلْكَ مَن تَشَاءُ وَتَنزِعُ المُلْكَ مِمَّن تَشَاءُ﴾$$

Say: "O Allâh! Possessor of the kingdom, You give the kingdom to whom You will, and You take the kingdom from whom You will..."[2]

As the One Who deserves worship alone, He is One, for there is none that deserves to be worshipped but Him. Allâh Almighty says:

$$﴿قُلْ إِنِّي أُمِرْتُ أَنْ أَعْبُدَ اللَّهَ مُخْلِصًا لَهُ الدِّينَ﴾$$

Say: "Verily, I am commanded to worship Allâh making religion purely for Him."[3]

There Are Three Categories Of *Tawhid*

1) *Tawhid Ar-Rububiyyah*

2) *Tawhid Al-Uluhiyyah*

3) *Tawhid Al-Asma' was-Sifat*

---

[1] (*Ash-Shura* 42:11)
[2] (*Aal 'Imran* 3:26)
[3] (*Az-Zumar* 39:11)

First, *Tawhid Ar-Rububiyyah*

It is to believe in the oneness of Allâh's actions, such as creating the creation, providing for them, giving life, causing death, sending down rain, causing crops to grow. The monotheistic Muslim believes that Allâh is the Creator, the Provider, the One Who brings benefit, and the only One Who can harm, the One Who brings to life, the One Who causes death, the King of the entire dominion — in His Hand are the reins of the heavens and the earth.

The polytheists believed in this category of *Tawhid*, for Allâh Almighty says about them:

﴿قُلْ مَن يَرْزُقُكُم مِّنَ ٱلسَّمَآءِ وَٱلْأَرْضِ أَمَّن يَمْلِكُ ٱلسَّمْعَ وَٱلْأَبْصَٰرَ وَمَن يُخْرِجُ ٱلْحَيَّ مِنَ ٱلْمَيِّتِ وَيُخْرِجُ ٱلْمَيِّتَ مِنَ ٱلْحَيِّ وَمَن يُدَبِّرُ ٱلْأَمْرَ فَسَيَقُولُونَ ٱللَّهُ فَقُلْ أَفَلَا تَتَّقُونَ﴾

Say: "Who provides for you from the sky and from the earth? Or who owns hearing and sight? And who brings out the living from the dead and brings out the dead from the living? And who disposes the affairs?" They will say: "Allâh." Say: "Will you not then be afraid of Allâh's punishment?"[1]

Second, *Tawhid Al-Uluhiyyah*

This means to single out Allâh with those actions that His worshipper performs as a form of worship — in ways that Allâh Almighty and His Messenger ﷺ have legislated. It means to believe that Allâh alone is the One Who has the right to be worshipped and obeyed, and that there is none that deserves to be worshipped other than Him. Therefore, all acts of worship must be performed purely for Him. So, when one prays, he must pray only to Allâh; when one supplicates, one must supplicate only to Him. When one slaughters an animal, it must be done by Allâh's Name only. When one makes a vow, one must do it only for Allâh. When one seeks help, one must seek it from Allâh — in those matters that only Allâh is capable of. When one calls out for help, one must call out for help from Allâh — in those matters that only Allâh is capable of. To believe and apply *Tawhid* in this sense requires one to:

---

[1] (*Yunus* 10:31)

- Worship none but Allâh.
- Fear none but Allâh.
- Submit to none but Allâh.
- Seek refuge in none but Allâh.
- Seek help from none but Allâh.
- Trust in none but in Allâh.
- Seek judgement from none but Allâh's Legislation.
- To not make permissible except that which Allâh has made permissible.
- To not make forbidden except that which Allâh has made forbidden.

In an authentic *Hadith*, 'Adi bin Hatim, may Allâh be pleased with him — who was a Christian in the Days of Ignorance — heard the Prophet ﷺ recite this verse:

﴿ٱتَّخَذُوٓاْ أَحْبَارَهُمْ وَرُهْبَٰنَهُمْ أَرْبَابًا مِّن دُونِ ٱللَّهِ وَٱلْمَسِيحَ ٱبْنَ مَرْيَمَ﴾

They (Jews and Christians) took their rabbis and their monks to be their lords besides Allâh, and (they also took as their Lord) Messiah, son of Maryam (Mary).[1]

'Adi said, "O Messenger of Allâh, they wouldn't worship them (i.e., the rabbis and monks)." The Messenger of Allâh ﷺ said,

«بَلَى إِنَّهُمْ حَرَّمُوا عَلَيْهِمُ الْحَلَالَ، وَأَحَلُّوا لَهُمُ الْحَرَامَ، فَاتَّبَعُوهُمْ. فَذَلِكَ عِبَادَتُهُمْ إِيَّاهُمْ»

"Indeed, they (the rabbis and monks) would forbid them from that which was lawful, and they would permit them to do that which was forbidden. They (the Christians and Jews) followed them (in that): that was their worship of them."

The *Tawhid* With Which The Messengers Were Sent

Tawhid Al-Uluhiyyah is the *Tawhid* that the Messengers invited people to accept, and it is that category of *Tawhid* that people

---

[1] (*At-Tawbah* 9:31)

rejected, from the time of Nuh, peace be upon him, until that of Muhammad ﷺ. Allâh Almighty says:

$$﴿وَمَآ أَرْسَلْنَا مِن قَبْلِكَ مِن رَّسُولٍ إِلَّا نُوحِىٓ إِلَيْهِ أَنَّهُ لَآ إِلَٰهَ إِلَّا أَنَا۠ فَٱعْبُدُونِ﴾$$

And We did not send any Messenger before you but We inspired him (saying): *Laa Ilaha Illa Ana* [none has the right to be worshipped but I], so worship Me.[1]

And Allâh Almighty says:

$$﴿وَلَقَدْ بَعَثْنَا فِى كُلِّ أُمَّةٍ رَّسُولًا أَنِ ٱعْبُدُواْ ٱللَّهَ وَٱجْتَنِبُواْ ٱلطَّٰغُوتَ﴾$$

And verily, We have sent among every *Ummah* (community, nation) a Messenger (proclaiming): "Worship Allâh, and avoid (or keep away from) *Taghut* (all false deities)."[2]

Whosoever worships Allâh alone, leaving the worship of all else, has indeed followed the straight path and has grasped the most trustworthy handhold:

$$﴿فَمَن يَكْفُرْ بِٱلطَّٰغُوتِ وَيُؤْمِنۢ بِٱللَّهِ فَقَدِ ٱسْتَمْسَكَ بِٱلْعُرْوَةِ ٱلْوُثْقَىٰ لَا ٱنفِصَامَ لَهَا﴾$$

Whoever disbelieves in *Taghut* and believes in Allâh, then he has grasped the most trustworthy handhold that will never break. [3]

And Allâh said:

$$﴿لَا تَتَّخِذُوٓاْ إِلَٰهَيْنِ ٱثْنَيْنِ إِنَّمَا هُوَ إِلَٰهٌ وَٰحِدٌ فَإِيَّٰىَ فَٱرْهَبُونِ﴾$$

(O mankind!): "Take not *Ilahain* (two gods in worship, etc.). Verily, He is (the) only One *Ilah* (God). Then, fear Me (Allâh) much."[4]

The polytheists among the Arabs acknowledged that Allâh created all things, while their gods neither created nor provided nor brought

---

[1] (*Al-Anbiya'* 21:25)
[2] (*An-Nahl* 16:36)
[3] (*Al-Baqarah* 2:256)
[4] (*An-Nahl* 16:51)

things to life nor caused death; Allâh says:

$$﴿وَلَئِن سَأَلْتَهُم مَّنْ خَلَقَ ٱلسَّمَٰوَٰتِ وَٱلْأَرْضَ لَيَقُولُنَّ خَلَقَهُنَّ ٱلْعَزِيزُ ٱلْعَلِيمُ﴾$$

And indeed if you ask them, "Who has created the heavens and the earth?" They will surely say: "The All-Mighty, the All-Knower created them."[1]

Nevertheless, they were polytheists because along with Allâh Almighty they worshipped other gods, gods that in their thinking, were intermediaries between them and Allâh. So, because they rejected *Tawhid Al-Uluhiyyah*, their belief in *Tawhid Ar-Rububiyyah* didn't benefit them at all:

$$﴿وَمَا يُؤْمِنُ أَكْثَرُهُم بِٱللَّهِ إِلَّا وَهُم مُّشْرِكُونَ﴾$$

And most of them believe not in Allâh except that they attribute partners to Him.[2]

They didn't single out Allâh for worship and for supplication and for seeking help; rather, they associated partners with Him in their worship:

$$﴿مَا نَعْبُدُهُمْ إِلَّا لِيُقَرِّبُونَآ إِلَى ٱللَّهِ زُلْفَىٰ﴾$$

"We worship them only that they may bring us near to Allâh."[3]

$$﴿هَٰٓؤُلَآءِ شُفَعَٰٓؤُنَا عِندَ ٱللَّهِ﴾$$

"These are our intercessors with Allâh."[4]

So again, it becomes clear that although one may believe in *Tawhid Ar-Rububiyyah*, one is a polytheist and not a Muslim as long as one doesn't believe in *Tawhid Al-Uluhiyyah*.

Who Is Allâh?

Indeed Allâh is the One True God: He has no partner and there is none that is equal or similar to Him, not similar to His Self, to His Attributes, or to His actions. With this belief, we are different from

[1] (*Az-Zukhruf* 43:9)
[2] (*Yusuf* 12:106)
[3] (*Az-Zumar* 39:3)
[4] (*Yunus* 10:18)

those who ascribe a wife or a child to Allâh:

﴿قُلْ هُوَ ٱللَّهُ أَحَدٌ ۝ ٱللَّهُ ٱلصَّمَدُ ۝ لَمْ يَلِدْ وَلَمْ يُولَدْ ۝ وَلَمْ يَكُن لَّهُۥ كُفُوًا أَحَدٌ﴾

Say: "He is Allâh, (the) One; *Allâhus-Samad* (Allâh – the Self-Sufficient Master, Whom all creatures need, He neither eats nor drinks). He begets not, nor was He begotten. And there is none coequal or comparable to Him."[1]

With our belief that is explained above, we are different from those who claim that Allâh is the third of three — far, far above is Allâh Almighty from the evil they ascribe to Him:

﴿لَّقَدْ كَفَرَ ٱلَّذِينَ قَالُوٓا۟ إِنَّ ٱللَّهَ ثَالِثُ ثَلَـٰثَةٍ وَمَا مِنْ إِلَـٰهٍ إِلَّآ إِلَـٰهٌ وَٰحِدٌ﴾

Surely, disbelievers are those who said: "Allâh is the third of the three." But there is no *Ilah* (god) (none who has the right to be worshipped) but One *Ilah* (God—Allâh).[2]

﴿وَإِلَـٰهُكُمْ إِلَـٰهٌ وَٰحِدٌ لَّآ إِلَـٰهَ إِلَّا هُوَ ٱلرَّحْمَـٰنُ ٱلرَّحِيمُ﴾

And your *Ilah* (God) is One *Ilah* (God - Allâh), *Laa Ilaha Illa Huwa* (there is none who has the right to be worshipped but He), the Most Beneficent, the Most Merciful.[3]

With that same belief, we are opposite of those who believe that a god other than Allâh Almighty has any power in the universe:

﴿لَوْ كَانَ فِيهِمَآ ءَالِهَةٌ إِلَّا ٱللَّهُ لَفَسَدَتَا فَسُبْحَـٰنَ ٱللَّهِ رَبِّ ٱلْعَرْشِ عَمَّا يَصِفُونَ﴾

Had there been therein (in the heavens and the earth) gods besides Allâh, then verily both would have been ruined. Glorified is Allâh, the Lord of the Throne, (High is He) above what they attribute to Him![4]

---

[1] (*Al-Ikhlas* 112:1-4)
[2] (*Al-Ma'idah* 5:73)
[3] (*Al-Baqarah* 2:163)
[4] (*Al-Anbiya'* 21:22)

Third, *Tawhid Al-Asma' was-Sifat* (Names and Attributes)

Under this category, we affirm for Allâh all that He has affirmed regarding Himself and all that His Messenger Muhammad ﷺ affirmed for Him — in terms of His Beautiful Names and the Attributes that those Names indicate; but we do not compare His Qualities to those of creation, we do not exemplify those qualities, we do not distort their meanings, and we do not effectively negate their implications.[1] What we do believe is that Allâh has Names and Attributes that indicate His Perfection and Greatness, and no one is similar to Him in those Names and Attributes.

Allâh's Names and Attributes are mentioned in the Qur'ân and in the authentic Sunnah of the Prophet ﷺ, and we must believe that they are real, for Allâh Almighty says:

$$﴿ لَيْسَ كَمِثْلِهِ شَيْءٌ وَهُوَ ٱلسَّمِيعُ ٱلْبَصِيرُ ﴾$$

There is nothing like Him, and He is the All-Hearer, the All-Seer.[2]

---

[1] Shaikh 'Abdur-Rahman bin Sa'di in *As-Suw'al wal-Jawab fee Ahammil-Muhimmat*, pg. 13.
[2] (*Ash-Shura* 42:11)

Examples Of Allâh's Names And Attributes

1) Some Of His Names: Ar-Rahman, Ar-Rahim, Al-Qahir, Al-Qadir, As-Sami', Al-Basir, Al-Quddus.

2) Some Of His Attributes: The Highness, the Hearing, the Seeing, the Ability, that He has a Face and Hand, and that He Descends (during the last third of every night).

The Messengers

After clarifying the different kinds of *Tawhid*, we move on to the Messengers and the wisdom behind their being sent. Allâh sent the Messengers ﷺ to the people, so that they could call them to His religion, to worshipping Him alone — without associating partners with Him, and to avoiding the worship of others. The first Messenger was Nuh, peace be upon him, and the last one was Muhammad ﷺ.

The Wisdom Behind Sending The Messengers

Allâh sent them as a proof upon mankind, to convey the message of the religion to the people, to give glad tidings of Paradise and of a great reward to the obedient one, and to warn the disobedient one of a severe punishment and the Hellfire. Allâh Almighty says:

$$﴿رُّسُلًا مُّبَشِّرِينَ وَمُنذِرِينَ لِئَلَّا يَكُونَ لِلنَّاسِ عَلَى ٱللَّهِ حُجَّةُۢ بَعْدَ ٱلرُّسُلِۚ﴾$$

Messengers as bearers of good news as well as of warning in order that mankind should have no plea against Allâh after the Messengers.[1]

---

[1] (*An-Nisa'* 4:165)

The Virtue Of *Tawhid*

It is a great virtue to have belief in *Tawhid*; indeed, Allâh made that belief to be a saving ship for His creatures in this life and in the Hereafter. As for this life — if one is from the people of *Tawhid*, living his life according to its implications, and not associating any partners with Allâh whatsoever, Allâh Almighty will shower him with safety, peace, guidance, and a good life, for He Almighty says:

﴿ ٱلَّذِينَ ءَامَنُوا۟ وَلَمْ يَلْبِسُوٓا۟ إِيمَٰنَهُم بِظُلْمٍ أُو۟لَٰٓئِكَ لَهُمُ ٱلْأَمْنُ وَهُم مُّهْتَدُونَ ﴾

It is those who believe and confuse not their belief with wrong, for them (only) there is security and they are the guided.[1]

"Wrong" here means to mix one's faith with the association of partners with Allâh. When one avoids that wrong, one will have achieved security and guidance. Allâh Almighty says:

﴿مَنْ عَمِلَ صَٰلِحًا مِّن ذَكَرٍ أَوْ أُنثَىٰ وَهُوَ مُؤْمِنٌ فَلَنُحْيِيَنَّهُۥ حَيَوٰةً طَيِّبَةً﴾

Whoever works righteousness, whether male or female, while he (or she) is a true believer verily, to him We will give a good life.[2]

As for the Hereafter — when one dies upon *Tawhid* and meets his Lord, not associating any partners with Him, He enters Paradise and Allâh saves him from the Hellfire. In an authentic *Hadith*, the Prophet ﷺ said:

«إِنَّ اللهَ حَرَّمَ عَلَى النَّارِ مَنْ قَالَ لَا إِلَهَ إِلَّا اللهُ يَبْتَغِي بِذَلِكَ وَجْهَ اللهِ»

Indeed, Allâh has forbidden upon the Fire the one who says, "None has the right to be worshipped but Allâh," seeking from that Allâh's Face.[3]

---

[1] (*Al-An'am* 6:82)

[2] (*An-Nahl* 16:97)

[3] Agreed upon. Recorded by Al-Bukhari (6:202) and Muslim, the Book of Faith (1:61) no. 54 from the *Hadith* of 'Itban bin Malik.

Shirk And Its Categories

There are two kinds of *Shirk*:

First, The Greater *Shirk*

The Greater *Shirk* means either to worship other than Allâh Almighty or to make partners with Allâh in something that is specifically His; for example, to take someone as His partner in worship, obedience, love, fear, supplication, and the seeking of help.

When one associates partners with Allâh — regardless of who that partner is, such as a man, animal, plant, or inanimate object — one has perpetrated the Greater *Shirk*, examples of which are as follows:

- To supplicate to that partner as one supplicates to Allâh.
- To love that partner as one loves Allâh.
- To hope from that partner as one hopes from Allâh.
- To submit oneself in obedience to that partner as one submits in obedience to Allâh.
- To fear that partner as one fears Allâh.
- To seek a ruling or judgement from other than Allâh's *Shari'ah*.

Allâh Almighty says:

﴿وَٱعْبُدُوا۟ ٱللَّهَ وَلَا تُشْرِكُوا۟ بِهِۦ شَيْـًٔا﴾

Worship Allâh and join none with Him in worship.[1]

Of course, the Greater *Shirk* is the worst and most severe kind of *Shirk*; indeed, it is the greatest sin with Allâh, for Allâh does not accept any deed from its perpetrator, regardless of how pious he may be otherwise. If one dies, associating partners with Allâh, Allâh will not forgive him, for He says:

﴿إِنَّ ٱللَّهَ لَا يَغْفِرُ أَن يُشْرَكَ بِهِۦ وَيَغْفِرُ مَا دُونَ ذَٰلِكَ لِمَن يَشَآءُ وَمَن يُشْرِكْ بِٱللَّهِ فَقَدِ ٱفْتَرَىٰٓ إِثْمًا عَظِيمًا﴾

Verily, Allâh forgives not that partners should be set up with him in worship, but He forgives except that (anything else) to

---

[1] (*An-Nisa'* 4:36)

whom He pleases, and whoever sets up partners with Allâh in worship, he has indeed invented a tremendous sin.[1]

Whoever dies upon this form of *Shirk* is from the dwellers of the Hellfire, for the Prophet ﷺ said:

«مَنْ مَاتَ وَهُوَ يَدْعُو مِنْ دُونِ اللهِ نِدًّا دَخَلَ النَّارَ»

Whoever dies calling upon other than Allâh as a rival, he enters the Hellfire.[2]

In another *Hadith*, the Prophet ﷺ said:

«مَنْ لَقِيَ اللهَ لَا يُشْرِكُ بِهِ شَيْئاً دَخَلَ الْجَنَّةَ. وَمَنْ لَقِيَهُ يُشْرِكُ بِهِ شَيْئاً دَخَلَ النَّارَ»

Whoever meets Allâh without associating any partner with Him enters Paradise. Whoever meets Him, associating any partner with Him enters the Hellfire.[3]

The Muslim, therefore, worships and invokes only Allâh, and submits only to Him, for Allâh Almighty says:

﴿قُلْ إِنَّ صَلَاتِي وَنُسُكِي وَمَحْيَايَ وَمَمَاتِي لِلَّهِ رَبِّ ٱلْعَٰلَمِينَ ۝ لَا شَرِيكَ لَهُۥ وَبِذَٰلِكَ أُمِرْتُ وَأَنَا۠ أَوَّلُ ٱلْمُسْلِمِينَ﴾

Say: "Verily, my *Salat* (prayer), my sacrifice, my living, and my dying are for Allâh, the Lord of the ʿAlamin (mankind, jinn and all that exists). He has no partner. And of this I have been commanded, and I am the first of the Muslims."[4]

Second, The Lesser *Shirk*

It consists of various categories:

1) A small amount of *Riya'* (doing good deeds for show); for example, when one prays, fasts, or gives charity, he is seeking other than Allâh's Face; hence, he is mixing good deeds with bad ones. The

[1] (*An-Nisa'* 4:48)
[2] Al-Bukhari in the Book of *Tafsir* (5:153) and Muslim (1:94) from Ibn Masʿud.
[3] Recorded by Muslim (1:94) from Jabir.
[4] *Al-Anʿam* 6:162,163. Included here is one whom people see doing a righteous deed, but he did not do it out of sincerity, and also one who does a righteous deed secretly but wants to let people know about it.

Prophet ﷺ said:

«أَخْوَفُ مَا أَخَافُ عَلَيْكُمُ الشِّرْكُ الأَصْغَرُ»

What I fear most for you is the Lesser *Shirk*.

When asked about it, he ﷺ said:

«الرِّيَاءُ»

Riya'.[1]

When one performs any good deed or act of worship to impress or please people thereby, then he has committed *Riya'*, which is forbidden. In another *Hadith* related by Shaddad bin 'Aws, may Allâh be pleased with him, the Prophet ﷺ said:

«مَنْ صَلَّى يُرَائِي فَقَدْ أَشْرَكَ، وَمَنْ صَامَ يُرَائِي فَقَدْ أَشْرَكَ، وَمَنْ تَصَدَّقَ يُرَائِي فَقَدْ أَشْرَكَ»

Whoever prays, showing off to others, he has indeed committed *Shirk*; whoever fasts, showing off to others, he has indeed committed *Shirk*; whoever gives charity, showing off to others, he has indeed committed *Shirk*.[2]

2) Another form of the lesser *Shirk* is to swear by anyone other than Allâh, for instance, to swear by the Prophet ﷺ, by the Ka'bah, or by one's parents. In an authentic *Hadith* related by Ibn 'Umar, may Allâh be pleased with them, the Prophet ﷺ said:

«إِنَّ اللهَ يَنْهَاكُمْ أَنْ تَحْلِفُوا بِآبَائِكُمْ. مَنْ كَانَ حَالِفاً فَلْيَحْلِفْ بِاللهِ أَوْ لِيَصْمُتْ»

Indeed, Allâh has forbidden you from swearing by your fathers; whoever makes an oath, let him swear by Allâh or remain silent.

3) Another form of the Lesser *Shirk* is for one to say the following expressions:

---

[1] Imam Ahmad (4:126) and Ibn Majah (2:1406) from Shaddad bin Aws. Ahmad also recorded it from a *Hadith* of Mahmud bin Lubaid (5:428).

[2] Agreed upon. Recorded by Al-Bukhari (3:195), Muslim (1:92) from Abu Hurairah, may Allâh be pleased with him.

- "What Allâh wills and what you will."
- "This is from Allâh and from you."
- "I am what I am because of Allâh and because of you."
- "I have no one but Allâh and you."
- "I place my trust upon Allâh and upon you."
- "Were it not for Allâh and you, such and such would (or wouldn't) have happened."

Based on one's intention when saying these phrases, this category may even become a form of the Greater *Shirk*.

Protecting The Belief In *Tawhid*

The Prophet ﷺ strove hard to keep the belief in *Tawhid* clean and pure in the hearts of Muslims, making every effort to prevent doubt or *Shirk* from entering those hearts. He ﷺ taught his Companions to turn with their hearts to Allâh only, to seek help in Him alone, and to put their trust in Him alone. As soon as the Prophet ﷺ saw anything that might weaken the relationship between the Muslims and their Lord, that might shake the belief of *Tawhid* in their hearts, he ﷺ raced to warn the Muslims regarding the effect of that matter on their faith. Some examples of such matters are as follows:

1) Magic:

Incantations, spells, or charms that are used to have an effect on hearts and bodies, intended to make them sick, to make people kill one another, to divide between a man and his wife, and so on. Magic is a matter that depends on secrecy and concealment. Magicians use the above-mentioned techniques to inflict harm on people, and in the plainest of terms, Islam forbade magic when the Prophet ﷺ said:

«اجْتَنِبُوا السَّبْعَ الْمُوبِقَاتِ»

"Stay away from the seven grave (and deadly) sins."

The Companions, may Allâh be pleased with them, asked, "And what are they, O Messenger of Allâh?" He ﷺ said:

«الشِّرْكُ بِاللهِ وَالسِّحْرُ وَقَتْلُ النَّفْسِ الَّتِي حَرَّمَ اللهُ إِلَّا بِالْحَقِّ. وَأَكْلُ الرِّبَا. وَأَكْلُ مَالِ الْيَتِيمِ. وَالتَّوَلِّي يَوْمَ الزَّحْفِ. وَقَذْفُ الْمُحْصَنَاتِ الْغَافِلَاتِ»

"Associating partners with Allâh, magic, taking a life that Allâh has forbidden unless it is by a right, consuming usury, consuming the wealth of an orphan, fleeing on the day of battle, and slandering chaste innocent women."[1]

In Islam, the magician's punishment is execution — by being struck on his neck with a sword. The Messenger of Allâh ﷺ said:

---

[1] Agreed upon. Recorded by Al-Bukhari (3:195), Muslim (1:92) from Abu Hurairah, may Allâh be pleased with him.

«حَدُّ السَّاحِرِ ضَرْبُهُ بِالسَّيْفِ»

The punishment of the magician is striking him with the sword.[1]

The one who is deceived by magicians, believing in them, going to them, and seeking a cure from an ailment or help in any matter that involves the unseen, has indeed disbelieved in what was revealed to Muhammad ﷺ.

The proof for that: The Prophet ﷺ said:

«لَيْسَ مِنَّا مَنْ تَطَيَّرَ أَوْ تُطُيِّرَ لَهُ أَوْ تَكَهَّنَ أَوْ تُكُهِّنَ لَهُ، أَوْ سَحَرَ أَوْ سُحِرَ لَهُ»

These are not from us: one who sees (and believes in) an evil omen or has someone else see it for him, one who predicts the future or has someone predict it for him, and one who performs magic or has it performed for him.[2]

Abu Hurairah, may Allâh be pleased with him, related that the Prophet ﷺ said:

«مَنْ أَتَى كَاهِناً فَصَدَّقَهُ بِمَا يَقُولُ فَقَدْ كَفَرَ بِمَا أُنْزِلَ عَلَى مُحَمَّدٍ»

Whoever goes to a soothsayer and believes in what he says, has indeed disbelieved in what has been revealed to Muhammad.

It was recorded by Abu Dawud and the remainder of the four *Sunan* Compilers.

2) *Ruqya* (Incantations):

From this category, Islam forbade that which involves *Shirk*, such as invoking anyone other than Allâh, seeking help from anyone other than Allâh, or seeking protection from anyone other than Allâh. Examples of such spells are those that use the names of angels, of devils, of jinn, and so on.

---

[1] Recorded by At-Tirmithi (4:60). Its chain contains Isma'il bin Muslim Al-Makki who was graded weak in *Hadith*. See the discussion of At-Tirmithi after the *Hadith*.

[2] Shaikh Muhammad bin 'Abdul-Wahhab mentioned this in his *Kitab At-Tawhid*, and he attributed it to Al-Bazzar, with a good (*Jayyid*) chain. See *Fathul-Majid* 237.

However, if, having the same purpose, one recites verses of the Qur'ân, says Allâh's Names or Attributes, or supplicates to Allâh alone, then that is permissible because it doesn't involve *Shirk*.

'Awf bin Malik, may Allâh be pleased with him, said that they used to recite incantations during the days of ignorance and so he asked, "O Messenger of Allâh, how do you view that?" The Prophet ﷺ answered, "Present to me your *Ruqya*; there is no harm in using *Ruqya* (incantations that are read over the sick) as long as there is no *Shirk* involved."[1]

The *Ruqya* Of The Prophet ﷺ:

The Messenger of Allâh ﷺ would use *Ruqya*; one form that is related to us from him is the following:

«اللَّهُمَّ رَبَّ النَّاسِ أَذْهِبِ الْبَاسَ، وَاشْفِ أَنْتَ الشَّافِي لَا شِفَاءَ إِلَّا شِفَاؤُكَ. شِفَاءً لَا يُغَادِرُ سَقَماً»

O Allâh, Lord of mankind, take away the severe sickness, and cure: You are the Curer; there is no cure except Your cure, a cure that leaves behind no sickness.[2]

3) *At-Tama'im*, the plural of *Tamimah* (An Amulet):

It is something that one hangs on the neck of children; it consists of beads or other materials. They claimed that it would protect them from evil and envy.

The Prophet ﷺ forbade the use of such things, because no one drives away evil and envy except Allâh. The Messenger of Allâh ﷺ said:

«مَنْ تَعَلَّقَ تَمِيمَةً فَلَا أَتَمَّ اللهُ لَهُ، وَمَنْ عَلَّقَ وَدَعَةً فَلَا وَدَّعَ اللهُ لَهُ»

Whoever wears a *Tamimah*, then may Allâh not complete for him his affair, and whoever wears a charm, Allâh will entrust him to it.[3]

According to the correct view, it is not only forbidden to wear a *Tamimah* around one's neck, but it is also forbidden to hang a small

---

[1] Recorded by Muslim and Abu Dawud.
[2] Al-Bukhari in the Book of Patients (5675), as well as Muslim (2191).
[3] Ahmad (4:154 and 156)

copy of the Qur'ân around one's neck, first because of the general prohibition, and second because we must block the door to further evils.[1]

To hang up other things around one's neck, seeking some sort of benefit is an act of *Shirk*. It has been reported that the Prophet ﷺ said:

«مَنْ عَلَّقَ تَمِيمَةً فَقَدْ أَشْرَكَ»

Whoever hangs a *Tamimah* has indeed committed *Shirk*.[2]

4) *At-Tiwalah* (Spells To Cause Love):

It is an item that a woman makes, thinking that it has power to make her more beloved to her husband. The Prophet ﷺ forbade this practice because through it, one seeks benefit or seeks to ward off harm from other than Allâh, which is why it has been related in a *Hadith*:

«إِنَّ الرُّقَى وَالتَّمَائِمَ وَالتِّوَلَةَ شِرْكٌ»

Indeed, *Ar-Ruqya*, *At-Tama'im*, and *At-Tiwalah* are *Shirk*.[3]

Whoever Depends On Something, Then He Is Entrusted to It

Whoever believes that some of the forbidden matters mentioned above have a special effect on things, such as the ability to cure the sick, to fulfill needs, to ward off evil, to bring back the lost, or so on, then Allâh forsakes that person, leaving him to what he believes. The Messenger of Allâh ﷺ said:

«مَنْ تَعَلَّقَ شَيْئاً وُكِلَ إِلَيْهِ»

Whoever depends upon something, he is left to it.

This means that whoever turns not to Allâh but to another, with his heart attached to that other, all the while forgetting Allâh, then Allâh forsakes that person, leaving him to the object of his trust or worship. But whoever trusts Allâh, entrusts Him his affairs, and his

---

[1] This opinion is held by Ibn Mas'ud, Ibn 'Abbas, may Allâh be pleased with them, some of the *Tabi'in*, and the noble Shaikh, 'Abdul-'Aziz bin Baz.

[2] *As-Silsilah As-Sahibah* no. 492 and *Sahih Al-Jami'* no. 6394.

[3] Abu Dawud (4:212) and Ibn Majah (2:1167), from Ibn 'Abbas.

heart is attached to Allâh, then Allâh suffices him, protecting him from all evil, making easy for him every difficult matter, and saving him from every trial. Allâh Almighty says:

$$﴿وَمَن يَتَوَكَّلْ عَلَى ٱللَّهِ فَهُوَ حَسْبُهُۥٓ﴾$$

And whosoever puts his trust in Allâh, then He will suffice him.[1]

Exaggerating Over the Righteous People

Islam forbids us from exceeding the proper bounds when it comes to praising people or glorifying them. Muslims know that no matter how high the level is of a person, he is still a creature of Allâh. Allâh Almighty says:

$$﴿إِن كُلُّ مَن فِى ٱلسَّمَٰوَٰتِ وَٱلْأَرْضِ إِلَّآ ءَاتِى ٱلرَّحْمَٰنِ عَبْدًا﴾$$

There is none in the heavens and the earth but comes to the Most Beneficent as a slave.[2]

Islam forbade us from exceeding the proper bounds in this matter so that *Tawhid* may remain pure and clean, and so that deeds may be performed purely for Allâh. Exaggerating the good qualities of people most definitely leads to associating partners with Allâh.

In this regard, we have the example of the Christians, who continued to exaggerate the qualities of 'Iesa, peace be upon him, until they made Him a god on one occasion, and the son of a god on another, and a part of a god on yet another occasion — all of which is disbelief itself. Allâh Almighty says:

$$﴿لَّقَدْ كَفَرَ ٱلَّذِينَ قَالُوٓا۟ إِنَّ ٱللَّهَ هُوَ ٱلْمَسِيحُ ٱبْنُ مَرْيَمَ﴾$$

Surely, they have disbelieved who say: "Allâh is the Messiah, son of Maryam."[3]

$$﴿لَّقَدْ كَفَرَ ٱلَّذِينَ قَالُوٓا۟ إِنَّ ٱللَّهَ ثَالِثُ ثَلَٰثَةٍ﴾$$

---

[1] (*At-Talaq* 65:3)

[2] (*Maryam* 19:93)

[3] (*Al-Ma'idah* 5:72)

Surely, disbelievers are those who said: "Allâh is the third of the three."[1]

They only deviated so far from the correct path because they exceeded the proper bounds regarding 'Iesa. Allâh clarified that fact and made clear to them the way of the truth, saying:

﴿يَٰٓأَهۡلَ ٱلۡكِتَٰبِ لَا تَغۡلُوا۟ فِى دِينِكُمۡ وَلَا تَقُولُوا۟ عَلَى ٱللَّهِ إِلَّا ٱلۡحَقَّ﴾

O People of the Scripture (Jews and Christians)! Do not exceed the limits in your religion, nor say of Allâh but the truth.[2]

So that the Muslims are saved from what other nations have fallen into; the Prophet ﷺ said:

«لَا تُطۡرُونِي كَمَا أَطۡرَتِ النَّصَارَى ابۡنَ مَرۡيَمَ. إِنَّمَا أَنَا عَبۡدٌ. فَقُولُوا: عَبۡدُ اللهِ وَرَسُولُهُ»

Do not praise me as the Christians praised the son of Maryam; indeed, I am only a slave, so say, "The slave of Allâh and His Messenger."[3]

Overexaggerating the Righteous People Is The Basis For The Worship Of Idols

It has been related that the names of the idols that were worshipped are the names of righteous people; they had followers who would glorify them, and when they died, those followers said, "Let us erect statues where they used to gather so that we may continue to remember them." When that generation died and when much time passed, future generations came, not knowing the purpose of the statues; the *Shaitan* seduced them into believing that their fathers and grandfathers used to worship the statues, and so they began to do the same.

---

[1] (*Al-Ma'idah* 5:73)
[2] (*An-Nisa'* 4:171)
[3] Recorded by Al-Bukhari in the Book of the Prophets.

The Second Pillar: Prayer

From its conditions is purity,[1] which is to be performed:

You must acquaint yourself with purification, which is of three kinds.

First, *Wudhu'* (Ablution):

It is a compulsory mode of purification that is performed after the lesser *Hadath* (matters that cause one to exit from a state of purity) occurs. Examples of the lesser *Hadath* occurring are when one urinates, defecates, passes wind, falls into a deep sleep, or eats the meat of a camel.

How To Perform *Wudhu'*

1) Make intention in your heart, and not with your tongue, to perform *Wudhu'*. The Prophet ﷺ wouldn't utter his intention — not for his *Wudhu'*, not for his prayer, and not any of his other acts of worship. And because Allâh Almighty knows what is in our hearts, He doesn't need to be informed of it verbally.

2) Begin with Allâh's Name, saying, "*Bismillâh* (In the Name of Allâh)."

3) Next, wash your hands three times.

4) Put water in your mouth, shake it, and then expel it. After you put a handful of water in your mouth, moving that hand upwards, inhale through your nose the water that remains in your hand (exaggerate when you inhale, unless you are fasting), and then blow the water out through your nose, slightly squeezing the two sides of your nose, making sure all of the water comes out. Repeat this process three times.

5) Wash your face three times — in terms of width, from one ear to the other; and in terms of length, from where the hair on your head begins to grow to the bottom of your beard.

6) Then wash your hands and forearms three times — from the tips of your fingers until — and including — your elbows. Begin with the right arm, and then move on to the left one.

7) Wipe your head once with your wet hands; pass them over your

---

[1] Taken from a dissertation by Shaikh Muhammad bin Salih Al-'Uthaimin.

head, moving from the front of your head until the back, and then returning. Then wipe your ears (without wetting your hands again).

8) Wash your feet, including your ankles, three times.

Second, *Al-Ghusl* (Bath):

It is performed after the greater kind of *Hadath* takes place. Examples of the greater kind of *Hadath* are menstruation and sexual intercourse. *Al-Ghusl* is performed as follows:

1) Make intention with your heart, and not with your tongue, to perform *Ghusl*.

2) Begin with Allâh's Name, saying, "*Bismillâh* (In the Name of Allâh)."

3) Perform the *Wudhu'* in its entirety.

4) Generously pour water over your head three times.

5) Finally, wash the rest of your body.

Third, *At-Tayammum* (Dry Ablution):

It is an obligatory form of purification that is performed using clean earth, and it is a substitute for *Wudhu'* and *Ghusl* — and it is performed by someone who cannot find water or who can find water, but will somehow be harmed by using it.

How To Perform *At-Tayammum*

Make intention to perform *Tayammum* as a replacement for either the *Wudhu'* or *Ghusl* (whichever of the two was obligatory upon you). Next, strike the earth — or whatever is connected to the earth, such as walls — and then wipe your face and hands.

How Does A Sick Person Purify Himself?

1) Like others, the sick person must purify himself with water, performing *Wudhu'* from the lesser *Hadath*, and performing *Ghusl* from the greater *Hadath*.

2) If he cannot purify himself using water — either because he is not able to, or because he fears that his sickness will intensify, or he fears that the healing process will be delayed — then he must perform *Tayammum*.

3) To perform *Tayammum*, he must strike the ground once. Then

he must wipe his entire face, and then finally, he wipes his hands, wiping one against the other.

4) If a sick person is not able to purify himself, then another person should administer *Wudhu'* or *Tayammum* (whichever applies) for him.

5) If some of the *Wudhu'* areas are injured, then one should wash those areas with water. If washing worsens the injury, one may pass wet hands over the affected area. If even wiping wet hands would worsen the injury, one may perform *Tayammum* over the affected area.

6) If some of the *Wudhu'* areas are injured and are bound in cloth or plaster, then rather than washing those areas, one may pass wet hands over them. In this instance, *Tayammum* is not necessary because wiping replaces washing.

7) It is permissible to perform *Tayammum* using a wall or anything pure that has dust on it. But if the wall is wiped over with a material other than what comes from the ground, such as paint, then *Tayammum* is not performed using it unless it has dust on it.

8) If *Tayammum* cannot be performed using the ground or wall or anything else that has dust, then there is no harm in putting dust in a container or on a handkerchief and then performing *Tayammum* using that dust.

9) When one performs *Tayammum* for prayer and then remains in a state of purity when the time for the next prayer arrives, then one may perform that second prayer based upon the *Tayammum* that he performed earlier. So because he remains in a state of purity, and because nothing takes him out of that state, he doesn't need to repeat the *Tayammum* for the second prayer.

10) The sick person must purify his body from all impurities, but in case that he is not able to remove those impurities, he may pray as he is: his prayer is correct and he doesn't have to repeat it.

11) The sick person must offer his prayer wearing a clean and pure garment. If the garment is soiled by an impurity, he must wash it or change into a clean and pure garment. In case that it is not

possible for him to change his clothing or clean the clothes he is wearing, he may pray as he is: his prayer is correct and he doesn't have to repeat it.

12) The sich person must pray on something pure. If the area became impure, then it is his duty to wash it or to put something pure over it.

13) The sick person may not delay the prayer until its time is over; his inability to purify himself is not an excuse. He must purify himself as much as he is able to and then he must pray his prayer in time, even if there is an impurity he is unable to remove — on his body, his garment, or the place where he is praying.

As-Salat: The Prayer

As-Salat is a form of worship that consists of both sayings and actions: it opens with the *Takbir* (saying, "*Allâhu Akbar*") and it ends with the *Taslim* (saying, "*As-Salaamu 'Alaikum wa-Rahmatullah*").

What follows is a description of the Prophet's prayer,[1] which we present to every male and female Muslim, so that all who read it may strive to follow the Prophet ﷺ, for he ﷺ said:

«صَلُّوا كَمَا رَأَيْتُمُونِي أُصَلِّي»

Offer *Salat* (prayer) as you have seen me praying.[2]

Here is how you should pray, based on the Prophet's prayer:

1) Completely perform the *Wudhu'* — meaning, perform it as Allâh Almighty ordered you to perform it, for Allâh says:

﴿يَٰٓأَيُّهَا ٱلَّذِينَ ءَامَنُوٓاْ إِذَا قُمۡتُمۡ إِلَى ٱلصَّلَوٰةِ فَٱغۡسِلُواْ وُجُوهَكُمۡ وَأَيۡدِيَكُمۡ إِلَى ٱلۡمَرَافِقِ وَٱمۡسَحُواْ بِرُءُوسِكُمۡ وَأَرۡجُلَكُمۡ إِلَى ٱلۡكَعۡبَيۡنِ﴾

O you who believe! When you intend to offer *As-Salat* (the

---

[1] From a dissertation written by the noble *Mufti* of the Kingdom of Saudi Arabia, Ash-Shaikh 'Abdul-'Aziz bin 'Abdullah bin Baz.

[2] Al-Bukhari no. (631), in a *Hadith* related by Malik bin Huwairith, may Allâh be pleased with him.

prayer), wash your faces and your hands (forearms) up to the elbows, rub (by passing wet hands over) your heads, and (wash) your feet up to the ankles.[1]

And the Prophet ﷺ said:

«لَا تُقْبَلُ صَلَاةٌ بِغَيْرِ طُهُورٍ»

The prayer is not accepted without purification.[2]

2)   Face the *Qiblah*, which is the Ka'bah (in Makkah); no matter where you are, you must turn toward it when you pray.

3)   Formulate the *Niyyah* (intention), intending in your heart to pray the prayer you are about to pray — whether it is obligatory or voluntary.

4)   Do not utter the *Niyyah* with your tongue because doing so is not legislated in Islam; rather it is an innovation, for neither the Prophet ﷺ nor his Companions, may Allâh be pleased with them, uttered their intention.

5)   Place a *Sutrah*[3] before you; whether one is an *Imam*, or praying alone.

6)   You must face the *Qiblah*, an act that is one of the conditions of prayer, except in certain situations that are well known and that are clarified in the books of the scholars.

7)   Make the sacred *Takbir (Takbiratul-Ihram)*, saying, "*Allâhu Akbar*" — sacred because with it one enters the sacred state of prayer. As you are saying the *Takbir*, your eyes should be fixed on the place of your prostration.

8)   As you are making the *Takbir*, your hands should be raised to the level of either your shoulders or ears.

9)   Then place your hands on your chest, placing the right arm on your left hand, wrist, and forearm, for this practice is established in the Sunnah of the Prophet ﷺ.[4]

---

[1] (*Al-Ma'idah* 5:6)

[2] Muslim, in a *Hadith* related by Abu Hurairah, may Allâh be pleased with him.

[3] A *Sutrah* means an obstacle or barrier to prevent one who is walking from passing in front of the one praying, so as not to interrupt his prayer.

[4] Related by Ahmad, Abu Dawud, At-Tirmithi, and Ibn Majah — in a *Hadith* narrated by Wa'il bin Hujr.

10) It is Sunnah for you to recite the opening supplication:

«اللَّهُمَّ بَاعِدْ بَيْنِي وَبَيْنَ خَطَايَايَ، كَمَا بَاعَدْتَ بَيْنَ الْمَشْرِقِ وَالْمَغْرِبِ، اللَّهُمَّ نَقِّنِي مِنْ خَطَايَايَ، كَمَا يُنَقَّى الثَّوْبُ الأَبْيَضُ مِنَ الدَّنَسِ، اللَّهُمَّ اغْسِلْنِي مِنْ خَطَايَايَ، بِالْمَاءِ، وَالثَّلْجِ، وَالْبَرَدِ»

Allâhumma Baa'id Bainee wa Baina Khataayaaya, Kamaa Baa'adta Bainal-Mashriqi wal-Maghribi. Allâhumma Naqqi-nee Min Khataayaaya, Kamaa Unaqqath-Thawbul-Abyadhu Minad-Danas. Allâhummaghsilnee Min Khataayaaya, Bil-Maa'i, wath-Thalji, wal-Barad.

O Allâh, distance me from my sins just as You have distanced the east from the west. O Allâh, purify me of my sins as a white robe is purified of filth. O Allâh, cleanse me of my sins with water snow, and hail.[1]

11) You may recite the previous supplication or you may replace it with the following one:

«سُبْحَانَكَ اللَّهُمَّ وَبِحَمْدِكَ، وَتَبَارَكَ اسْمُكَ، وَتَعَالَى جَدُّكَ، وَلَا إِلَهَ غَيْرُكَ»

Subhaanaka Allâhumma wa Bihamdika, wa Tabaarak-asmuka, wa Ta'alaa Jadduka, wa Laa Ilaha Ghairuka.

How perfect You are, O Allâh, and I praise You. Blessed is Your Name, and lofty is Your position and none has the right to be worshipped except You.[2]

12) It is also permissible to read other opening invocations, as long as they are authentically established in the Sunnah of the Prophet ﷺ. It is best, however, to change, reciting one opening invocation during one prayer and another invocation during another prayer; by doing so, you are more complete in your following of the Sunnah.

13) Then recite:

---

[1] Al-Bukhari (744), Muslim (598) — in a *Hadith* related by Abu Hurairah, may Allâh be pleased with him.

[2] Related by Muslim, from the practice of 'Umar. *Sharh Muslim* (4:111).

«أَعُوذُ بِاللهِ مِنَ الشَّيْطَانِ الرَّجِيمِ، بِسْمِ اللهِ الرَّحْمٰنِ الرَّحِيمِ»

A'oothu Billâhi Minash-Shaitaanir-Rajeem, Bismillâhhir-Rahmaanir-Raheem.

"I take protection in Allâh from the accursed *Shaitan*. In the Name of Allâh, the Most Beneficent, the Most Merciful."

14) Next, recite *Surat Al-Fatihah*, for the Prophet ﷺ said:

«لَا صَلَاةَ لِمَنْ لَمْ يَقْرَأْ بِفَاتِحَةِ الْكِتَابِ»

There is no prayer for the one who doesn't read the Opening of the Book.[1]

15) After you finish reciting *Al-Fatihah*, say:

«آمِينَ»

"Aameen"

out loud for the spoken prayers and to yourself in the quiet prayers.

16) Then recite what is easy for you from the Qur'ân.

17) After *Al-Fatihah*, it is best to recite from the middle *Mufassil Surahs* in the *Zuhr*, *'Asr*, and *'Isha'* prayers.

18) In *Fajr* Prayer, read the longer *Surahs*.

19) In the *Maghrib* prayer, sometimes read the longer *Surahs* and sometimes the short ones, so as to apply every *Hadith* that is related to this issue.

20) Next comes the bowing position (*Ruku'*).

21) As you are about to bow, raise your hands to the level of your shoulders or ears, and say, "*Allâhu Akbar* (Allâh is the Most Great)". In the *Ruku'*, make sure that your head is parallel to your back. Place your hands on your knees, separating your fingers. Reach a level of calmness and tranquility in your *Ruku'*.

22) While in *Ruku'*, say:

«سُبْحَانَ رَبِّيَ الْعَظِيمِ»

---

[1] Al-Bukhari (756), Muslim (394) (38) — in a *Hadith* narrated by 'Ubadah bin As-Samit, may Allâh be pleased with him.

Subhaana Rabbiyal-'Atheem.

How perfect my Lord is, the Supreme.

23) It is best to recite that phrase three or more times.

24) In addition to that phrase, it is recommended for you to also say:

«سُبْحَانَكَ اللَّهُمَ رَبَّنَا وَبِحَمْدِكَ اللَّهُمَّ اغْفِرْ لِي»

Subhaanaka Allâhumma, Rabbana wa Bihamdika, Allâhummaghfir lee.

How perfect You are, O Allâh, our Lord and I praise You. O Allâh, forgive me.[1]

25) Next, one rises from the *Ruku'*.

26) Rise from the *Ruku'*, raising your hands to the level of either your shoulders or ears, saying (whether *Imam* or individual worshipper):

«سَمِعَ اللهُ لِمَنْ حَمِدَهُ»

Sami' Allâhu Liman Hamidah.

Allâh listens to those who praise Him.

27) As soon as you reach the standing position, say:

«رَبَّنَا وَلَكَ الْحَمْدُ حَمْدًا كَثِيرًا طَيِّبًا مُبَارَكًا فِيهِ مِلْءَ السَّمَاوَاتِ، وَمِلْءَ الْأَرْضِ، وَمِلْءَ مَا بَيْنَهُمَا، وَمِلْءَ مَاشِئْتَ مِنْ شَيْءٍ بَعْدُ»

Rabbana wa Lakal-Hamdu, Hamdan Katheeran Tayyiban, Mubaarakan Feeh, Mil'as-Samaawaati wa Mil'al-Ardhi, wa Mil'a Ma Bainahuma wa Mil'a Maa Shi'ta Min Shay'in Ba'd.

Our Lord, for You is all praise, an abundant beautiful blessed praise. The heavens and the earth and all between them abound with Your praises and all that You will abound with Your praise.[2]

Because it is established in the Sunnah of the Prophet ﷺ, it is also good for you to continue, saying:

---

[1] Al-Bukhari (484), in a *Hadith* related by 'Aishah, may Allâh be pleased with her.
[2] Muslim (476) from 'Abdulluah bin Abi Awfa.

«أَهْلَ الثَّنَاءِ وَالْمَجْدِ، أَحَقُّ مَا قَالَ الْعَبْدُ، وَكُلُّنَا لَكَ عَبْدٌ، اللَّهُمَّ لَا مَانِعَ لِمَا أَعْطَيْتَ وَلَا مُعْطِيَ لِمَا مَنَعْتَ، وَلَا يَنْفَعُ ذَا الْجَدِّ مِنْكَ الْجَدُّ»

Ahlath-Thana'i wal-Majdi, Ahaqqu Maa Qaalal-'Abdu, wa Kullunaa Laka 'Abdun, Allâhumma Laa Maani'a Limaa A'taita wa Laa Mu'tiya Limaa Man'ata, wa Laa Yanfa'u Thal-Jaddi Minkal-Jadd.

O Possessor of praise and majesty, the truest thing a worshipper has said (of You) and we are all Your worshippers. O Allâh, none can prevent what You have willed to bestow and none can bestow what You have willed to prevent, and no wealth or majesty can benefit anyone, as from You is all wealth and majesty.[1]

28) If you are following an *Imam*, then say:

«رَبَّنَا وَلَكَ الْحَمْدُ»

Rabbana wa Lakal-Hamd

Our Lord, and for You is all praise

until the end of what has preceded.

29) It is recommended for you to then place your hands on your chest, just as you did before bowing, for it is a practice that is established in the Sunnah of the Prophet ﷺ; it is related by Wa'il bin Hujr and Sahl bin Sa'd, may Allâh be pleased with them.

30) Next comes the prostration (*Sajdah*).

31) As you are going down for *Sajdah*, say the *Takbir*. When you go down, let your knees touch the ground before your hands do — if that is possible for you.

32) If doing the above is difficult for you, you may allow for your hands to precede your knees in touching the ground.

33) During the *Sajdah*, your fingers, hands and feet should be facing the *Qiblah*; also, your fingers should be joined and stretched.

---

[1] Muslim (477) (205).

34) Make sure that seven body parts are touching the ground: your forehead along with your nose (this is considered as one), your two hands, your knees, and the bottom of the toes of your feet.

35) While prostrating, say:

«سُبْحَانَ رَبِّيَ الأَعْلَى»

Subhaana Rabbiyal-A'laa.

How Perfect my Lord is, the Most High.

36) It is Sunnah to say that phrase three times or more.

37) Along with that phrase, it is recommended to say:

«سُبْحَانَكَ اللَّهُمَّ رَبَّنَا وَبِحَمْدِكَ اللَّهُمَّ اغْفِرْلِي»

Subhaanaka Allâhumma, Rabbana wa Bihamdika, Allâhummaghfir lee.

How perfect You are, O Allâh, our Lord, and I praise You. O Allâh, forgive me.[1]

38) While in *Sajdah*, you should make much supplication, for the Prophet ﷺ said,

«أَمَّا الرُّكُوعُ؛ فَعَظِّمُوا فِيهِ الرَّبَّ؛ وَأَمَّا السُّجُودُ؛ فَاجْتَهِدُوا فِي الدُّعَاءِ؛ فَإِنَّه قَمِنٌ أَنْ يُسْتَجَابَ لَكُمْ»

As for the bowing, glorify your Lord therein; and as for the prostration, be diligent in supplication, for it is a time when you are worthy of being answered.[2]

39) Ask your Lord for good in both this world and the Hereafter — regardless of whether you are praying an obligatory prayer or a voluntary one.

40) Distance your upper arms from your sides, your stomach from your thighs, and your thighs from your calves. And raise your elbows above the ground, for the Prophet ﷺ said:

«اعْتَدِلُوا فِي السُّجُودِ، وَلَا يَبْسُطْ أَحَدُكُمْ ذِرَاعَيْهِ انْبِسَاطَ الْكَلْبِ»

---

[1] Al-Bukhari (817, 417), in a *Hadith* related by 'Aishah, may Allâh be pleased with her.

[2] Muslim (479) (207), in a *Hadith* related by Ibn 'Abbas, may Allâh be pleased with them.

Be balanced while prostrating, and let not one of you flatten and extend your arms as a dog does.[1]

41) Next, rise from the *Sajdah*.

42) As you are rising from *Sajdah*, say the *Takbir*. Rest your left foot on the ground and sit on it. Make your right foot stand erect, and place your hands on your thighs and knees.

43) While seated, say:

«رَبِّ اغْفِرْ لِي، وَارْحَمْنِي، وَاهْدِنِي، وَارْزُقْنِي، وَعَافِنِي وَاجْبُرْنِي»

Rabbighfir lee, warhamnee, wahdinee, warzuqnee, wa 'Aafinee, wajburnee.

My Lord forgive me, have mercy upon me, guide me, grant me sustenance, pardon me, and console me.[2]

44) Achieve calmness in this seated position.

45) Then go down for the second *Sajdah*, after which you stand up for the second unit.

46) As you are going down for the second *Sajdah*, say the *Takbir*, and do in that second *Sajdah* what you did in the first one.

47) As you are rising from the second *Sajdah*, say the *Takbir*, and sit down for a very brief amount of time; this is called the "*Jalsatul Istirahah* (the sitting of rest)''. It is recommended, and so if one does not perform it, there is no harm. During this brief seated position, there is no invocation or supplication that you should read.

48) Then stand up for the second unit, rising not with your hands, but with your knees.

49) Recite *Al-Fatihah*, followed by whatever is easy for you from the Qur'ân.

50) Until the second prostration, do as you did in the first unit.

51) How to sit for the *Tashahhud*:

---

[1] Al-Bukhari (722), and Muslim (893) (223), in a *Hadith* related by Anas, may Allâh be pleased with him.

[2] Recorded by Ahmad (1:371) Abu Dawud (850) At-Tirmithi (284, 285) Ibn Majah (898) and Al-Hakim (1:271) and he graded it *Sahih*, from Ibn 'Abbas, may Allâh be pleased with them.

If you are praying a prayer that comprises of two units only — such as the *Fajr*, *Jumu'ah*, and *'Eid* prayers — you will remain seated after the second prostration, with your right foot erected, your left foot rested on the ground, and your right hand placed on your right thigh. Clench all of the fingers of your right hand into the shape of a fist, except for the index finger, with which you will point indicating *Tawhid*. It is also correct to clench only your pinkie and ring finger, while you make a ring shape using your middle finger and thumb, all the while indicating *Tawhid* with your index finger. Both ways are established in the Sunnah of the Prophet ﷺ.

52) Because both of the previous ways are established in the Sunnah, it is best to apply each, sometimes applying the first method and sometimes applying the second one.

53) For the sitting position, place your left hand on your left thigh and knee.

54) Reciting *At-Tashahhud* and sending blessing upon the Prophet ﷺ:

55) Recite the *Tashahhud*:

«التَّحِيَّاتُ للهِ وَالصَّلَوَاتُ وَالطَّيِّبَاتُ، السَّلَامُ عَلَيْكَ أَيُّهَا النَّبِيُّ وَرَحْمَةُ اللهِ وَبَرَكَاتُهُ، السَّلَامُ عَلَيْنَا وَعَلَى عِبَادِ اللهِ الصَّالِحِينَ، أَشْهَدُ أَنْ لَا إِلَهَ إِلَّا اللهُ، وَأَشْهَدُ أَنَّ مُحَمَّدًا عَبْدُهُ وَرَسُولُهُ»

At-Tahiyyatu-lillaahi was-Salawaatu wat-Tayyibaatu, As-Salaamu 'Alaika Ayyuhan-Nabiyyu, wa Rahmatullâhi wa Barakaatuhu. As-Salaamu 'Alainaa wa 'Alaa 'Ibaadillahis-Saaliheen. Ash-hadu An laa Ilaha Illallâhu, wa Ash-hadu Anna Muhammadan 'Abduhu wa Rasooluhu.

Greetings to Allâh, and blessings and goodness. Peace and the mercy and blessings of Allâh be upon you O Prophet. Peace be upon us and all of Allâh's righteous servants. I bear witness that none has the right to be worshipped except Allâh and I bear witness that Muhammad is His servant and Messenger.[1]

---

[1] Related by Al-Bukhari (6230), Muslim (402) (55), narrated by Ibn Mas'ud, may Allâh be pleased with him.

56) Then send the blessings saying:

«اللَّهُمَّ صَلِّ عَلَى مُحَمَّدٍ وَعَلَى آلِ مُحَمَّدٍ، كَمَا صَلَّيْتَ عَلَى إِبْرَاهِيمَ وَآلِ إِبْرَاهِيمَ، إِنَّكَ حَمِيدٌ مَجِيدٌ، وَبَارِكْ عَلَى مُحَمَّدٍ وَعَلَى آلِ مُحَمَّدٍ، كَمَا بَارَكْتَ عَلَى إِبْرَاهِيمَ وَآلِ إِبْرَاهِيمَ، إِنَّكَ حَمِيدٌ مَجِيدٌ»

Allâhumma Salli 'Alaa Muhammadin wa 'Alaa Aali Muhammadin, Kamaa Sallaita 'Alaa Ibraheema wa Aali Ibraheema, Innaka Hameedun Majeed. Wa Baarik 'Alaa Muhammadin wa 'Alaa Aali Muhammadin, Kamaa Baarakta 'Alaa Ibraheema wa Aali Ibraheema, Innaka Hameedun Majeed.

O Allâh, bestow Your favor upon Muhammad and the family of Muhammad, just as You bestowed Your favor upon Ibrahim and upon the family of Ibrahim. Verily, You are full of praise, Most Glorious. And send blessings upon Muhammad and upon the family of Muhammad, just as You sent blessings upon Ibrahim and upon the family of Ibrahim. Verily, You are full of praise, Most Glorious.[1]

57) Next, seek protection in Allâh from four, saying,

«اللَّهُمَّ إِنِّي أَعُوذُ بِكَ مِنْ عَذَابِ جَهَنَّمَ، وَمِنْ عَذَابِ الْقَبْرِ، وَمِنْ فِتْنَةِ الْمَحْيَا وَالْمَمَاتِ، وَمِنْ فِتْنَةِ الْمَسِيحِ الدَّجَّالِ»

Allâhumma Inee A'oothu Bika Min 'Athaabi Jahannam, wa Min 'Athaabil-Qabr, wa Min Fitnatil-Mahyaa wal-Mamaat, wa Min Fitnatil-Maseehid-Dajjaal.

O Allâh, I take refuge in You from the punishment of the grave, from the torment of the Fire, from the trials and tribulations of life and death and from the evil affliction of Al-Masih Ad-Dajjal.[2]

58) Then supplicate, asking for whatever you wish, in terms of good in this life and the Hereafter. It is correct here to also supplicate

---

[1] Related by Al-Bukhari (3370) and Muslim (406) (66), narrated by Ka'b bin 'Ujrah, may Allâh be pleased with him.
[2] Related by Muslim (590,) (134) from Abu Hurairah, may Allâh be pleased with him.

for one's parents or for anyone else – regardless of whether it is a compulsory or voluntary prayer, for in a *Hadith* related by Ibn Mas'ud, may Allâh be pleased with him, the Prophet ﷺ said:

«ثُمَّ لِيَتَخَيَّرْ مِنَ الدُّعَاءِ أَعْجَبَهُ إِلَيْهِ، فَيَدْعُو»

Then let him choose that supplication which pleases him most, and let him supplicate (with it).[1]

And in another wording:

«ثُمَّ لْيَخْتَرْ بَعْدُ مِنَ الْمَسْأَلَةِ مَا شَاءَ»

Then, afterwards, let him choose to ask what he pleases.

59) Finally, turn to your right and left, each time saying:

«السَّلَامُ عَلَيْكُمْ وَرَحْمَةُ اللهِ»

As-Salaamu 'Alaikum wa Rahmatullâh.

May the peace and mercy of Allâh be upon you.

A description of the three-unit and four-unit prayer:

60) If the prayer comprises of three units – such as the *Maghrib* prayer – or four units – such as the *Zuhr*, *'Asr*, or *'Isha'* prayers – recite the *Tashahhud* that is mentioned above and send blessings upon the Prophet ﷺ.

61) Then stand up, rising not with your hands, but with your knees.

62) As soon as you are standing, raise your hands to the level of your ears or shoulders, saying, *"Allâhu Akbar."*

63) Then, as before, place your hands on your chest.

64) Recite only *Al-Fatihah*.

65) In the third and fourth units of prayer, if you sometimes recite more than *Al-Fatihah*, then that is also correct, for a *Hadith* related by Abu Sa'id, may Allâh be pleased with him, indicates its that this is correct.[2]

66) In the seated position of the third unit of *Maghrib* or the fourth unit of *Zuhr*, *'Asr*, or *'Isha'*, recite exactly those invocations that

---

[1] Al-Bukhari (835), Muslim (502) (55).

[2] The *Hadith* is related in Muslim (752) (156)

you recite in the sitting position of the two-unit prayer.

67) Then turn to your right and left, each time making *Taslim* (i.e., saying, "*As-Salaamu 'Alaikum wa-Rahmatullah*"). When you finish making your second *Taslim*, say, "*Astaghfirullâh* (I seek forgiveness from Allâh)'' three times.

68) Then say:

«اللَّهُمَّ أَنْتَ السَّلَامُ وَمِنْكَ السَّلَامُ، تَبَارَكْتَ يَا ذَا الْجَلَالِ وَالْإِكْرَامِ»

Allâhumma Antas-Salaam, wa Minkas-Salaam, Tabaarakta Yaa Thal-Jalaali wal-Ikram.

O Allâh, You are peace and from You is all peace, You have blessed us, O Possessor of majesty and honor.[1]

69) Also say:

«لَا إِلَهَ إِلَّا اللهُ وَحْدَهُ لَا شَرِيكَ لَهُ، لَهُ الْمُلْكُ وَلَهُ الْحَمْدُ، وَهُوَ عَلَى كُلِّ شَيْءٍ قَدِيرٌ، اللَّهُمَّ لَا مَانِعَ لِمَا أَعْطَيْتَ، وَلَا مُعْطِيَ لِمَا مَنَعْتَ، وَلَا يَنْفَعُ ذَا الْجَدِّ مِنْكَ الْجَدُّ»

Laa Ilaha Illallâhu Wahdahu Laa Shareeka Lahu, Lahul-Mulku wa Lahul-Hamdu, wa Huwa 'Alaa Kulli Shay'in Qadeer. Allâhumma Laa Maani'a Limaa 'A'taita, wa Laa Mu'tiya Limaa Mana'ta, wa Laa Yunfa'u Thal-Jaddi Minkal-Jadd.

None has the right to be worshipped except Allâh, alone, without partner, to Him belongs all sovereignty and praise and He has power over all things. O Allâh, none can prevent what You have willed to bestow and none can bestow what You have willed to prevent, and no wealth or majesty can benefit anyone, as from You is all wealth and majesty.[2]

70) Then say:

«لَا حَوْلَ وَلَا قُوَّةَ إِلَّا بِاللهِ، لَا إِلَهَ إِلَّا اللهُ، وَلَا نَعْبُدُ إِلَّا إِيَّاهُ، لَهُ

---

[1] Related by Muslim (592) (136) from Thawban, may Allâh be pleased with him.
[2] Al-Bukhari (844), Muslim (593) (137), from Al-Mughirah bin Shu'bah, may Allâh be pleased with him.

النِّعْمَةُ وَلَهُ الْفَضْلُ وَلَهُ الثَّنَاءُ الْحَسَنُ، لَا إِلَهَ إِلَّا اللهُ، مُخْلِصِينَ لَهُ الدِّينَ وَلَوْ كَرِهَ الْكَافِرُونَ»

Laa Hawla wa Laa Quwwata Illa Billâh, Laa Ilaha Illallâh, wa Laa Na'budu 'Illa Iyyaah, Lahun-Ni'matu wa Lahul-Fadhlu, wa Lahuth-Thanaa'ul-Hasan. Laa Ilaha Illallâh, Mukhliseena Lahud-Deena wa Law Karihal-Kaafiroon.

There is neither might nor power except with Allâh, none has the right to be worshipped except Allâh and we worship none except Him. For Him is all favor, grace, and glorious praise. None has the right to be worshipped except Allâh and we are sincere in faith and devotion to Him although the disbelievers detest it.[1]

71) After that, say:

«سُبْحَانَ اللهِ»

Subhaanallâh (How perfect Allâh is!) thirty-three times,

«الْحَمْدُ للهِ»

Al-Hamdulillâh (All praise is for Allâh) thirty-three times,

«اللهُ أَكْبَرُ»

Allâhu Akbar (Allâh is the Most Great) thirty-three times, completing one hundred by saying once:

«لَا إِلَهَ إِلَّا اللهُ وَحْدَهُ لَا شَرِيكَ لَهُ، لَهُ الْمُلْكُ، وَلَهُ الْحَمْدُ وَهُوَ عَلَى كُلِّ شَيْءٍ قَدِيرٌ»

Laa Ilaha Illallâhu Wahdahu Laa Shareeka Lahu, Lahul-Mulku wa Lahul-Hamdu, wa Huwa 'Alaa Kulli Shay'in Qadeer.

None has the right to be worshipped except Allâh, alone, without partner, to Him belongs all sovereignty and praise and He has power over all things.[2]

---

[1] Muslim (593) (139) from 'Abdullah bin Az-Zubair, may Allâh be pleased with him.
[2] Muslim (597) (146) from Abu Hurairah, may Allâh be pleased with them.

72) Then recite *Ayatul-Kursi.*[1]

73) Follow *Ayatul-Kursi* by reciting the last three *Surahs* of the Qur'ân. Do so after every prayer.[2]

74) Because doing so is related from the Sunnah of the Prophet ﷺ, recite the last three *Surahs* of the Qur'ân three times each after the *Fajr* and *Maghrib* prayers.

All of the above-mentioned invocations are Sunnah and not *Fardh* (obligatory).

Sunnah And *Rawatib* Prayers:

75) It is legislated for every male and female Muslim to pray four units before *Zuhr*, and two units after it; two units after *Maghrib*; two units after *'Isha'*; two units before *Fajr*, making a total of 12 units.

76) The units referred to above are called *Ar-Rawatib* (regular *Sunnah* prayers; when he wasn't traveling, the Prophet ﷺ would consistently perform those prayers.

77) During travel, he wouldn't pray those units, except for the Sunnah (two units) of the *Fajr* prayer and the *Witr* prayer (odd number of units prayed either after the *'Isha'* prayer or after the late-night voluntary prayer). The Prophet ﷺ would make sure to perform these prayers when at home and when traveling.

78) It is best to perform the *Rawatib* and *Witr* prayers at home.

79) If you pray them in the *Masjid*, then that is good as well, for the Prophet ﷺ said:

«أَفْضَلُ صَلَاةِ الْمَرْءِ فِي بَيْتِهِ إِلَّا الْمَكْتُوبَةَ»

The best prayer of someone is to pray in his house except for the prescribed prayer.[3]

80) Praying the *Rawatib* units can help one enter Paradise, for the

---

[1] (*Al-Baqarah* 2:255) An-Nasa'i in *'Amalul-Yawm wal-Lailah* (123) with an authentic chain.

[2] Ahmad (4:155), Abu Dawud and Ibn Hibban in his *Sahih*, as mentioned in *Al-Mawarid* no. (2348).

[3] Al-Bukhari (7290), Muslim (781) (213), in a *Hadith* related by Zaid bin Thabit, may Allâh be pleased with him.

Prophet ﷺ said:

«مَنْ صَلَّى اثْنَتَيْ عَشَرَةَ رَكْعَةً فِي يَوْمِهِ وَلَيْلَتِهِ تَطَوُّعاً؛ بَنَى اللهُ لَهُ بَيْتاً فِي الْجَنَّةِ»

Whoever prays twelve units in a day and night, Allâh builds a house for him in Paradise.[1]

81) Four units before the *'Asr* prayer, two units before the *Maghrib* prayer, and two units before the *'Isha'* prayer – it is good for you to perform these prayers because authentic *Hadiths* indicate that they are legislated.

---

[1] Muslim, in his *Sahih* (728) (101), in a *Hadith* related by Umm Habibah, may Allâh be pleased with her.

The Prescribed Prayers And The Number Of Their Units

The Prescribed Prayer	Number of Units	The *Ratibah* (Singular of *Rawatib*) *Sunnah*
Zuhr Prayer	4 units	2 units before and 2 units after. It has also been said that there are four units before the *Zuhr* prayer.
'Asr Prayer	4 units	It is Sunnah to either pray 2 or 4 units before *'Asr* prayer; however, they are not from the *Rawatib* prayers
Maghrib Prayer	3 units	2 units after
'Isha' Prayer	4 units	2 units after
Fajr Prayer	2 units	2 units before

That Which Is *Makruh* (Hated or Extremely Disliked) During The Prayer[1]

1) It is *Makruh* for one to turn his head or avert his gaze during prayer, and raising one's eyes to the sky is forbidden.

2) It is *Makruh* to make frivolous movements or unnecessary actions during prayer.

3) While praying, it is *Makruh* for one to carry something that is distracting – such as something heavy – or to wear something that is distracting – such as a multi-colored shirt.

4) During prayer it is *Makruh* to rest one's hands on one's sides.

Matters That Nullify One's Prayer

1) Speaking, even if one does so briefly.

2) Turning away from the *Qiblah* with one's entire body.

3) Passing wind or doing anything that necessitates *Wudhu'* or *Ghusl*.

---

[1] From a dissertation by Shaikh Ibn 'Uthaimin.

4) Many and continuous unnecessary movements.

5) Laughing, even if it is a brief one.

6) On purpose, standing or sitting more than is legislated or making an extra *Ruku'* or *Sajdah*.

7) Preceding the *Imam* on purpose.

Rulings Related To The Prostration Of Forgetfulness During Prayer

1) If one forgets during prayer and performs an extra *Ruku'* or *Sajdah*, for example, then he makes the *Taslim* as he normally does, performs two prostrations for forgetfulness, and then makes *Taslim* again. For example, if one prays *Zuhr* (a 4-unit prayer), and by mistake stands up for the fifth unit, but then remembers or is reminded, he should return to the sitting position without making *Takbir*. He then reads the final *Tashahhud*, after which he makes *Taslim*, 2 prostrations of forgetfulness, and then *Taslim* again. Even if he only remembered the extra unit after finishing his prayer, he should make two prostrations and then make *Taslim*.

2) If one forgetfully makes *Taslim* before he completes his prayer, but then later remembers or is reminded of his mistake, he may continue the prayer from where he left off, as long as he remembers after a short period of time. Then when he finishes the prayer, he must make the two prostrations of forgetfulness, followed by the *Taslim*.

For example, one is praying the *Zuhr* prayer, and due to forgetfulness, makes *Taslim* in the third unit, ending his prayer. However, he then remembers his mistake or is reminded of it. In this case, he must perform the fourth unit, make *Taslim*, perform two prostrations for forgetfulness, and then make *Taslim* again. But if he only remembers after a long period of time, he must repeat the prayer from its beginning.

3) If one forgets to make the first *Tashahhud* or any of the other obligatory actions of prayer, he must perform two prostrations for forgetfulness before he makes the *Taslim*, and there is nothing else required from him. If he remembers before leaving the position he is in, he must perform what he forgot, and there

is nothing else required from him. And if he remembers after leaving his position but before reaching his next position in prayer, he must return to the previous position and perform what he forgot.

For example, one forgets to perform the first *Tashahhud*, standing without pause to the third unit of prayer. If he reaches an upright position, he doesn't return to the *Tashahhud*, but rather he must perform two prostrations of forgetfulness before making *Taslim*. If he sits for the *Tashahhud* but forgets to say the *Tashahhud* and remembers to say it before standing, he should make the *Tashahhud*, complete the prayer, and there is nothing else required from him. Similarly, if he begins to stand but remembers to sit before reaching an upright position: he should return to the *Tashahhud* and finish his prayer. However, the people of knowledge have mentioned that he should perform two prostrations for forgetfulness, because of the extra movement he made in his prayer when he began to stand. And Allâh knows best.

4) If one is doubtful as to whether he prayed three or four units, without being surer of one over the other, he must base his prayer on certainty – which means the lower number. Before making *Taslim*, he must perform two prostrations for forgetfulness and then make *Taslim*.

For example, one is praying *Zuhr* and in the second unit, he is not sur whether it is the second unit or the third; in fact, he is not surer regarding one over the other. He must continue to pray as if he is in the second unit, and then before making *Taslim*, he must perform two prostrations for forgetfulness, followed by the *Taslim*.

5) If one is doubtful in his prayer, not knowing for sure whether he prayed two or three units, but is surer regarding one over the other, then he must base his prayer on what he is surer of – regardless of whether it is the smaller or larger number. Then after making one *Taslim*, he should perform two prostrations for forgetfulness, followed by the *Taslim*.

For example, if one is praying *Zuhr*, and in the second unit, he is doubtful as to whether he is in the second unit or the third, but he is sure of being in the third. In this case, he must continue his prayer as if he is in the third unit. Then after making one *Taslim*, he must perform two prostrations for forgetfulness, followed by the *Taslim*.

If doubt creeps into his mind after he has completed his prayer, then he must ignore that doubt, only taking it into consideration when it becomes certainty. And if one doubts very often, he must disregard his doubt, for in his situation, it is a case of whispering (from the Devil).

How A Sick Person Prays

1) A sick person must perform the obligatory prayers in a standing position, even if he has to lean forward or lean on a wall or stick.

2) Nonetheless, if he is not able to stand, the sick person may pray in a seated position. In such a situation, it is best for him to pray, sitting cross-legged for the standing and bowing positions.

3) If he is not able to sit, he may pray, lying on his side – the right side is preferable – facing the *Qiblah*. If he is not able to face the *Qiblah*, he may pray as is, and his prayer is correct: he does not have to repeat it later.

4) And if he cannot pray on his side, he may pray lying down on his back, with his legs facing the *Qiblah*. It is best for him to slightly raise his head, so that he faces the *Qiblah*. If he cannot even have his legs facing the *Qiblah*, he may pray as is, and he doesn't have to repeat his prayer.

5) The sick person must perform the bowing and prostration position in his prayer. If he is not able to do so, then he must make a gesture with his head for both, allowing for his head to fall lower in the prostration. If he can bow but not prostrate, he must perform the former and make a gesture for the latter. And if he is able to prostrate but not bow, he must prostrate, and gesture for the bowing position.

6) In case that one's sickness prevents one from gesturing with one's head for the bowing and prostration positions, then one should make a signal with one's eyes, closing them slightly for the bowing and closing them further for the prostration. As for signaling with one's finger as some sick people do, it is not

correct and I know of no basis in the Qur'ân, the Sunnah, or the sayings of the people of knowledge for that practice.

7) If one's sickness is so severe that one can neither signal with his head or eyes, he must pray with his heart, reciting, and intending in his heart to bow, prostrate, to stand, and to sit: "For every person is that which he intended."

8) The sick person must pray every prayer on time, and furthermore must perform as much as he can from the obligatory elements of prayer. If it is truly difficult for him to pray every prayer in its time, he may combine the *Zuhr* and *'Asr* prayers, and combine the *Maghrib* and *'Isha'* prayers, either by praying in the earlier time, meaning he prays *'Asr* in the time of *Zuhr* and *'Isha'* in the time of *Maghrib*, or in the later time, delaying *Zuhr* until the time of *'Asr*, and *Maghrib* until the time of *'Isha'*. Based on what is easiest for him, he may do either. The *Fajr* prayer, however, may not be combined, not to the prayer that precedes it, nor to the prayer that follows it.

9) If a sick person travels abroad for treatment, he may shorten the four-unit prayers – *Zuhr*, *'Asr*, and *'Isha'* – praying two units instead until he returns home,[1] regardless of whether he is abroad for a long or a short period of time.[2]

---

[1] Some of the people of knowledge hold that he may only shorten his prayer if he is abroad for four days or less; if he is abroad for a longer period of time, he must perform the prayers, always completing four units.

[2] Taken from a work written by Shaikh Muhammad bin Salih Al-'Uthaimin.

The Rulings For Congregational Prayer And For The *Imam*[1]

First, The Congregational Prayer

1) Its Ruling: Congregational prayer is obligatory upon every (male) believer who has no excuse that prevents him from attending it. This ruling is based on the Prophet's saying:

«مَا مِنْ ثَلَاثَةٍ فِي قَرْيَةٍ وَلَا بَدْوٍ لَا تُقَامُ فِيهِمْ صَلَاةُ الْجَمَاعَةِ إِلَّا اسْتَحْوَذَ عَلَيْهِمُ الشَّيْطَانُ، فَعَلَيْكُمْ بِالْجَمَاعَةِ، فَإِنَّمَا يَأْكُلُ الذِّئْبُ مِنَ الْغَنَمِ الْقَاصِيَةَ»

There are not three in a village or desert who do not establish the congregational prayer except that the *Shaitan* (Devil) overpowers them. Upon you, then, is the congregation, for indeed, the wolf eats the lone sheep.[2]

The Prophet ﷺ also said:

«وَالَّذِي نَفْسِي بِيَدِهِ، لَقَدْ هَمَمْتُ أَنْ آمُرَ بِحَطَبٍ فَيُحْتَطَبَ، ثُمَّ آمُرَ بِالصَّلَاةِ فَيُؤَذَّنُ لَهَا، ثُمَّ آمُرَ رَجُلاً فَيَؤُمَّ النَّاسَ، ثُمَّ أُخَالِفَ إِلَى رِجَالٍ لَايَشْهَدُونَ الصَّلَاةَ فَأُحَرِّقَ عَلَيْهِمْ بُيُوتَهُمْ»

By the One Who has my soul in His Hand, I resolved to order for firewood to be gathered, to order the call to prayer, and then to order a man to lead the people (in prayer). Then I would go back to the men who wouldn't attend the prayer and burn down their houses.[3]

In another *Hadith*, a blind man said, "O Messenger of Allâh, I have no one to lead me to the *Masjid*." The Prophet ﷺ permitted him to remain behind from the congregational prayer, but when the man turned around to leave, the Prophet ﷺ called him back and said,

---

[1] Taken from the book *Minhajul-Muslim*, by Abu Bakr Al-Jaza'iri
[2] Ahmad, Abu Dawud, An-Nasa'i, and Al-Hakim; it is an authentic *Hadith*.
[3] Agreed upon.

«هَلْ تَسْمَعُ النِّدَاءَ بِالصَّلَاةِ؟ فَقَالَ: نَعَمْ، قَالَ: فَأَجِبْ»

"Do you hear the call to prayer?" The man said, "Yes." The Prophet ﷺ said, "Then respond to it."[1]

Ibn Mas'ud, may Allâh be pleased with him, once said, "Not one of us would remain behind from the congregational prayer except for the hypocrite who was known to be a hypocrite. A (sick) man would be brought to the prayer and guided between two men until he stood in the line."[2]

2) Its Virtues: The virtues of congregational prayer are great and so are its rewards, for the Prophet ﷺ said:

«صَلَاةُ الْجَمَاعَةِ تَفْضُلُ صَلَاةَ الْفَذِّ بِسَبْعٍ وَعِشْرِينَ دَرَجَةً»

The congregational prayer surpasses the individual prayer by twenty-seven degrees.

He ﷺ also said:

«صَلَاةُ الرَّجُلِ فِي جَمَاعَةٍ، تَزِيدُ عَلَى صَلَاتِهِ فِي بَيْتِهِ، وَصَلَاته فِي سُوقِهِ بِضْعاً وَعِشْرِينَ دَرَجَةً، وَذَلِكَ أَنَّ أَحَدَهُمْ إِذَا تَوَضَّأَ فَأَحْسَنَ الْوُضُوءَ، ثُمَّ أَتَى الْمَسْجِدَ لَا يُرِيدُ إِلَّا الصَّلَاةَ، فَلَمْ يَخْطُ خُطْوَةً إِلَّا رَفَعَهُ اللهُ بِهَا دَرَجَةً، وَحَطَّ عَنْهُ بِهَا خَطِيئَةً حَتَّى يَدْخُلَ الْمَسْجِدَ، وَإِذَا دَخَلَ الْمَسْجِدَ كَانَ فِي صَلَاةٍ مَا كَانَتِ الصَّلَاةُ تَحْبِسُهُ، وَالْمَلَائِكَةُ يُصَلُّونَ عَلَى أَحَدِكُمْ مَا دَامَ فِي مَجْلِسِهِ الَّذِي صَلَّى فِيهِ يَقُولُونَ: اللَّهُمَّ اغْفِرْ لَهُ، اللَّهُمَّ ارْحَمْهُ مَالَمْ يُحْدِثْ»

The prayer of a man in congregation excels his prayer in his home or in his store by twenty-seven degrees. That is because if one of them were to perform *Wudhu'* and perform it well, then go to the *Masjid* not intending other than the prayer, he would not take a step except that Allâh would raise him one rank because of that step and remove from him one sin, until he entered the *Masjid*. When he enters the *Masjid*, he

---
[1] Muslim
[2] Related by Muslim

continues to be in prayer as long as he awaits it. The angels pray over one of you as long as he is in the place he prayed in. They say, "O Allâh, forgive him, O Allâh have mercy on him," as long as he remains in a state of purity.[1]

Second, Rulings Regarding The *Imam*

1) The Conditions Of Being *Imam* (The One Who Leads The Prayer): The *Imam* must be male, pious (meaning that he neither commits the major sins nor persists in the minor ones), and fully knowledgeable regarding the rulings of the prayer. A woman may not lead men in prayer, nor may a *Fasiq* (evil-doer) known for his wickedness, unless he is a feared leader. An illiterate ignorant person may not lead others unless the others are like him, for the Prophet ﷺ said:

«لَا تَؤُمَّنَّ امْرَأَةٌ وَلَا فَاجِرٌ مُؤْمِناً، إِلَّا أَنْ يَقْهَرَهُ بِسُلْطَانٍ، أَوْ يُخَافُ سَوْطُهُ أَوْ سَيْفُهُ»

The woman and the evildoer may not lead the believer unless he (the believer) is forced by the leader or fears his whip or sword. (It was reported by Ibn Majah but it is weak.)

2) Who Is More Deserving To Be *Imam*? The worthiest person to lead the prayer is the one who knows more from Allâh's Book, followed by the one who is most knowledgeable in Allâh's religion, followed by the one who is most pious, and then followed by the one who is most senior in age. The Prophet ﷺ said:

«يَؤُمُّ الْقَوْمَ أَقْرَؤُهُمْ لِكِتَابِ اللهِ، فَإِنْ كَانُوا فِي الْقِرَاءَةِ سَوَاءً فَأَعْلَمُهُمْ بِالسُّنَّةِ، فَإِنْ كَانُوا فِي السُّنَّةِ سَوَاءً، فَأَقْدَمُهُمْ هِجْرَةً، فَإِنْ كَانُوا فِي الْهِجْرَةِ سَوَاءً، فَأَكْبَرُهُمْ سِنًّا»

The one who knows more of Allâh's Book should lead the people (in prayer). If there are more than one who are equal in their reading of the Qur'ân, then the one who is most knowledgeable regarding the Sunnah. If they are equal regarding the Sunnah, then the one who emigrated first. If

---

[1] Related by Muslim in the chapter, "Prayer of the Traveler": (1:478)

they are equal in their emigration, then the oldest of them.[1]
The leader and the owner of a house are exceptions in this ruling, for they are preferred over others in being *Imam*. The Prophet ﷺ said:

«لَا يُؤَمَّنَّ الرَّجُلُ فِي أَهْلِهِ وَلَا سُلْطَانِهِ إِلَّا بِإِذْنِهِ»

A man should not be led in prayer among his family nor in a place that he has authority over, unless his permission is taken.

Sa'id bin Mansur – may Allâh have mercy on him – related this part with the previous *Hadith*.

The *Athan* and *Iqamah*

First, The *Athan*

1) Its Definition: An announcement using specific words that the time of prayer has entered.

2) Its Ruling: The *Athan* is a communal obligation upon the inhabitants of cities and villages, for the Prophet ﷺ said:

«إِذَا حَضَرَتِ الصَّلَاةُ فَلْيُؤَذِّنْ لَكُمْ أَحَدُكُمْ، وَلْيَؤُمَّكُمْ أَكْبَرُكُمْ»

When the (time of) prayer arrives, then one of you must call the *Athan*, and let the eldest among you lead the rest of you.[2]

Regarding the traveler and the nomad, it is Sunnah for them to call *Athan*. The Prophet ﷺ said:

«إِذَا كُنْتَ فِي غَنَمِكَ أَوْ بَادِيَتِكَ فَأَذَّنْتَ بِالصَّلَاةِ فَارْفَعْ صَوْتَكَ بِالنِّدَاءِ، فَإِنَّهُ لَا يَسْمَعُ مَدَى صَوْتِ الْمُؤَذِّنِ جِنٌّ وَلَا إِنْسٌ، وَلَا شَيْءٌ إِلَّا شَهِدَ لَهُ يَوْمَ الْقِيَامَةِ»

If you are with your sheep or in the desert, raise your voice with the call (to prayer), for indeed, the calling voice of the *Mu'aththin* (one who makes *Athan*) is not heard by a jinn or

---

[1] Muslim
[2] Agreed upon.

human but he will bear witness for him on the Day of judgement.[1]

3) Its Wording: The wording of the *Athan*, as the Prophet ﷺ taught Bilal, may Allâh be pleased with him, is as follows:

Allâhu Akbar, Allâhu Akbar (Allâh is the Most Great, Allâh is the Most Great) – two times.

Ashhadu Al-Laa Ilaha Illallâh (I bear witness that none has the right to be worshipped but Allâh) – twice.

Ashhadu Anna Muhammadar-Rasoolullâh (I bear witness that Muhammad is the Messenger of Allâh) – twice.

Hayya 'Alas-Salaah (Hasten to prayer) – twice.

Hayya 'Alal-Falaah (Hasten to success) – twice.

If it is the call to *Fajr*, the *Mu'aththin* calls here, "*As-Salaatu Khairum-Minan-Nawm*" (The prayer is better than sleep) – twice.

Allâhu Akbar, Allâhu Akbar.

Laa Ilaha Illallâh (None has the right to be worshipped but Allâh) – once.

Second, the *Iqamah*

1) Its Ruling: The *Iqamah* is Sunnah for the five obligatory prayers, whether one is a resident or traveler. The Prophet ﷺ said:

«مَا مِنْ ثَلَاثَةٍ فِي قَرْيَةٍ وَلَا بَدْوٍ لَا تُقَامُ فِيهِمُ الصَّلَاةُ إِلَّا اسْتَحْوَذَ عَلَيْهِمُ الشَّيْطَانُ، فَعَلَيْكُمْ بِالْجَمَاعَةِ، فَإِنَّمَا يَأْكُلُ الذِّئْبُ مِنَ الْغَنَمِ الْقَاصِيَةَ»

There are not three in a village or desert who do not establish the congregational prayer except that the *Shaitan* (Devil) overpowers them. Upon you, then, is the congregation, for indeed, the wolf eats the lone sheep.[2]

Anas, may Allâh be pleased with him, said that Bilal was ordered to say the *Athan* with even–numbered phrases, and the *Iqamah* with

---

[1] Al-Bukhari.

[2] Ahmad, Abu Dawud, An-Nasa'i, and Al-Hakim; it is an authentic *Hadith*.

odd.[1]

2) Its Wording: As in a *Hadith* related by 'Abdullah bin Zaid, the wording of the *Iqamah* is as follows:

Allâhu Akbar, Allâhu Akbar (Allâh is the Most Great, Allâh is the Most Great) once.

Ashhadu Al-Laa Ilaha Illallâh (I bear witness that none has the right to be worshipped but Allâh) – once.

Ashhadu Anna Muhammadar-Rasoolullâh (I bear witness that Muhammad is the Messenger of Allâh) – once.

Hayya 'Alas-Salaah (Hasten to prayer) – once.

Hayya 'Alal-Falaah (Hasten to success) – once.

Qad Qaamatis-Salaat (Indeed the prayer is about to begin) – twice.

Allâhu Akbar, Allâhu Akbar – once.

Laa Ilaha Illallâh (None has the right to be worshipped but Allâh) – once.

Shortening The Prayer, Combining Prayers, And The Fear Prayer

1) The Meaning Of Shortening: What this means is to shorten a four-unit prayer, making it two units. As for the *Maghrib* and *Fajr* prayers, they are not shortened because the former consists of three units while the latter consists of two.

2) Its Ruling: The shortened prayer is legislated in Islam, for Allâh Almighty says:

﴿وَإِذَا ضَرَبْتُمْ فِي ٱلْأَرْضِ فَلَيْسَ عَلَيْكُمْ جُنَاحٌ أَن تَقْصُرُوا۟ مِنَ ٱلصَّلَوٰةِ﴾

And when you (Muslims) travel in the land, there is no sin on you if you shorten your *Salat* (prayer).[2]

When the Prophet ﷺ was asked about shortening the prayer, he ﷺ said:

«صَدَقَةٌ تَصَدَّقَ اللهُ بِهَا عَلَيْكُمْ فَاقْبَلُوا صَدَقَتَهُ»

---

[1] Muslim.
[2] (*An-Nisa'* 4:101).

It is charity that Allâh has bestowed upon you, so accept His charity.[1]

Since the Prophet ﷺ was consistent in shortening the prayer while traveling, making it a compulsory Sunnah (*Sunnat Mu'akkadah*). The Prophet ﷺ never traveled except that he ﷺ and his Companions, may Allâh be pleased with them, would shorten their prayers.

3) The Minimum Distance Of Travel For Shortening The Prayer: The Prophet ﷺ did not specify a minimum distance of travel for shortening the prayer; rather, the vast majority of Companions, *Tabi'in* (companions of the Prophet's Companions), and the Imams of past generations have studied the Prophet's travels, noting at what distance he shortened the prayer. They found that the shortest distance in which the Prophet ﷺ shortened the prayer is forty-eight miles, which makes it the minimum distance for shortening the prayer. So, it is Sunnah for whoever travels at least that distance – on a journey that is not meant for sinning – to shorten his prayer; he may perform two units for each of the *Zuhr*, *'Asr*, and *'Isha'* prayers.

4) When Shortening The Prayer Begins And When It Ends: The traveler may begin to shorten his prayer when he leaves the dwellings of his town, and he may continue to perform shortening it until he returns to his region, no matter how long the journey is, unless he intends to remain more than four days in any given city, for he must then perform the complete prayer without shortening it. This is because his mind is at rest when he intends to remain in a specific place, so the grounds for which the shortened prayer was legislated no longer apply, the grounds being the nervousness of the traveler and his preoccupation with the duties related to his journey. However, there is another opinion as well; because when the Prophet ﷺ stayed for twenty days in Tabuk, he always shortened his prayer.[2] Yet it is said that he ﷺ did so because he didn't intend to stay there.

5) The Shortened Prayer Applies To Travelers In General: There is no difference between the traveler who is riding or walking;

---

[1] Agreed upon.
[2] Recorded by Ahmad in *Al-Musnad*.

between the one traveling by camel and the one traveling by car or plane: the shortened prayer applies to them all. The exception here is the sea-voyager who (1) is always traveling and (2) has his family with him on his ship. The shortened prayer is not legislated for him; rather, he must complete the prayers because, just like an inhabitant of a given land, he is an inhabitant of his ship.

Second, Combining The Prayers:

It is permissible to combine between *Zuhr* and *'Asr* and between *Maghrib* and *'Isha'*. The exception is the *Zuhr* and *'Asr* prayers on the day of *'Arafah* and the *Maghrib* and *'Isha'* prayers on the night of Al-Muzdalifah for the one performing *Hajj*, for it is a Sunnah in which he has no choice: he must combine those prayers. In an authentic *Hadith*, a Companion of the Prophet ﷺ said the following: "Indeed, he prayed *Zuhr* and *'Asr* in 'Arafat with one *Athan* and two *Iqamahs*. When he reached Al-Muzdalifah, he prayed *Maghrib* and *'Isha'* with one *Athan* and two *Iqamahs*."[1]

1) How To Combine The Prayers: The traveler may combine the prayers in two ways:

i) Praying the later prayer in the earlier prayer's time. Therefore the traveler may combine *Zuhr* and *'Asr*, praying both together in the time of *Zuhr*, and he may combine *Maghrib* and *'Isha'*, praying both together in the time of *Maghrib*.

ii) Praying the earlier prayer in the later prayer's time: The traveler may combine *Zuhr* and *'Asr*, praying both together in the time of *'Asr*, and combine *Maghrib* and *'Isha'*, praying both together in the time of *'Isha'*. It is related that the Prophet ﷺ delayed the prayer in Tabuk, coming out and praying *Zuhr* and *'Asr* together. Then he ﷺ prayed *Maghrib* and *'Isha'* together while camping at Tabuk.[2]

If it is raining, it is extremely cold, or the winds are severe, and if it is difficult for people to return to the *Masjid* for *'Isha'*, they may combine the *Maghrib* and *'Isha'* prayer in the *Masjid*. On one night when it was raining profusely, the Prophet ﷺ combined the *Maghrib* and *'Isha'* prayers.[3]

---

[1] Muslim.

[2] Agreed upon.

[3] Related by Al-Bukhari

Similarly, the sick person may combine both the two afternoon and the two night prayers if it is difficult for him to perform each prayer in its time – for the basis upon which combining is legislated is hardship. So, whenever there is hardship, it is permissible to combine. Even when not traveling, a Muslim may face severe trials, such as fear for himself, his family, or his wealth: in all of those instances he may combine. It has authentically been related from the Prophet ﷺ that he once combined when at home, and not because of rain. Ibn 'Abbas, may Allâh be pleased with him, said, "Indeed the Prophet ﷺ prayed seven and eight in Al-Madinah: *Zuhr*, *'Asr*, *Maghrib*, and *'Isha'*."[1]

As Ibn 'Abbas said, it was perhaps to avoid creating hardship for his nation. One may perform it by delaying *Zuhr* and advancing *'Asr* to its earliest time, and by delaying *Maghrib* and advancing *'Isha'* to its earliest time, this is when two of the prayer times meet.

Third, The Fear Prayer:

1) Its Legislation: The fear prayer is legislated by the following verse:

﴿وَإِذَا كُنتَ فِيهِمْ فَأَقَمْتَ لَهُمُ ٱلصَّلَوٰةَ فَلْتَقُمْ طَآئِفَةٌ مِّنْهُم مَّعَكَ وَلْيَأْخُذُوٓاْ أَسْلِحَتَهُمْ فَإِذَا سَجَدُواْ فَلْيَكُونُواْ مِن وَرَآئِكُمْ وَلْتَأْتِ طَآئِفَةٌ أُخْرَىٰ لَمْ يُصَلُّواْ فَلْيُصَلُّواْ مَعَكَ وَلْيَأْخُذُواْ حِذْرَهُمْ وَأَسْلِحَتَهُمْ﴾

When you (O Muhammad ﷺ) are among them, and lead them in *As-Salat* (the prayer), let one party of them stand up [in *Salat* (prayer)] with you, taking their arms with them; when they finish their prostrations, let them take their positions in the rear and let the other party come up which has not yet prayed, and let them pray with you, taking all the precautions and bearing arms.[2]

2) The Description Of The Fear Prayer During Travel: There are different forms of the Fear Prayer that have been related, indicating that it may be performed in a state of fear, be it strong or weak. The most famous of its forms is during battle while traveling. The *Imam*

---

[1] Agreed upon
[2] (*An-Nisa'* 4:102)

should divide his army into two groups, one group facing the enemy and the second group lining up behind him, praying one unit behind him. In the second unit, the *Imam* should remain standing while those behind him pray their second unit and make *Taslim*. Then they should go and stand in the place of the second group, who come and pray one unit behind the *Imam*. The *Imam* should remain in a seated position, while the second group finishes their second unit. Then, as their *Imam*, they should make *Taslim* with them following him.

This form is supported by the *Hadith* of Sahl bin Abu Hathamah: "One group lined up with the Prophet ﷺ while a second group faced the enemy. He ﷺ prayed one unit with the group that was with him, and then he remained in the standing position as they completed (the second unit) for themselves. Then they went to face the enemy. The second group came, and the Prophet ﷺ prayed the unit that remained with them; then he remained seated, while they finished (their second unit) for themselves. Then he ﷺ made *Taslim* for them."

3) The Fear Prayer When At Home: If a battle takes place in one's own city where prayer is not shortened, the first group prays two units with the *Imam* and two units by themselves. After the second unit, the *Imam* remains in a standing position. The second group comes and prays two units behind the *Imam*, who then remains seated, waiting for them to finish their last two units by themselves, after which he makes *Taslim* with them.[1]

4) When It Is Not Possible To Divide The Army Because The Fighting Is Fierce: If the fighting is fierce and it is not possible to divide the army, then everyone should pray individually – in any situation that they are in: walking or riding, facing the *Qiblah* or not facing the *Qiblah*, going from one position to the next by making gestures. Allâh Almighty says:

$$﴿ فَإِنْ خِفْتُمْ فَرِجَالًا أَوْ رُكْبَانًا ﴾$$

And if you fear (an enemy), perform *Salat* (prayer) on foot or riding.[2]

---

[1] Related by Muslim
[2] (*Al-Baqarah* 2:239)

And the Prophet ﷺ said:

$$«وَإِنْ كَانُوا أَكْثَرَ مِنْ ذَلِكَ فَلْيُصَلُّوا قِيَاماً وَرُكْبَاناً»$$

And if they are more than that, then let them pray standing or riding.[1]

"And if they are more than that" means, "If fear increases, the two armies clash, and the Muslim army is mixed in the enemy's army."

5) When Chasing The Enemy Or When Fleeing From The Enemy: When one is chasing the enemy, fearing that he will get away, or when one is being chased by the enemy, fearing that he will catch up with him, he may pray in any way that he can – walking, running, facing or not facing the *Qiblah*. This applies to all who fear being attacked by man, animal, or otherwise. The way he performs the Fear Prayer is based on his situation. Allâh Almighty says:

$$﴿فَإِنْ خِفْتُمْ فَرِجَالًا أَوْ رُكْبَانًا﴾$$

And if you fear (an enemy), perform *Salat* (prayer) on foot or riding.[2]

When the Prophet ﷺ sent 'Abdullah bin Unais, may Allâh be pleased with him, to seek out Al-Huthali, this situation occurred. 'Abdullah later said, "When I feared that between him and I was what would make me delay the prayer, I continued to walk, praying by making gestures toward him. And when I got close to him..."[3]

---

[1] Related by Al-Bukhari.
[2] (*Al-Baqarah* 2:239).
[3] Related by Al-Bukhari.

Al-Jumu'ah (The Friday) Prayer

The Virtue Of Friday

Friday is a blessed day; indeed, it is the best day of this world, the best day of the week. Because Allâh Almighty gave it such an important status, it should be honored. It is a day in which we should perform many good deeds, avoiding all evil ones. It is a day in which we should send many prayers upon the Prophet ﷺ. Abu Hurairah, may Allâh be pleased with him, related that the Prophet ﷺ said:

«خَيْرُ يَوْم طَلَعَتْ عَلَيْهِ الشَّمْسُ، يَوْمُ الْجُمُعَةِ، فِيهِ خُلِقَ آدَمُ، وَفِيهِ أُدْخِلَ الْجَنَّةَ، وَفِيهِ أُخْرِجَ مِنْهَا، وَلَا تَقُومُ السَّاعَةُ إِلَّا فِي يَوْمِ الْجُمُعَةِ»

The best day that the sun has risen upon is Friday; in it Adam was created, and during it he was made to enter Paradise, and on it he left Paradise. And the Hour will not arrive except on Friday.[1]

In a *Hadith* related by Abu Lubabah Al-Badri, may Allâh be pleased with him, the Prophet ﷺ said:

«سَيِّدُ الْأَيَّام يَوْمُ الْجُمُعَةِ، وَأَعْظَمُهَا عِنْدَ اللهِ تَعَالَى، مِنْ يَوْمِ الْفِطْرِ، وَيَوْمِ الْأَضْحَى . . .»

The master of all days is Friday, and it is the greatest day with Allâh, (greater) than the day of *Al-Fitr* and the day of *Al-Adhha*.[2]

In *Hadith* related by Abu Hurairah, may Allâh be pleased with him, the Messenger of Allâh ﷺ said:

«مَنِ اغْتَسَلَ يَوْمَ الْجُمُعَةِ غُسْلَ الْجَنَابَةِ، ثُمَّ رَاحَ فِي السَّاعَةِ الْأُولَى، فَكَأَنَّما قَرَّبَ بَدَنَةً، وَمَنْ رَاحَ فِي السَّاعَةِ الثَّانِيَةِ، فَكَأَنَّمَا قَرَّبَ بَقَرَةً،

---

[1] Related by Muslim; this narration is based on his wording. It is also related by Ahmad and At-Tirmithi.

[2] Ahmad and Ibn Majah. Al-'Iraqi said, "Its chain is *Hasan*."

وَمَنْ رَاحَ فِي السَّاعَةِ الثَّالِثَةِ، فَكَأَنَّمَا قَرَّبَ كَبْشًا أَقْرَنَ، وَمَنْ رَاحَ فِي
السَّاعَةِ الرَّابِعَةِ فَكَأَنَّمَا قَرَّبَ دَجَاجَةً، وَمَنْ رَاحَ فِي السَّاعَةِ الْخَامِسَةِ
فَكَأَنَّمَا قَرَّبَ بَيْضَةً، فَإِذَا خَرَجَ الْإِمَامُ حَضَرَتِ الْمَلَائِكَةُ يَسْتَمِعُونَ
الذِّكْرَ»

Whoever performs *Ghusl* on Friday, the *Ghusl* for sexual
impurity, and then goes in the first hour (to the Friday prayer),
it is as if he sacrificed a camel; whoever goes in the second
hour, it is as if he sacrificed a cow; whoever goes in the third
hour, it is as if he sacrificed a horned male sheep; whoever
goes in the fourth hour, it is as if he sacrificed a chicken;
whoever goes in the fifth hour, it is as if he sacrificed an egg.
And when the *Imam* comes out, the angels attend, listening to
the remembrance.[1]

In yet another *Hadith*, both Abu Sa'id and Abu Hurairah, may Allâh
be pleased with them, related that the Prophet ﷺ said,

«إِنَّ فِي الْجُمُعَةِ سَاعَةً، لَا يُوَافِقُهَا عَبْدٌ مُسْلِمٌ، يَسْأَلُ اللهَ عَزَّ وَجَلَّ
فِيهَا خَيْرًا، إِلَّا أَعْطَاهُ إِيَّاهُ، وَهِيَ بَعْدَ الْعَصْرِ»

Indeed there is an hour on Friday: no Muslim worshipper
finds it, asking Allâh good during it, except that He gives that
thing to him. And that hour is after *Al-'Asr*.[2]

Its Ruling

The *Jumu'ah* (Friday) prayer is obligatory based on this verse:

﴿يَٰٓأَيُّهَا ٱلَّذِينَ ءَامَنُوٓاْ إِذَا نُودِيَ لِلصَّلَوٰةِ مِن يَوْمِ ٱلْجُمُعَةِ فَٱسْعَوْاْ إِلَىٰ ذِكْرِ ٱللَّهِ
وَذَرُواْ ٱلْبَيْعَ﴾

O you who believe (Muslims)! When the call is proclaimed for
the *Salat* (prayer) on the day of Friday (*Jumu'ah* prayer), come
to the remembrance of Allâh [*Jumu'ah* religious talk (*Khutbah*) and *Salat* (prayer)] and leave off business (and every

---

[1] Malik and Al-Bukhari; the wording is from the latter.
[2] Related by Ahmad. Al-'Iraqi declared it to be authentic

other thing).[1]

Based on this saying of the Messenger of Allâh ﷺ:

«لَيَنْتَهِيَنَّ أَقْوَامٌ عَنْ وَدَعِهِمُ الْجُمُعَاتِ، أَوْ لَيَخْتِمَنَّ اللهُ عَلَى قُلُوبِهِمْ، ثُمَّ لَيَكُونُنَّ مِنَ الغَافِلِينَ»

People should desist from abandoning Friday prayers, or indeed Allâh will seal their hearts, and they will become from the heedless ones.

The Prophet ﷺ said:

«الْجُمُعَةُ حَقٌّ وَاجِبٌ عَلَى كُلِّ مُسْلِمٍ فِي جَمَاعَةٍ إِلَّا أَرْبَعَةً: عَبْدٌ مَمْلُوكٌ، أَوِ امْرَأَةٌ، أَوْ صَبِيٌّ، أَوْ مَرِيضٌ»

The *Jumu'ah* (prayer) is an obligatory right upon every Muslim in a community, except for four: an owned slave, a woman, a child, and a sick person.[2]

The Manners And Necessary Actions Of Friday Prayer

1) Everyone who attends the prayer must first perform *Ghusl*; the Prophet ﷺ said:

«غُسْلُ الْجُمُعَةِ وَاجِبٌ عَلَى كُلِّ مُحْتَلِمٍ»

The shower of *Jumu'ah* is obligatory upon every adult.[3]

2) One (male) should wear a clean garment and apply perfume, for the Prophet ﷺ said:

«عَلَى كُلِّ مُسْلِمٍ الْغُسْلُ يَوْمَ الْجُمُعَةِ، وَيَلْبَسُ مِنْ صَالِحِ ثِيَابِهِ، وَإِنْ كَانَ لَهُ طِيبٌ مَسَّ مِنْهُ»

Upon every Muslim is a shower on Friday; he wears from his best garments, and if he has perfume, he should apply it on himself.[4]

---

[1] (*Al-Jumu'ah* 62:9)
[2] Related by Abu Dawud from Tariq bin Shihab, who never heard anything from the Prophet ﷺ.
[3] Agreed upon.
[4] Recorded by Ahmad and Abu Dawud and its basis is in the Two *Sahihs*.

3) One should make an effort to arrive early for the prayer, even earlier than its time begins, for the Prophet ﷺ said:

«مَنِ اغْتَسَلَ يَوْمَ الْجُمُعَةِ غُسْلَ الْجَنَابَةِ، ثُمَّ رَاحَ فِي السَّاعَةِ الْأُولَى، فَكَأَنَّمَا قَرَّبَ بَدَنَةً، وَمَنْ رَاحَ فِي السَّاعَةِ الثَّانِيَةِ، فَكَأَنَّمَا قَرَّبَ بَقَرَةً، وَمَنْ رَاحَ فِي السَّاعَةِ الثَّالِثَةِ، فَكَأَنَّمَا قَرَّبَ كَبْشًا أَقْرَنَ، وَمَنْ رَاحَ فِي السَّاعَةِ الرَّابِعَةِ فَكَأَنَّمَا قَرَّبَ دَجَاجَةً، وَمَنْ رَاحَ فِي السَّاعَةِ الْخَامِسَةِ فَكَأَنَّمَا قَرَّبَ بَيْضَةً، فَإِذَا خَرَجَ الْإِمَامُ حَضَرَتِ الْمَلَائِكَةُ يَسْتَمِعُونَ الذِّكْرَ»

Whoever performs *Ghusl* on Friday, the *Ghusl* for sexual impurity, and then goes in the first hour (to the Friday prayer), it is as if he sacrificed a camel; whoever goes in the second hour, it is as if he sacrificed a cow; whoever goes in the third hour, it is as if he sacrificed a horned male sheep; whoever goes in the fourth hour, it is as if he sacrificed a chicken; whoever goes in the fifth hour, it is as if he sacrificed an egg. And when the *Imam* comes out, the angels attend, listening to the remembrance.[1]

4) When one enters the *Masjid* for the Friday prayer, one should pray as much voluntary prayers as are easy for him. The Prophet ﷺ said:

«لَا يَغْتَسِلُ رَجُلٌ يَوْمَ الْجُمُعَةِ، وَيَتَطَهَّرُ بِمَا اسْتَطَاعَ مِنْ طُهْرٍ، وَيَدَّهِنُ مِنْ دُهْنِهِ أَوْ يَمَسُّ مِنْ طِيبِ بَيْتِهِ، ثُمَّ يَرُوحُ إِلَى الْمَسْجِدِ لَا يُفَرِّقُ بَيْنَ اثْنَيْنِ، ثُمَّ يُصَلِّي مَا كُتِبَ لَهُ، ثُمَّ يُنْصِتُ لِلْإِمَامِ إِذَا تَكَلَّمَ إِلَّا غُفِرَ لَهُ مِنَ الْجُمُعَةِ إِلَى الْجُمُعَةِ الْأُخْرَى مَالَمْ يَغْشَ الْكَبَائِرَ»

When a man performs *Ghusl* on Friday, purifies himself as much as he is able, applies some of his oils or applies the perfume of his house, then goes to the *Masjid*, not separating two (worshippers), then prays what is written for him, then

---

[1] Recorded by Malik, with an authentic chain of narration, and Al-Bukhari reported it with a chain to Malik (1:212).

listens to the *Imam* when he speaks – he will be forgiven from one *Jumu'ah* to the next, so long as he does not perpetrate the major sins.[1]

5) When the *Imam* comes out to deliver the *Khutbah* (Friday sermon), one must avoid talking, making frivolous movements, or playing with pebbles and the like. So important it is to remain quiet that the Prophet ﷺ said:

«إِذَا قُلْتَ لِصَاحِبِكَ يَوْمَ الْجُمُعَةِ وَالإِمَامُ يَخْطُبُ : أَنْصِتْ فَقَدْ لَغَوْتَ»

When you say to your companion, "pay attention" as the *Imam* is delivering the *Khutbah*, then you have indeed spoken nonsense.[2]

Again, regarding the *Khutbah* on Friday, the Prophet ﷺ also said:

«مَنْ مَسَّ الْحَصَى فَقَدْ لَغَا، وَمَنْ لَغَا فَلَا جُمُعَةَ لَهُ»

Whoever touches pebbles, then he has perpetrated nonsense; whoever perpetrates nonsense, then there is no *Jumu'ah* for him.[3]

6) If one enters the *Masjid* as the *Imam* is delivering *Khutbah*, then he should perform two brief units upon entering the *Masjid*. The Prophet ﷺ said:

«إِذَا دَخَلَ أَحَدُكُمْ يَوْمَ الْجُمُعَةِ وَالإِمَامُ يَخْطُبُ فَلْيَرْكَعْ رَكْعَتَيْنِ وَلْيَتَجَوَّزْ فِيهَا»

If one of you enters on Friday as the *Imam* is delivering his *Khutbah*, then let him perform two units (of prayer), and let him perform them quickly.[4]

7) It is disliked to walk over the necks of those who are seated or to separate two people who are seated together. When the Prophet ﷺ saw a man walking over the necks of people, he ﷺ said:

«اجْلِسْ فَقَدْ آذَيْتَ»

---

[1] Al-Bukhari.
[2] Muslim.
[3] Abu Dawud.
[4] Muslim.

Sit, for indeed you have caused harm.[1]

He ﷺ also said:

«وَلَا يُفَرِّقْ بَيْنَ اثْنَيِن»

And two people (seated together) should not be separated.

8) As soon as the second call to Friday prayer is made, it is forbidden to buy and sell; indeed, Allâh Almighty says:

﴿يَٰٓأَيُّهَا ٱلَّذِينَ ءَامَنُوٓاْ إِذَا نُودِيَ لِلصَّلَوٰةِ مِن يَوْمِ ٱلْجُمُعَةِ فَٱسْعَوْاْ إِلَىٰ ذِكْرِ ٱللَّهِ وَذَرُواْ ٱلْبَيْعَ﴾

O you who believe! When the call is proclaimed for the *Salat* (prayer) on the day of Friday (*Jumu'ah* prayer), come to the remembrance of Allâh [*Jumu'ah* religious talk (*Khutbah*) and *Salat* (prayer)] and leave off business (and every other thing).[2]

9) It is recommended to recite *Surat Al-Kahf* on Thursday night or during the day of Friday. The following saying is related from the Prophet ﷺ:

«مَنْ قَرَأَ سُورَةَ الْكَهْفِ فِي يَوْمِ الْجُمُعَةِ أَضَاءَ لَهُ مِنَ النُّورِ مَا بَيْنَ الْجُمُعَتَيْنِ»

Whoever recites *Surat Al-Kahf* on Friday, it will furnish light for him between the two Fridays.[3]

Our pious predecessors would assiduously apply this *Hadith*.

10) On Friday, one should send many blessings upon the Prophet ﷺ, for he ﷺ said:

«أَكْثِرُوا عَلَيَّ مِنَ الصَّلَاةِ يَوْمَ الْجُمُعَةِ وَلَيْلَةَ الْجُمُعَةِ، فَمَنْ فَعَلَ ذَلِكَ كُنْتُ لَهُ شَهِيدًا وَشَفِيعًا يَوْمَ الْقِيَامَةِ»

Increase sending blessings upon me on Friday and the night (before) Friday; whoever does that, I will be his witness and

---

[1] Abu Dawud.

[2] (*Al-Jumu'ah* 62:9).

[3] Recorded by Al-Hakim who graded it *Sahih*.

intercessor on the Day of Judgement.[1]

11) One should supplicate much on Friday, for on that day there is an hour when supplications are answered. Whoever's supplication corresponds to that hour, Allâh will answer him and give him what he asked. The Prophet ﷺ said:

«إِنَّ فِي يَوْمِ الْجُمُعَةِ لَسَاعَةً لَا يُوَافِقُهَا عَبْدٌ مُسْلِمٌ يَسْأَلُ اللهَ عَزَّ وَجَلَّ فِيهَا خَيْرًا إِلَّا أَعْطَاهُ إِيَّاهُ»

Indeed there is an hour on Friday: no Muslim worshipper finds it, asking Allâh good during it, except that He gives that thing to him.[2]

That hour has been related to be the time between the *Imam* coming out and the time when the Friday prayer is finished; it is also said to be after *Al-'Asr*.

Conditions For Its Validity

1) One must be living in a city or village, because the *Jumu'ah* prayer is not correct in the desert nor is it correct to perform when one is traveling. During the life of the Prophet ﷺ, *Jumu'ah* was only performed in cities, towns, and villages; the Messenger of Allâh ﷺ didn't order the inhabitants of the desert to perform it. Despite his many travels, it has not been authentically established that the Prophet ﷺ ever performed the Friday prayer when traveling.

2) *Jumu'ah* is only correct and acceptable inside a *Masjid* and in the courtyards of *Masjids*, so that Muslims are not harmed by heat or cold or rain.

3) The *Jumu'ah* prayer must include a *Khutbah*; indeed, *Jumu'ah* was legislated only for the *Khutbah*.

4) *Jumu'ah* is not obligatory upon one who lives far from any city in which *Jumu'ah* prayer is held. The meaning of far is more than three miles because the Prophet ﷺ said:

«الْجُمُعَةُ عَلَى مَنْ سَمِعَ النِّدَاءَ»

---

[1] Related by Al-Baihaqi with a *Hasan* chain
[2] Muslim

Al-Jumu'ah is upon he who hears the call.[1]

5) If one is late but arrives in time for the second unit, he should only perform an additional unit after the *Imam* makes *Taslim* and that is enough for him. This is because the Prophet ﷺ said:

«مَنْ أَدْرَكَ مِنَ الصَّلَاةِ رَكْعَةً، فَقَدْ أَدْرَكَهَا كُلَّهَا»

Whoever catches the prayer, being able to perform at least one unit, then he has caught the entire prayer.[2]

But as for one who catches the prayer, being able to perform less than one unit, such as one who arrives at the prayer when the *Imam* is making the final prostrations, then he should make an intention for praying *Zuhr*, and not *Jumu'ah*, and then complete the four units after the *Imam* makes *Taslim*.

6) How is *Jumu'ah* performed? After midday, the *Imam* should come out, ascend the *Minbar*, give greetings of peace to the people, and then sit down. Then the *Mu'aththin* should call the *Athan*, and when he is finished, the *Imam* stands and delivers a *Khutbah*, beginning by praising Allâh and mentioning the two testimonies of faith. Next, he should send blessings and salutations upon the Prophet ﷺ. Then he should admonish the people and remind them, raising his voice while doing so. He should order by Allâh and His Messenger's commands and forbid by their prohibitions.

He should encourage people to do good, reminding them of Allâh's reward and warn them against perpetrating evil, reminding them of Allâh's punishment. Then he should sit down briefly before delivering the second sermon. Continuing into the second *Khutbah*, he should praise Allâh and then continue in the same tone of voice – the voice of a man warning of an approaching army. Then without prolonging his speech, he should finish it off and then descend. Next, the *Mu'aththin* calls the *Iqamah* and the *Imam* leads the people in two units of prayer, reading out loud in both units. After reciting *Al-Fatihah*, it is Sunnah in the first unit to recite *Surat Al-A'la* and in the second unit *Al-Ghashiyah*, or *Surahs* similar in length.

---

[1] Abu Dawud and Ad-Daraqutni, but the *Hadith* is weak.
[2] Agreed upon

Miscellaneous Prayers

Al-Witr Prayer

Its Ruling And Definition: *Al-Witr* is a compulsory Sunnah; a Muslim should never abandon it. The *Witr* is one unit of prayer that is performed after the last voluntary prayer performed after the *'Isha'* prayer. The Messenger of Allâh ﷺ said:

«صَلَاةُ اللَّيْلِ مَثْنَى مَثْنَى، فَإِذَا خَشِيَ أَحَدُكُمُ الصُّبْحَ صَلَّى رَكْعَةً وَاحِدَةً تُوتِرُ لَهُ مَا قَدْ صَلَّى»

The night prayer is two units at a time; if one of you fears that the morning is about to arrive, he should pray one unit, making the number he prayed odd.[1]

What Sunnah Precedes *Al-Witr*: Before performing the *Witr* prayer, it is Sunnah to pray two units or more and then pray the *Witr*, for this practice is authentically related from the Prophet ﷺ in the *Sahihs*.

The Time For *Witr*: *Witr* may be performed from after the *'Isha'* prayer until just before *Fajr*; performing it at the end of the night is better than performing it at the beginning of it, except for the one who is afraid that he won't wake up at the end of the night to perform it. The Prophet ﷺ said:

«مَنْ ظَنَّ مِنْكُمْ أَنْ لَا يَسْتَيْقِظَ آخِرَ اللَّيْلِ فَلْيُوتِرْ أَوَّلَهُ، وَمَنْ ظَنَّ مِنْكُمْ أَنَّهُ يَسْتَيْقِظُ آخِرَهُ، فَلْيُوتِرْ آخِرَهُ، فَإِنَّ صَلَاةَ آخِرِ اللَّيْلِ مَحْضُورَةٌ وَهِيَ أَفْضَلُ»

Whoever among you thinks that he will not wake up at the end of the night, then let him perform *Al-Witr* in its beginning. And whoever among you thinks that he will wake up at the end of the night, then let him perform the *Witr* at the end of it. Indeed, the prayer at the end of the night is attended and it is better.[2]

The meaning of "attended" is that the angels attend it.

---

[1] Al-Bukhari
[2] Ahmad, and the wording is his. It is also related in meaning by Muslim.

Sleeping Until The Morning Without Having Performed *Al-Witr*:
When a Muslim sleeps without performing *Al-Witr*, and when he
doesn't wake up until the morning, he should make up for it,
praying it before the *Zuhr* prayer. The Prophet ﷺ said:

«مَنْ نَامَ عَنْ وِتْرِهِ أَوْ نَسِيَهُ، فَلْيُصَلِّهِ إِذَا ذَكَرَهُ»

Whoever sleeps, leaving the *Witr*, or whoever forgets it, let him
pray it when he remembers.[1]

In case that one forgets it, he should perform it with an even number
in the morning; for example, if he habitually performs *Witr* with
three units, he should perform it with four.

Recitation In *Al-Witr*: It is recommended to recite *Al-A'la* and *Al-
Kafirun* in the two units before *Al-Witr*, and then in the unit of *Al-
Witr* to recite the three last *Surahs* of the Qur'ân after *Al-Fatihah*;[2]
however, this should be done only sometimes. For the most part,
one should read only *Surat Al-Ikhlas* after *Al-Fatihah*.

It Is Disliked To Perform *Al-Witr* More Than Once: In a single
night, it is disliked to perform more than one *Witr*, for the Prophet
ﷺ said:

«لَا وِتْرَانِ بلَيْلَةٍ»

There are no two *Witrs* in one night.[3]

The Sunnah Of *Fajr*

Its Ruling: Like the *Witr*, the Sunnah prayer (two units) before *Al-
Fajr* is a compulsory Sunnah, for it is the first prayer of a Muslim
during the day, while the *Witr* is the last prayer of the Muslim at
night. The Prophet ﷺ further stressed the importance of this Sunnah
prayer by performing it consistently, never leaving it. The Prophet ﷺ
encouraged Muslims to perform it, saying:

«رَكْعَتَا الْفَجْرِ خَيْرٌ مِنَ الدُّنْيَا وَمَا فِيهَا»

The two units of *Fajr* are better than the world and all that is in it.[4]

---

[1] Abu Dawud, and the *Hadith* is authentic
[2] Ahmad, Abu Dawud, and An-Nasa'i, with a *Hasan* chain
[3] At-Tirmithi, who said it is *Hasan*.
[4] Muslim

He ﷺ also said:

«لَا تَدَعُوا رَكْعَتَيِ الْفَجْرِ وَإِنْ طَارَدَتْكُمُ الْخَيْلُ»

Do not abandon the two units of *Fajr* even if you are being chased by horses.[1]

When The Sunnah Prayer Of *Fajr* Is Performed: It is performed in the time between dawn and the actual *Fajr* prayer. Whoever sleeps until the sun rises, or forgets to pray it, then he should perform it when he remembers, unless midday arrives, in which case one should not perform it. The Prophet ﷺ said:

«مَنْ لَمْ يُصَلِّ رَكْعَتَيِ الْفَجْرِ حَتَّى تَطْلُعَ الشَّمْسُ فَلْيُصَلِّهِمَا»

Whoever doesn't pray the two units of *Fajr* until the sun rises should then perform them.[2]

During days of battle, the Prophet ﷺ and his Companions once slept until the sun had risen; they moved a little, leaving their place, and then the Prophet ﷺ ordered Bilal to call the *Athan* for prayer. He ﷺ then prayed two units before the *Fajr* prayer, after which the *Iqamah* was called and he ﷺ prayed *Fajr*.[3]

How The Two Sunnah Units Of *Fajr* Are Performed: The Sunnah of *Fajr* consists of two light units; after reading *Al-Fatihah* in each unit, one should recite *Surat Al-Kafirun* in the first unit and *Al-Ikhlas* in the second unit, reading both units quietly. If one reads only *Al-Fatihah* in each unit, then that is sufficient for him. 'Aishah, may Allâh be pleased with her, said, "The Messenger of Allâh ﷺ would pray two units before the early morning, and he would perform them so lightly that I doubted whether he even recited the Opening of the Book or not."[4]   She also said, "In the two units of *Fajr*, the Messenger of Allâh ﷺ used to read "*Qul Yaa Ayyuhal-Kaafiroon*" and "*Qul Huwallâhu Ahad*," and he would be satisfied with them."[5]

---

[1] Ahmad and Abu Dawud.

[2] Al-Baihaqi, with a *Hasan* chain.

[3] Related by Al-Bukhari.

[4] Related by Al-Bukhari (2:52 in the Book of *Tahajjud*), and by Muslim (1:500).

[5] Muslim (1:502)

Sometimes in the first unit he would recite:

$$﴿قُولُوٓاْ ءَامَنَّا بِٱللَّهِ وَمَآ أُنزِلَ إِلَيْنَا﴾$$

Say (O Muslims), "We believe in Allâh and that which has been sent down to us..."[1]

And in the second unit:

$$﴿قُلْ يَٰٓأَهْلَ ٱلْكِتَٰبِ تَعَالَوْاْ إِلَىٰ كَلِمَةٍ سَوَآءٍ﴾$$

Say (O Muhammad): "O People of the Scripture (Jews and Christians): Come to a word that is just between us and you..."[2]

And sometimes he would recite:

$$﴿ءَامَنَّا بِٱللَّهِ وَٱشْهَدْ بِأَنَّا مُسْلِمُونَ﴾$$

We believe in Allâh, and bear witness that we are Muslims.[3]

Voluntary Prayers In General

Their Superiority: There are many great virtues attached to voluntary prayers. The Prophet ﷺ said:

$$«مَا أُذِنَ لِعَبْدٍ فِي شَيْءٍ أَفْضَلَ مِنْ رَكْعَتَيْنِ يُصَلِّيهِمَا، وَإِنَّ الْبِرَّ لَيُذَرُّ عَلَى رَأْسِ الْعَبْدِ مَا دَامَ فِي صَلَاتِهِ»$$

The best thing in which Allâh listens to His worshipper are two units that he prays, for indeed good is showered over his head as long as he is in his prayer.[4]

When a Companion asked the Prophet ﷺ for his companionship in Paradise, the Prophet ﷺ said:

$$«أَعِنِّي عَلَى نَفْسِكَ بِكَثْرَةِ السُّجُودِ»$$

Help me to help you by performing a lot of prostrations.[5]

The Wisdom Behind The Voluntary Prayers: The voluntary prayer

---

[1] (*Al-Baqarah* 2:136)
[2] (*Aal 'Imran* 3:64)
[3] (*Aal 'Imran* 3:52) See Muslim (1:502).
[4] Related by At-Tirmithi, and the *Hadith* is authentic.
[5] Muslim

makes up for obligatory prayers if they are deficient. The Messengers of Allâh ﷺ said:

«إِنَّ أَوَّلَ مَا يُحَاسَبُ النَّاسُ بِهِ يَوْمَ الْقِيَامَةِ مِنْ أَعْمَالِهِمُ الصَّلَاةُ، يَقُولُ رَبُّنَا لِلْمَلَائِكَةِ - وَهُوَ أَعْلَمُ -: انْظُرُوا فِي صَلَاةِ عَبْدِي أَتَمَّهَا أَمْ نَقَصَهَا؟ فَإِنْ كَانَتْ تَامَّةً كُتِبَتْ لَهُ تَامَّةٌ، وَإِنْ كَانَ انْتَقَصَ مِنْهَا..

Indeed, the first deed for which people will be held accountable on the Day of Judgement is the prayer. Our Lord says to the angels – and He is more knowledgeable thereof, "Look at the prayer of my servant – did he complete it or did he leave it deficient?" If it is complete, then it is written for him as complete. And if it is deficient...

The *Hadith* goes on to mention that if the obligatory prayers are deficient, then the voluntary prayers can make up for them.

The Two 'Eid Prayers

Their Rulings And Timings: The two 'Eid Prayers – *Al-Fitr* and *Al-Adhha* – are Sunnahs that are compulsory like obligations.[1] Allâh ordered Muslims to perform this prayer when He said:

﴿إِنَّا أَعْطَيْنَاكَ ٱلْكَوْثَرَ ۝ فَصَلِّ لِرَبِّكَ وَٱنْحَرْ﴾

Verily, We have granted you (O Muhammad) *Al-Kawthar* (a river in Paradise); therefore turn in prayer to your Lord and sacrifice (to Him only).[2]

And Allâh Almighty made the success of the believer conditional upon it in this verse:

﴿قَدْ أَفْلَحَ مَن تَزَكَّىٰ ۝ وَذَكَرَ ٱسْمَ رَبِّهِ فَصَلَّىٰ﴾

Indeed whosoever purifies himself shall achieve success. And remembers the Name of his Lord, and prays....[3]

The Prophet ﷺ always prayed the two 'Eid prayers and he ordered

---

[1] Indeed, some of the people of knowledge have said that the two 'Eid prayers are obligatory upon the same people as those that the *Jumu'ah* prayer is obligatory upon, and that it is recommended for women.

[2] (*Al-Kawthar* 108:1,2)

[3] (*Al- A'la* 87:14,15)

others to do so as well; he ﷺ even ordered women and children to come out and attend. The *'Eid* prayer is one of the religious practices of Islam, one of its outward aspects through which faith and piety are manifest.

The Time Of The *'Eid* Prayer: When the sun rises the length of a spear, Muslims should perform the *'Eid* prayer; this means that it can be performed fifteen minutes after the sun rises until midday. It is best to perform *Al-Adhha* at its earliest time, allowing people to slaughter their sacrifices. And it is best to delay the *Fitr* prayer, allowing people extra time to pay their *Fitr* charity, because that is what the Prophet ﷺ did. Jundub, may Allâh be pleased with him, said, "The Prophet ﷺ would pray the *Fitr* when the sun was up the length of two spears and *Al-Adhha* when the sun was up the length of a single spear."[1]

Manners Related To The *'Eid* Prayer:

1) One should perform *Ghusl*, apply perfume, and wear beautiful clothing. Anas, may Allâh be pleased with him, said, "For the two *'Eids*, the Messenger of Allâh ﷺ ordered us to wear the best that we could find, to wear perfume with the best we could find, and to sacrifice with the most expensive that we could find."[2] "And the Messenger of Allâh ﷺ used to wear a stripped robe every *'Eid*."[3]

2) Before going to the *'Eidul-Fitr* prayer, one should eat; and after the *'Eidul-Adhha* prayer, one should eat from the sacrifice, rulings about that are based on the following saying of Buraidah, may Allâh be pleased with him, "The Prophet ﷺ wouldn't leave early in the morning on the day of *Al-Fitr* until he ate, and he wouldn't eat on the day of *Al-Adhha* until he returned, and then he would eat from his sacrifice."[4]

3) One should say the *Takbir* on the nights before both *'Eids*, and for *Adhha*, one should continue to do so until the end of the days of

---

[1] Refer to *Talkhis Al-Habir*, by Ibn Hajr.

[2] Related by Al-Hakim, and there is no harm in its chain.

[3] Related by Ash-Shafi'i, and there is no harm in its chain due to supporting narrators.

[4] Related by Tirmithi and others, and declared to be authentic by Ibn Al-Qattan.

Tashriq – when the sun sets on the thirteenth (of Thul-Hijjah). And one should continue to say the *Takbir* on *Al-Fitr* until the *Imam* comes out for the *'Eid* prayer. The wording of this special *Takbir* is as follows:

"*Allâhu Akbar, Allâhu Akbar* (Allâh is the Most Great, Allâh is the Most Great). *Laa Ilaha Illallâh* (None has the right to be worshipped but Allâh). *Allâhu Akbar, Allâhu Akbar* (Allâh is the Most Great, Allâh is the Most Great), *Wa lillâhil-Hamd* (And to Allâh belongs all praise)."

It especially becomes significant to say the *Takbir* when one leaves for the place of prayer, and after the obligatory prayers.

Also, in the days of *Tashriq*, based on Allâh's saying:

﴿ وَٱذۡكُرُواْ ٱللَّهَ فِىٓ أَيَّامٖ مَّعۡدُودَٰتٖ ﴾

And remember Allâh during the appointed Days.[1]

And:

﴿ وَذَكَرَ ٱسۡمَ رَبِّهِۦ فَصَلَّىٰ ﴾

And remembers the Name of his Lord, and prays.[2]

And:

﴿ لِتُكَبِّرُواْ ٱللَّهَ عَلَىٰ مَا هَدَىٰكُمۡ ﴾

That you may exalt Allâh for His guidance to you.[3]

4) One should go to the *'Eid* prayer, taking one route, and return, taking another, for that is what the Prophet ﷺ did. Jabir, may Allâh be pleased with him, said, "On the day of *'Eid*, the Prophet ﷺ would take different routes."[4]

5) The *'Eid* prayers should be performed in open areas unless rain or something similar prevents that from happening, in which case they may be performed in a *Masjid*, as has been related in the *Sahihs*.

6) One should congratulate his brother Muslim, saying, "May Allâh

[1] (*Al-Baqarah* 2:203)
[2] (*Al- A'la* 87:15)
[3] (*Al-Hajj* 22:37)
[4] Al-Bukhari

accept from me and you.'' When the Companions would meet one another on the day of *'Eid*, they would say, "May Allâh accept from us and from you.''[1]

7) There is no harm on these days to eat and drink abundantly and to play those games or sports that are permissible in Islam. On the day of *'Eidul-Adhha*, the Prophet ﷺ said:

«أَيَّامُ التَّشْرِيقِ أَيَّامُ أَكْلٍ وَشُرْبٍ، وَذِكْرِ اللهِ عَزَّ وَجَلَّ»

The days of *Tashriq* are days for eating and drinking and remembering Allâh.[2]

Anas, may Allâh be pleased with him, said, "When the Prophet ﷺ came to Al-Madinah, its inhabitants had two days that they would play in. The Messenger of Allâh ﷺ said,

«قَدْ أَبْدَلَكُمُ اللهُ تَعَالَى بِهِمَا خَيْرًا مِنْهُمَا، يَوْمَ الْفِطْرِ وَيَوْمَ الْأَضْحَى»

Indeed, Allâh Almighty has replaced those two days with that which is better than them: the day of *Al-Fitr* and the day of *Al-Adhha*.''[3]

On the day of *'Eid*, Abu Bakr, may Allâh be pleased with him, scolded two girls for reciting poetry in the house of 'Aishah, and the Prophet ﷺ said:

«يَا أَبَا بَكْرٍ، إِنَّ لِكُلِّ قَوْمٍ عِيدًا، وَإِنَّ الْيَوْمَ عِيدُنَا»

O Abu Bakr, indeed every people have an *'Eid* (festival holiday), and indeed today is our *'Eid*.[4]

How It Is Performed: People go out to the place of the *'Eid* prayer, declaring Allâh's Greatness. When the sun rises a few meters, the *Imam* stands and leads the people in a prayer of two units that has neither *Athan* nor *Iqamah*. In the first unit, he makes the *Takbir* (saying, "*Allâhu Akbar*") seven times with the opening *Takbir*. The people follow him, making the *Takbir* for each of his *Takbirs*. Then he recites *Surat Al-Fatihah*, followed by *Al-A'la* out loud. In the

---

[1] Recorded by Ahmad with a good (*Jayyid*) chain of narration.
[2] Muslim
[3] Related by An-Nasa'i with an authentic chain.
[4] Al-Bukhari

second unit, he should make *Takbir* six times with the *Takbir* of standing up. After reading *Al-Fatihah*, he should recite either *Surat Al-Ghashiyah* or *Wash-Shamsi wadh-Dhuhaha*. Then after making the final *Taslim*, he should rise and give a sermon to the people, dividing it into two by sitting for a brief period of time during it. He should admonish, advise, and remind the people, interposing *Takbirs* during the sermon. He should open his sermon by praising and extolling Allâh, and if it is *'Eidul-Fitr*, he should advise people to pay the *Fitr* charity, clarifying for them some of its rulings. And if it is *'Eidul-Adhha*, he should encourage people to follow the Sunnah of the sacrifice (*Udhhiyah*), clarifying the minimum age of the animal for it to be correct. When he finishes his sermon, he and the people leave, since there is neither a Sunnah prayer before it or after it. The exception is the person who comes late and misses the *'Eid* prayer, for he should pray four units. Ibn Mas'ud, may Allâh be pleased with him, said, "Whoever misses the *'Eid* prayer, then let him pray four, but as for him who catches a portion of the prayer with the *Imam*, even if it is only the *Tashahhud*, he should stand up after the *Imam* makes *Taslim* and perform two units of prayer..."[1]

The Eclipse Prayer

Its Ruling And Time: The Eclipse Prayer is a compulsory Sunnah for both men and women. The Prophet ﷺ ordered Muslims to perform it when he ﷺ said:

«إِنَّ الشَّمْسَ وَالْقَمَرَ آيَتَانِ مِنْ آيَاتِ اللهِ، لَا يَخْسِفَانِ لِمَوْتِ أَحَدٍ وَلَا لِحَيَاتِهِ، فَإِذَا رَأَيْتُمْ ذَلِكَ فَصَلُّوا»

Indeed the sun and the moon are two signs from Allâh's signs; they do not become eclipsed for the death or life of anyone; so if you see an eclipse, then pray.[2]

The time for the Eclipse Prayer begins when either the moon or the sun becomes eclipsed, and its time finishes when the sun or the

---

[1] In *Al-Fatwa* (4:507) compiled by Dr. 'Abdullah At-Tayyar and Shaikh Ahmad bin Baz, his eminence Shaikh 'Abdul-'Aziz bin Baz said, "If one misses the *'Eid* prayer, he should make it up for just as he does for the obligatory prayers."

[2] Related by Al-Bukhari

moon – depending on which is eclipsed – appears again. But if an eclipse occurs at the end of the day, a time when it is extremely disliked to perform voluntary prayers, the Eclipse Prayer is replaced by remembrance of Allâh, seeking His forgiveness, and supplication. This ruling applies to one who deems voluntary prayers to be categorically prohibited during the forbidden times. But if one is of the view that prayer for a reason is permissible during the forbidden times, then he may pray the Eclipse Prayer – and this latter view is correct.

What It Is Recommended To Do During An Eclipse: It is recommended to do as much of the following as one can: Remembering Allâh Almighty, seeking His forgiveness, supplicating to Him, giving charity, freeing a slave, performing good deeds in general, and establishing ties with relatives. The Prophet ﷺ said:

«إِنَّ الشَّمْسَ وَالْقَمَرَ آيَتَانِ مِنْ آيَاتِ اللهِ، لَا يَخْسِفَانِ لِمَوْتِ أَحَدٍ وَلَا لِحَيَاتِهِ، فَإِذَا رَأَيْتُمْ ذَلِكَ فَادْعُوا اللهَ وَكَبِّرُوا وَتَصَدَّقُوا وَصَلُّوا»

Indeed the sun and the moon are two signs from Allâh's signs; they do not become eclipsed for the death or life of anyone; so if you see an eclipse, then invoke Allâh, say the *Takbir*, give charity, and pray.[1]

How To Perform The Eclipse Prayer: The people gather in the *Masjid* without *Athan* or *Iqamah*, yet there is no harm in announcing it by saying, "Prayer in congregation." The *Imam* then leads the congregation in two units, performing two bowings and standing twice in each unit. He should prolong the following – his recitation, bowing, and prostration. If the eclipse finishes during the prayer, then they may complete it in the form of the normal voluntary prayer. Unlike the *'Eid* prayers, it is not Sunnah to have a *Khutbah* during the Eclipse prayer; but if the *Imam* wishes to do so he may remind and admonish the people, and he does well if he does remind them. 'Aishah, may Allâh be pleased with her, said,

"The sun was eclipsed during the life of the Messenger of Allâh ﷺ, and the Messenger of Allâh ﷺ went to the *Masjid*. He stood and then

---

[1] Related by Al-Bukhari

made *Takbir*; next, he made the people line up behind him. He prolonged his recitation, after which he made the *Takbir*, followed by a long bowing, though it was shorter than his recitation. Then he raised his head, saying, "Allâh listens to those who praise Him; O our Lord, to You belongs all praise." Then, standing for a second time in the same unit, he prolonged his recitation, but made it shorter than the first recitation. Next, he made the *Takbir* followed by the bowing, which was shorter than the first bowing. Then he ﷺ said, "Allâh listens to those who praise Him; O our Lord, to You belongs all praise." Then he prostrated, after which he did the same in the second unit as he did in the first, until he had completed four bowings and four prostrations. Before he parted, the sun appeared; he stood, addressed the people, praising Allâh Almighty with the best praise he could. Then he ﷺ said:

«إِنَّ الشَّمْسَ وَالْقَمَرَ آيَتَانِ مِنْ آيَاتِ اللهِ، عَزَّ وَجَلَّ لَا يَخْسِفَانِ لِمَوْتِ أَحَدٍ وَلَا لِحَيَاتِهِ، فَإِذَا رَأَيْتُمُوهُمَا فَافْزَعُوا لِلصَّلَاةِ»

Indeed the sun and the moon are two signs from Allâh's signs; they do not become eclipsed for the death or life of anyone; so if you see an eclipse, then take recourse in the prayer.

A Lunar Eclipse

The Eclipse Prayer is the same for both the solar and lunar eclipses, for the Prophet ﷺ said:

«فَإِذَا رَأَيْتُمُوهُمَا فَافْزَعُوا لِلصَّلَاةِ»

Then if you see it (i.e., an eclipse), then seek shelter in the prayer.

However, some of the people of knowledge hold that the Lunar Eclipse Prayer is the same as all other voluntary prayers, in that individuals should pray it in their homes or the *Masjid*. They hold that people should not gather and pray together because the Prophet ﷺ only gathered the people for prayer during a solar eclipse.

Therefore there is leeway in this issue: those who wish to gather to pray may do so and those who wish to pray individually may do so as well. The main point to keep in mind is that Muslims – both males and females – should seek shelter in the prayer, so that Allâh Almighty may remove them from that state.

The Rain Prayer

Its Ruling: The Rain Prayer is a compulsory Sunnah; the Prophet ﷺ performed it and announced it to the people, who gathered with him in their place of prayer. 'Abdullah bin Zaid, may Allâh be pleased with him, said, "The Prophet ﷺ went out supplicating for rain; he turned to the *Qiblah* and inverted his garment; he then prayed two units, reading out loud in them.[1]

What Is The Rain Prayer: When a drought occurs, people ask for forgiveness, pray, and invoke Allâh Almighty to provide them with rain for the land and for His slaves.

The Time for The Rain Prayer: The time for the Rain Prayer is just like the time for the *'Eid* prayer: when the sun is up the length of a spear – approximately fifteen minutes after the sun rises. 'Aishah, may Allâh be pleased with her, said, "The Messenger of Allâh ﷺ went out for it when the edge of the sun appeared."[2] Yet it is permitted to perform it any time, except for the disliked times, those times when the prayer is forbidden.

What Is Recommended To Do Before The Rain Prayer: It is recommended for the *Imam* to announce it before its appointed date by days; he should also exhort the people to repent from their sins and to desist in their transgressions against others. He should encourage them to fast and give charity, as well as to avoid any quarrels. He does the above because sins cause droughts to take place, just as obedience to Allâh Almighty causes blessings and good things to occur.

The Rain Prayer Described: The *Imam* and the people come out to the place of prayer, and he leads them in two units, making seven *Takbirs* in the first unit with the opening *Takbir*. In the second unit, he makes five *Takbirs* after the *Takbir* for standing, just as he does in the *'Eid* prayer. In the first unit, he reads out loud, reciting "*Sabbih-isma Rabbikal-A'la*" after *Surat Al-Fatihah*, and in the second unit,

---

[1] Agreed upon
[2] Abu Dawud and Al-Hakim, who declared it to be authentic.

Al-Ghashiyah. Then he faces the people, giving them a sermon, seeking much forgiveness from Allâh during it. Next, he should supplicate, and the people should say, "*Aameen*" after his supplications. Then, facing the *Qiblah*, he should invert his garment, making what was on the right to be on the left, and vice versa. The people should also invert their garments, after which they supplicate and leave.

Abu Hurairah said, "Allâh's Prophet ﷺ went out asking for rain, and he prayed two units with us, with neither *Athan* nor *Iqamah*. He then gave us a sermon and invoked Allâh. Raising his hands, he changed direction, facing the *Qiblah*. Next, he inverted his garment, putting the right side on the left, and the left side on the right."[1]

Some Of The Wordings Related To Us Regarding Supplication For Rain: It has been related that the Prophet ﷺ would say the following supplication for rain:

«اللَّهُمَّ اسْقِنَا غَيْثًا مَرِيئًا مَرِيعاً غَدَقاً مُجَلَّلاً عَامًّا طَبَقًا سَحًّا دَائِمًا . اللَّهُمَّ بِالْعِبَادِ وَالْبِلَادِ وَالْبَهَائِمِ وَالْخَلْقِ مِنَ اللَّأْوَاءِ وَالْجَهْدِ وَالضَّنْكِ مَا لَا نَشْكُوهُ إِلَّا إِلَيْكَ. اللَّهُمَّ أَنْبِتْ لَنَا الزَّرْعَ وَأَدِرَّ لَنَا الضَّرْعَ، وَاسْقِنَا مِنْ بَرَكَاتِ السَّمَاءِ، وَأَنْبِتْ لَنَا مِنْ بَرَكَاتِ الْأَرْضِ. اللَّهُمَّ ارْفَعْ عَنَّا الْجَهْدَ وَالْجُوعَ وَالْعُرْيَ، وَاكْشِفْ عَنَّا مِنَ الْبَلَاءِ مَا لَا يَكْشِفُهُ غَيْرُكَ. اللَّهُمَّ إِنَّا نَسْتَغْفِرُكَ، إِنَّكَ كُنْتَ غَفَّارًا، فَأَرْسِلِ السَّمَاءَ عَلَيْنَا مِدْرَارًا، اللَّهُمَّ اسْقِ عِبَادَكَ وَبَهَائِمَكَ، وَانْشُرْ رَحْمَتَكَ، وَأَحْيِ بَلَدَكَ الْمَيِّتَ»

O Allâh! Quench us with a shower that is wholesome and fertile, abundant and vital, covering all around and flowing steadily. O Allâh! Quench us with a shower and do not make us among those who despair! O Allâh! For the worshippers, the land, the animals, and the creatures, for their suffering, struggling and hardships that we do not complain of except to You. O Allâh! Cause our farms to sprout growth, and the

---

[1] Ahmad, Ibn Majah, Al-Baihaqi; the narrators of this *Hadith* are all trustworthy.

udders of our animals to flow. Quench us from the blessings of the heavens and sprout the blessings of the earth for us. O Allâh! Remove the suffering, the hunger, and the affliction from us, deliver us from a trial that none can deliver from besides You. O Allâh! We indeed seek Your forgiveness, You are certainly forgiving, so send the skies pouring forth upon us. O Allâh! Quench the thirst of Your worshippers and Your animals, spread Your mercy and enliven Your dying city.[1]

It has also been related that the Prophet ﷺ would say the following supplication when it would rain:

«اللَّهُمَّ سُقْيَا رَحْمَةٍ لَا سُقْيَا عَذَابٍ، وَلَا بَلَاءٍ، وَلَا هَدْمٍ وَلَا غَرَقٍ. اللَّهُمَّ عَلَى الضِّرَابِ وَمَنَابِتِ الشَّجَرِ. اللَّهُمَّ حَوَالَيْنَا وَلَا عَلَيْنَا»

O Allâh, make it be a rain of mercy, not a rain of punishment, trial, destruction, or drowning. O Allâh, (make it fall) in the streets and to the roots of the trees. O Allâh, around us and not upon us.[2]

The *Istikharah* Prayer

When one wants something that is permissible and is confused regarding the choice he should make, not knowing what option is better for him, it is Sunnah for him to pray two units – outside of the obligatory prayers, units that he may pray at any time during the day or night, and in which he may recite whatever he pleases after *Al-Fatihah*. After saying the *Taslim* from this two-unit prayer, he should praise Allâh, send blessings upon the Prophet ﷺ, and continue by invoking Allâh, using the invocation that is related in Al-Bukhari, and that is narrated by Jabir, may Allâh be pleased with him, who said, "The Prophet ﷺ would instruct us to make the *Istikharah* (to pray for guidance) in all of our affairs; (he taught it to us) just as he would teach us a *Surah* from the Qur'ân, saying:

«إِذَا هَمَّ أَحَدُكُمْ بِالْأَمْرِ، فَلْيَرْكَعْ رَكْعَتَيْنِ مِنْ غَيْرِ الْفَرِيضَةِ، ثُمَّ لِيَقُلْ: اللَّهُمَّ إِنِّي أَسْتَخِيرُكَ بِعِلْمِكَ، وَأَسْتَقْدِرُكَ بِقُدْرَتِكَ، وَأَسْأَلُكَ مِنْ

---

[1] Recorded by Ibn Majah and its narrators are trustworthy.

[2] Related by Ash-Shafi'i, and most of it is found in Al-Bukhari and Muslim.

فَضْلِكَ الْعَظِيمِ، فَإِنَّكَ تَقْدِرُ وَلَا أَقْدِرُ، وَتَعْلَمُ وَلَا أَعْلَمُ، وَأَنْتَ عَلَّامُ الْغُيُوبِ. اللَّهُمَّ إِنْ كُنْتَ تَعْلَمُ أَنَّ هَذَا الْأَمْرَ (وَيُسَمِّي حَاجَتَهُ) خَيْرٌ لِي فِي دِينِي، وَمَعَاشِي وَعَاقِبَةِ أَمْرِي - أَوْ قَالَ: عَاجِلِ أَمْرِي وَآجِلِهِ - فَاقْدُرْهُ لِي، وَيَسِّرْهُ لِي، ثُمَّ بَارِكْ لِي فِيهِ. وَإِنْ كُنْتَ تَعْلَمُ أَنَّ هَذَا الْأَمْرَ، شَرٌّ لِي فِي دِينِي وَمَعَاشِي، وَعَاقِبَةِ أَمْرِي –أَوْ قَالَ: عَاجِلِ أَمْرِي وَآجِلِهِ- فَاصْرِفْهُ عَنِّي وَاصْرِفْنِي عَنْهُ، وَاقْدُرْ لِيَ الْخَيْرَ حَيْثُ كَانَ، ثُمَّ أَرْضِنِي بِهِ»

If one of you is worried about a matter, then let him pray two units of prayer other than the obligatory; then let him say, "O Allâh, I seek Your Counsel by Your Knowledge, and strength by Your Power, and I ask You from Your immense favor, for verily You are Able while I am not, and verily You know while I do not, and You are the Knower of the Unseen. O Allâh, if You know this affair – and here he mentions his need – to be good for me in relation to my religion, my life, and end, then decree and facilitate it for me, and bless me with it, and if You know this affair to be bad for me towards my religion, my life, and end, then remove it from me and remove me from it, and decree for me what is good wherever it be, and make me satisfied with that.''

An-Nawawi said, "After the *Istikharah*, one should do that which his heart opens to, so one should not depend on what his heart was open to based on his desires before he performed the *Istikharah*. Before performing the two units of *Istikharah*, the worshipper should empty his mind of biases toward one choice over the other, because otherwise, he is not really seeking guidance from Allâh, in which case he is not truthful when he claims to be seeking that which is best for him, and when he ascribes ignorance to himself, while ascribing ability and knowledge to Allâh, for if he was sincere in saying those things, he would absolve himself from having any power or ability and he would leave off choosing for himself.''

The Rulings For Funerals

1. The Muslim Must Be Patient When Hardships Afflict Him

When hardships afflict the Muslim, he must be patient, not showing anger or vexation, for both Allâh Almighty and His Messenger ﷺ ordered Muslims to be patient. Even though one must be patient, there is no harm in the sick person describing his situation, such as when he says, "I am sick," or "I am in pain," or, "In all situations, all praise is for Allâh."

2. It Is Compulsory To Visit The Sick

When his brother is afflicted with sickness, a Muslim must visit him, for the Prophet ﷺ said:

«أَطْعِمُوا الْجَائِعَ وَعُودُوا الْمَرِيضَ، وَفُكُّوا الْعَانِيَ -الْأَسِيرَ-»

Feed the hungry, visit the sick, and ransom the captive.[1]

When a Muslim visits his sick brother, he should invoke Allâh Almighty to cure him, advise his brother to be patient, and speak to him such words as will comfort him. It is also recommended not to sit for a long time with him. When the Messenger of Allâh ﷺ would visit a sick person, he would say to him:

«لَا بَأْسَ، طَهُورٌ إِنْ شَاءَ اللهُ»

It's all right; this is purification (from your sins) – if Allâh wills.[2]

A Muslim should say this phrase when he visits his sick brother.

3. It Is Compulsory To Have Good Thoughts About Allâh When One Is Sick

When a Muslim is sick – and especially when he is on the verge of death – he should have good thoughts about Allâh Almighty, that Allâh will have mercy on Him and forgive him, that His forgiveness is vast, and that His mercy encompasses all things. The Prophet ﷺ said:

«لَا يَمُوتَنَّ أَحَدُكُمْ إِلَّا وَهُوَ يُحْسِنُ بِاللهِ الظَّنَّ»

---

[1] Related by Al-Bukhari.
[2] Related by Al-Bukhari.

Let not one of you die except that he has good thoughts about Allâh.[1]

4. Prompting One Who Is About To Die

When a Muslim is present during the last moments of his brother's life, he should gently prompt him to say the phrase of sincerity, saying to him, *Laa Ilaha Illallâh* (None has the right to be worshipped but Allâh). He should remind him to say it until he remembers and says it. If the sick person says it, then he should leave him alone. But if the sick person then says something else, he should return to prompting him, hoping that his last words will be *Laa Ilaha Illallâh*, so that he enters Paradise, for the Prophet ﷺ said:

«لَقِّنُوا مَوْتَاكُمْ لَا إِلَهَ إِلَّا اللهُ»

Prompt to say *Laa Ilaha Illallâh* those who are dying.[2]

And the Prophet ﷺ said:

«مَنْ كَانَ آخِرُ كَلَامِهِ لَا إِلَهَ إِلَّا اللهُ»

Whoever's last words are "*Laa Ilaha Illallâh*," enters Paradise.[3]

5. Paying Off The Debts Of The Deceased

Those who remain behind should hasten to pay off any debts that the deceased may have incurred. The Prophet ﷺ said:

«نَفْسُ الْمُؤْمِنِ مُعَلَّقَةٌ بِدَيْنِهِ، حَتَّى يُقْضَى عَنْهُ»

The soul of the believer is suspended by his debt, until it is paid off for him.[4]

6. *Al-Istirja'*, Supplication, And Patience

The family of the deceased should hold fast to patience, especially in the period immediately following the loss of their relative. The Prophet ﷺ said:

---

[1] Related by Muslim
[2] Related by Muslim
[3] Recorded by Abu Dawud and it is authentic.
[4] Related by Al-Bukhari

«إِنَّمَا الصَّبْرُ عِنْدَ الصَّدْمَةِ الْأُولَى»

Indeed patience is only during the initial shock.[1]

He should supplicate as much as he can and say the *Istirja'* – *Istirja'* is to say, "Indeed we belong to Allâh and indeed to Him we are returning." The Prophet ﷺ said:

«مَا مِنْ عَبْدٍ تُصِيبُهُ مُصِيبَةٌ فَيَقُولُ: إِنَّا للهِ وَإِنَّا إِلَيْهِ رَاجِعُونَ، اللَّهُمَّ أُجْرْنِي فِي مُصِيبَتِي وَأَخْلِفْ لِي خَيْرًا مِنْهَا، إِلَّا آجَرَهُ اللهُ تَعَالَى فِي مُصِيبَتِهِ، وَأَخْلِفْ لَهُ خَيْرًا مِنْهَا»

Whenever a worshipper is afflicted by a hardship and then says, "Indeed, we belong to Allâh and indeed to Him is our return. O Allâh: reward me in my affliction, and replace for me that which is better than it (i.e., the thing that he lost)," Allâh rewards him in his affliction and replaces for him that which is better than it.[2]

The Prophet ﷺ also said:

«يَقُولُ اللهُ تَعَالَى: مَا لِعَبْدِي الْمُؤْمِنِ عِنْدِي جَزَاءٌ، إِذَا قَبَضْتُ صَفِيَّهُ مِنْ أَهْلِ الدُّنْيَا ثُمَّ احْتَسَبَهُ إِلَّا الْجَنَّةُ»

Allâh Almighty says, "When I take the precious one of My worshipper from this world, and then when he seeks his reward with Me, my worshipper has no reward with Me other than Paradise.[3]

7. It Is Obligatory To Wash The Body

When a Muslim dies – be he young or old, his body remaining fully intact or partially intact – it is obligatory to perform *Ghusl* on his body. The only exception for this ruling is the martyr who died in a battle – in *Jihad* in the way of Allâh – at the hands of the disbelievers because the Prophet ﷺ said regarding such martyrs:

---

[1] Related by Al-Bukhari
[2] Related by Muslim
[3] Related by Ahmad with an authentic chain.

«لَا تَغْسِلُوهُمْ فَإِنَّ كُلَّ جُرْحٍ، أَوْ كُلَّ دَمٍ يَفُوحُ مِسْكاً يَوْمَ الْقِيَامَةِ»

Do not wash them, for from each injury or all of his blood, musk will emanate on the Day of Judgement.[1]

8. How To Wash The Dead

In terms of what is sufficient for the washing to be considered correct, water may be poured over the body, so that it reaches all of its parts.

The More Complete And Recommended Way Of Washing The Body: The deceased should be placed on an elevated surface, and a trustworthy righteous person should attend the washing. He should lightly squeeze the stomach of the body in the hope that that will facilitate the discharge of any harmful matter. Next, he should wrap a rag around his hand, making intention to wash the body. He begins by washing the private parts, cleaning away any harmful matter. Then, taking off the rag, he should perform the ablution for prayer on the deceased, after which he washes the rest of the body, beginning from the top, going down until he reaches the feet. He should wash the body three times, but if cleanliness is not achieved, then five times. On the last washing, he should apply camphor or *Sidr* or the like.

If the deceased is a female Muslim, then her braids should be undone and her hair washed, after which her braids should be done again. The Prophet ﷺ ordered, for such to be done with the hair of his daughter.[2]

A trustworthy and righteous female washes the female Muslim's body. Then perfume or the like is applied. The husband may wash the body of his wife just as a wife may wash the body of her husband.

9. *Tayammum* Replaces The *Ghusl* When Necessary

When water cannot be found to wash the deceased or when a man dies in a place populated by women only, or a woman dies in a place populated by men only – in these instances, *Tayammum* is performed on the deceased and the deceased is then enshrouded.

---

[1] Ahmad, with an authentic chain
[2] Al-Bukhari

This is similar to the situation of the *Junub* (for example, one who has had sexual intercourse) who cannot find water: he must perform *Tayammum* and then pray. That is because the Prophet ﷺ said:

«إِذَا مَاتَتِ الْمَرْأَةُ مَعَ رِجَالٍ لَيْسَ مَعَهُمُ امْرَأَةٌ غَيْرُهَا، وَالرَّجُلُ مَعَ نِسَاءٍ لَيْسَ مَعَهُنَّ رَجُلٌ غَيْرُهُ، فَإِنَّهُمَا يُتَيَمَّمَانِ وَيُدْفَنَانِ»

If a woman dies among men, and there is not a single woman among them, and if a man dies among woman, and there is not a single man among them, then *Tayammum* is performed on them, after which they are buried.[1]

They are of the status of one who cannot find water.

10. Enshrouding The Body Is Compulsory

After the deceased Muslim is washed, it is obligatory to enshroud him with enough material to cover his entire body. Mus'ab bin 'Umair, one of the martyrs of the battle of Uhud, was enshrouded in a very short garment, and so the Prophet ﷺ ordered the Companions to cover his head and body with that garment and to cover his legs with *Ithkhir* (lemon grass).[2] This shows that it is compulsory to cover the entire body and that *Ithkhir* is resorted to when there is not enough cloth to cover the rest of the body.

11. Prayer Upon The Deceased

When a Muslim dies, it is a communal obligation to pray over the deceased, the same ruling that is given to the washing, the enshrouding, and the burying of the deceased. As long as some Muslims perform it, the rest of the community is absolved from the obligation. The Prophet ﷺ used to pray over those Muslims who died; however, he would not pray over someone who died having outstanding debts without having someone pay those debts for him after his death; instead, the Prophet ﷺ would say to his Companions:

«صَلُّوا عَلَى صَاحِبِكُمْ»

Pray over your companion.[3]

---

[1] Abu Dawud in his *Maraseel* and Al-Baihaqi.
[2] Related by Al-Bukhari
[3] Related by Al-Bukhari

12. The Conditions Of Prayer Over The Deceased

The same conditions that apply to a regular prayer also apply to the Funeral Prayer: so the worshipper, for instance, must be in a state of purity, he must cover his *'Awrah*, and he must face the *Qiblah*. All of the above and other conditions apply because the Prophet ﷺ called the Funeral Prayer a prayer when he said:

«صَلُّوا عَلَى صَاحِبِكُمْ»

Pray over your companion.

Therefore it falls under the rulings of prayer in terms of its conditions.

13. The Obligatory Elements Of The Funeral Prayer Are As Follows

1) Standing, for whoever is able to do so.

2) Making intention, for the Prophet ﷺ said:

«إِنَّمَا الْأَعْمَالُ بِالنِّيَّاتِ»

Indeed deeds are based on intentions.

3) Recitation of *Surat Al-Fatihah*, or at least praising and extolling Allâh.

4) Sending blessings and salutations upon the Prophet ﷺ.

5) Making the four *Takbirs*.

6) Supplication.

7) The *Taslim*.

14. How To Perform It

1) The body of the deceased – or the bodies – should be placed so that it is facing the *Qiblah*.

2) The *Imam* stands, with the people behind him, making at least three rows, for the Prophet ﷺ said,

«مَنْ صَلَّى عَلَيْهِ ثَلَاثَةُ صُفُوفٍ فَقَدْ أَوْجَبَت»

Whoever is prayed upon by three rows then it (Paradise) becomes binding.[1]

---

[1] At-Tirmithi, who declared it to be *Hasan*.

3) The worshipper raises his hands, intending prayer over one dead person or more – depending on the situation – saying, "*Allâhu Akbar* (Allâh is the Most Great)."

4) Next, he recites *Al-Fatihah*, after which he says, "*Allâhu Akbar*," raising his hands if he wishes, or leaving them on his chest, with the right hand over the left one. Then he sends blessings upon the Prophet ﷺ, using the same wording that he uses in the *Tashahhud*.

5) Next, he makes *Takbir* and supplicates for the deceased.

6) Then he makes another *Takbir*.

7) At this point – after the fourth *Takbir* – he may either supplicate and make one *Taslim* or he may make one *Taslim* immediately. It has been related that the Sunnah in the prayer is for the *Imam* to make *Takbir*, to recite *Al-Fatihah*, silently to himself, to send blessings upon the Prophet ﷺ, to sincerely supplicate for the deceased in the *Takbirs*. Then, without reciting anything from the Qur'ân, he makes *Taslim* silently to himself.[1]

15. The Supplication

The supplication made during the Funeral Prayer has been related with a number of different wordings; it is sufficient for one to use any of those supplications that are related; here are some of them:

«اللَّهُمَّ إِنَّ فُلَاناً ابْنَ فُلَانٍ فِي ذِمَّتِكَ وَحَبْلِ جِوَارِكَ فَقِهِ مِنْ فِتْنَةِ الْقَبْرِ وَعَذَابِ النَّارِ، وَأَنْتَ أَهْلُ الْوَفَاءِ وَالْحَقِّ. اللَّهُمَّ فَاغْفِرْ لَهُ وَارْحَمْهُ فَإِنَّكَ أَنْتَ الْغَفُورُ الرَّحِيمُ. اللَّهُمَّ اغْفِرْ لِحَيِّنَا وَمَيِّتِنَا، وَصَغِيرِنَا وَكَبِيرِنَا، وَذَكَرِنَا وَأُنْثَانَا، وَحَاضِرِنَا وَغَائِبِنَا. اللَّهُمَّ مَنْ أَحْيَيْتَهُ مِنَّا فَأَحْيِهِ عَلَى الْإِسْلَامِ، وَمَنْ تَوَفَّيْتَهُ مِنَّا فَتَوَفَّهُ عَلَى الْإِيمَانِ. اللَّهُمَّ لَا تَحْرِمْنَا أَجْرَهُ، وَلَا تُضِلَّنَا بَعْدَهُ»

O Allâh, so-and-so is under Your care and protection, so protect him from the trial of the grave and torment of the Fire. Indeed You are the Guardian of faithful and truthful. Forgive and have mercy upon him, surely You are the Oft-Forgiving,

---

[1] Related by Ash-Shafi'i, and its chain is declared authentic by Al-Hafiz.

the Most Merciful. O Allâh, forgive our living and our dead, those present and those absent, our young and our old, our males and our females. O Allâh, whom among us You keep alive, then let such a life be upon Islam, and whom among us You take unto Yourself, then let such a death be upon faith. O Allâh, do not deprive us of his reward and do not let us stray after him.

If the deceased is a child, then the worshipper says:

«اللَّهُمَّ اجْعَلْهُ لِوَالِدَيْهِ سَلَفًا وَذُخْرًا وَفَرَطًا وَثَقِّلْ بِهِ مَوَازِينَهُمْ وَأَعْظِمْ بِهِ أُجُورَهُمْ، وَلَا تَحْرِمْنَا وَإِيَّاهُمْ أَجْرَهُ وَلَا تَفْتِنَّا وَإِيَّاهُمْ بَعْدَهُ. اللَّهُمَّ أَلْحِقْهُ بِصَالِحِ سَلَفِ الْمُؤْمِنِينَ فِي كَفَالَةِ إِبْرَاهِيمَ وَأَبْدِلْهُ دَارًا خَيْرًا مِنْ دَارِهِ، وَأَهْلًا خَيْرًا مِنْ أَهْلِهِ، وَعَافِهِ مِنْ فِتْنَةِ الْقَبْرِ، وَمِنْ عَذَابِ جَهَنَّمَ»

O Allâh, make him a preceding reward, a predecessor, and a stored treasure for his parents. O Allâh, through him, make heavy their Scales and magnify their reward. O Allâh, do not deprive us and them of his reward, and do not put us and them to trial after him. O Allâh, unite him with the righteous believing predecessors, and place him under the care of Ibrahim. Exchange his home for a better home, and his family for a better family, and keep him safe from the trial of the grave and the punishment of the Hellfire.

16. Following the Funeral until the Burial

It is from the Sunnah to go out with the funeral procession, for the Prophet ﷺ said:

«عُودُوا الْمَرِيضَ وَامْشُوا مَعَ الْجَنَازَةِ تُذَكِّرْكُمُ الآخِرَةَ»

Visit the sick and walk with the funeral, for they remind you of the Hereafter.[1]

It is also Sunnah to hasten the body to its grave because the Prophet ﷺ said:

---

[1] Related by Muslim

«أَسْرِعُوا فَإِنْ تَكُ صَالِحَةً فَخَيْرٌ تُقَدِّمُونَهَا إِلَيْهِ، وَإِنْ تَكُ سِوَى ذَلِكَ
فَشَرٌّ تَضَعُونَهُ عَنْ رِقَابِكُمْ»

Hurry, because if it (the soul) is righteous, then it is something
good you are taking it to, and if it is otherwise, then it is evil
that you are ridding yourselves of.[1]

It is also recommended to walk in front of the funeral procession
because the Prophet ﷺ, Abu Bakr, and 'Umar walked in front of
it.[2]

As for the virtues of following a funeral, the Prophet ﷺ said:

«مَنِ اتَّبَعَ جَنَازَةَ مُسْلِمٍ إِيمَاناً وَاحْتِسَابًا، وَكَانَ مَعَهَا حَتَّى يُصَلَّى
عَلَيْهَا وَيُفْرَغَ مِنْ دَفْنِهَا، فَإِنَّهُ يَرْجِعُ مِنَ الْأَجْرِ بِقِيرَاطَيْنِ، كُلُّ قِيرَاطٍ
مِثْلُ أُحُدٍ (وَهُوَ جَبَلٌ عَظِيمٌ قُرْبَ الْمَدِينَةِ)، وَمَنْ صَلَّى عَلَيْهَا ثُمَّ
رَجَعَ قَبْلَ أَنْ تُدْفَنَ فَإِنَّهُ يَرْجِعُ بِقِيرَاطٍ»

Whoever follows the funeral of a Muslim, with faith, expecting
his reward (from Allâh), and continues with it from the time
the deceased is prayed upon until the burial is completed,
then he returns with two *Qirats*, and each *Qirat* is like Uhud.
And whoever prays upon the deceased but returns before it is
buried, then he returns with one *Qirat* (of reward).[3]

17. The Burial

The burial – completely covering the body with dirt – is a communal
obligation, which means that if some people do it, the rest of the
community is absolved from the obligation. Allâh Almighty says:

﴿ثُمَّ أَمَاتَهُ فَأَقْبَرَهُ﴾

Then He causes him to die, and puts him in his grave;[4]

There are certain rulings related to the burial; here are some of
them:

---

[1] Al-Bukhari
[2] Related by Abu Dawud, An-Nasa'i, and others.
[3] Related by Al-Bukhari
[4] ('Abasa 80:21)

1) The grave should be deep enough to prevent predators and birds from reaching the body; it should also be made deep to prevent any odor from causing harm. The Prophet ﷺ said:

«احْفِرُوا وَأَعْمِقُوا وَأَحْسِنُوا وَادْفِنُوا الاثْنَيْنِ وَالثَّلَاثَةَ فِي قَبْرٍ وَاحِدٍ»

Dig, and dig deep, and perform it well, and bury two or three in a single grave.

The Companions asked, "Whom do we give precedence to, O Messenger of Allâh?"

He ﷺ said:

«قَدِّمُوا أَكْثَرَهُمْ قُرْآناً»

Put in first the one from them who knows the most from the Qur'ân.[1]

2) A hole should be dug in the right side of the grave, and that hole is called a *Lahd*. A *Lahd* is better than a *Shaqq*, which is a hole dug in the center of the grave, even though the *Shaqq* is permissible. The Prophet ﷺ said:

«اللَّحْدُ لَنَا وَالشَّقُّ لِغَيْرِنَا»

The *Lahd* is for us and the *Shaqq* is for other than us.[2]

3) It is recommended for one who attends the burial to pour three handfuls of dirt into the grave, from the direction of the head of the deceased. This was the practice of the Prophet ﷺ, as mentioned by Ibn Majah, with a chain in which there is no harm.

4) If possible, the body should be inserted from the back of the grave; then he should be made to face the *Qiblah* and is placed on his right side. The straps of the shroud should be undone but the face must not be exposed. Because the Prophet ﷺ did so, the one who places the deceased in the grave should say,

---

[1] Related by At-Tirmithi; he declared it to be authentic. No more than one body should be buried per grave unless there is a necessity, such as when there are a great many bodies.

[2] Ahmad, Abu Dawud, At-Tirmithi; there are disparaging remarks regarding its chain; however, some of the people of knowledge have declared it to be authentic.

«بِسْمِ اللهِ وَعَلَى مِلَّةِ رَسُولِ اللهِ»

In the Name of Allâh and upon the religion of the Messenger of Allâh.[1]

5) While a female body is being placed in her grave, the grave should be covered with a cloth. Our pious predecessors would cover the grave of a woman but they wouldn't do so for a man.

[1] Related by Abu Dawud and Al-Hakim, who said it is authentic.

The Third Pillar: *Zakat*
(Compulsory Charity)[1]

Zakat is not only obligatory in Islam, but it is also one of Islam's pillars, ranking third in importance after the two testimonies of faith and the prayer. Allâh's Book, the Prophet's Sunnah, and the consensus of the Muslims attest to *Zakat* being obligatory. Whoever denies that it is obligatory to give *Zakat* is a disbeliever, an apostate from whom repentance is demanded. If he repents, then that is well; otherwise, he is killed. Whoever is stingy regarding the *Zakat*, giving less than what is due from him, then he is from the wrongdoers who deserves the punishment of Allâh. Allâh Almighty says:

﴿وَلَا يَحْسَبَنَّ ٱلَّذِينَ يَبْخَلُونَ بِمَآ ءَاتَىٰهُمُ ٱللَّهُ مِن فَضْلِهِۦ هُوَ خَيْرًا لَّهُم بَلْ هُوَ شَرٌّ لَّهُمْ سَيُطَوَّقُونَ مَا بَخِلُواْ بِهِۦ يَوْمَ ٱلْقِيَٰمَةِ وَلِلَّهِ مِيرَٰثُ ٱلسَّمَٰوَٰتِ وَٱلْأَرْضِ وَٱللَّهُ بِمَا تَعْمَلُونَ خَبِيرٌ﴾

And let not those who covetously withhold of that which Allâh has bestowed on them of His bounty (wealth) think that it is good for them (and so they do not pay the obligatory *Zakat*). Nay, it will be worse for them; the things which they covetously withheld shall be tied to their necks like a collar on the Day of Resurrection. And to Allâh belongs the heritage of the heavens and the earth; and Allâh is Well-Acquainted with all that you do.[2]

In a *Hadith* related by Abu Hurairah, may Allâh be pleased with him, the Prophet ﷺ said:

«مَنْ آتَاهُ اللهُ مَالًا فَلَمْ يُؤَدِّ زَكَاتَهُ مُثِّلَ لَهُ يَوْمَ الْقِيَامَةِ شُجَاعًا أَقْرَعَ لَهُ زَبِيبَتَانِ يُطَوِّقُهُ يَوْمَ الْقِيَامَةِ ثُمَّ يَأْخُذُ بِلِهْزِمَتَيْهِ (يَعْنِي شِدْقَيْهِ) يَقُولُ: أَنَا مَالُكَ أَنَا كَنْزُكَ»

---

[1] Taken from a dissertation on *Zakat*, written by Shaikh Muhammad bin Salih Al-'Uthaimin
[2] (*Aal 'Imran* 3:180)

Whomsoever Allâh gives wealth to but doesn't pay *Zakat* for it, a bald-headed poisonous male snake with two black dots above its eyes will take form for him – it will have no fur on its scalp – and will squeeze him on the Day of Judgement. Then the snake will take him by the corners of his mouth and say, "I am your wealth, I am your treasure."[1]

And Allâh Almighty says:

﴿وَٱلَّذِينَ يَكْنِزُونَ ٱلذَّهَبَ وَٱلْفِضَّةَ وَلَا يُنفِقُونَهَا فِى سَبِيلِ ٱللَّهِ فَبَشِّرْهُم بِعَذَابٍ أَلِيمٍ ٣٤ يَوْمَ يُحْمَىٰ عَلَيْهَا فِى نَارِ جَهَنَّمَ فَتُكْوَىٰ بِهَا جِبَاهُهُمْ وَجُنُوبُهُمْ وَظُهُورُهُمْ هَٰذَا مَا كَنَزْتُمْ لِأَنفُسِكُمْ فَذُوقُوا۟ مَا كُنتُمْ تَكْنِزُونَ﴾

And those who hoard up gold and silver (*Al-Kanz*: the money, the *Zakat* of which has not been paid), and spend it not in the way of Allâh, announce unto them a painful torment. On the Day when that (*Al-Kanz*: money, gold and silver, etc., the *Zakat* of which has not been paid) will be heated in the fire of Hell and with it will be branded their foreheads, their flanks, and their backs, (and it will be said to them): "This is the treasure which you hoarded for yourselves. Now taste of what you used to hoard."[2]

In yet another *Hadith* related by Abu Hurairah, may Allâh be pleased with him, the Prophet ﷺ said:

«مَا مِنْ صَاحِبِ ذَهَبٍ وَلَا فِضَّةٍ لَا يُؤَدِّي مِنْهَا حَقَّهَا إِلَّا إِذَا كَانَ يَوْمُ الْقِيَامَةِ صُفِّحَتْ لَهُ صَفَائِحُ مِنْ نَارٍ فَأُحْمِيَ عَلَيْهَا مِنْ نَارِ جَهَنَّمَ فَيُكْوَى بِهَا جَنْبُهُ وَجَبِينُهُ وَظَهْرُهُ كُلَّمَا بَرَدَتْ أُعِيدَتْ فِي يَوْمٍ كَانَ مِقْدَارُهُ خَمْسِينَ أَلْفَ سَنَةٍ حَتَّى يُقْضَى بَيْنَ الْعِبَادِ»

Any owner of gold or silver who does not pay their due (i.e., *Zakat*) will have plates of fire prepared for him on the Day of Judgement. They will be heated in the Fire, and then his side,

[1] Related by Al-Bukhari
[2] (*At-Tawbah* 9:34,35)

his forehead, and his back will be ironed (by those plates). Each time he becomes cool again, the process is repeated on him in a day whose measure is equal to fifty thousand years, until finally judgements will have been passed among (Allâh's) worshippers."[1]

Some Of The Benefits Of *Zakat*

Zakat has many individual, social, and religious benefits; we will begin by mentioning some of its religious benefits:

1) By paying *Zakat*, one fulfills one of the pillars of Islam, around which revolves happiness for Allâh's worshippers both in this world and the Hereafter.

2) By giving *Zakat*, one gets closer to his Lord, and just as in other acts of obedience, his faith increases.

3) The rewards for giving charity are great; Allâh Almighty says:

$$﴿يَمْحَقُ ٱللَّهُ ٱلرِّبَوٰا۟ وَيُرْبِي ٱلصَّدَقَٰتِ﴾$$

Allâh will destroy *Riba* (usury) and will give increase for *Sadaqat* (deeds of charity, alms, etc.).[2]

And:

$$﴿وَمَآ ءَاتَيْتُم مِّن رِّبًا لِّيَرْبُوَا۟ فِىٓ أَمْوَٰلِ ٱلنَّاسِ فَلَا يَرْبُوا۟ عِندَ ٱللَّهِ وَمَآ ءَاتَيْتُم مِّن زَكَوٰةٍ تُرِيدُونَ وَجْهَ ٱللَّهِ فَأُو۟لَٰٓئِكَ هُمُ ٱلْمُضْعِفُونَ﴾$$

And that which you give in gift (to others), in order that it may increase (your wealth by expecting to get a better one in return) from other people's property, has no increase with Allâh, but that which you give in *Zakat* seeking Allâh's Face then those, they shall have manifold increase[3]

And the Prophet ﷺ said:

«مَنْ تَصَدَّقَ بِعَدْلِ تَمْرَةٍ- أَيْ بِمَا يُعَادِلُ تَمْرَةً - مِنْ كَسْبٍ طَيِّبٍ، وَلَا يَقْبَلُ اللهُ إِلَّا الطَّيِّبَ، فَإِنَّ اللهَ يَأْخُذُهَا بِيَمِينِهِ ثُمَّ يُرَبِّيهَا لِصَاحِبِهَا

---

[1] Related by Muslim
[2] (*Al-Baqarah* 2:276)
[3] (*Ar-Rum* 30:39)

«كَمَا يُرَبِّي أَحَدُكُمْ فَلُوَّهُ فَلُوَّهُ حَتَّى تَكُونَ مِثْلَ الْجَبَلِ»

Whoever gives charity from his good and lawful earnings in the
amount equal to a date – and Allâh accepts only that which is
good and pure – then indeed Allâh will take it with His Right
and will raise it for its giver, just as one of you raises his colt
until it becomes like a mountain.[1]

4) Allâh wipes out the sins of His worshippers with their charity; the
Prophet ﷺ said:

«وَالصَّدَقَةُ تُطْفِىءَ الْخَطِيئَةَ كَمَا يُطْفِىءَ الْمَاءُ النَّارَ»

And charity extinguishes a sin just as water extinguishes fire.

"Charity" in this *Hadith* embraces both *Zakat* and voluntary charity.

The Benefits Of *Zakat* On Manners And Morals

1) The giver of *Zakat* joins the ranks of the generous ones, those
who give freely from their wealth.

2) The giver of *Zakat* is described as being merciful and
compassionate to his poor Muslim brothers. It is the merciful ones
upon whom Allâh shows mercy.

3) Those who give financial or physical support to their Muslim
brothers gain a sense of joy and peace in their hearts and souls,
which further results in one being loved in proportion to that which
he expends.

4) *Zakat* purifies the character of its giver – purifies him from
miserliness, for Allâh says:

﴿خُذْ مِنْ أَمْوَالِهِمْ صَدَقَةً تُطَهِّرُهُمْ وَتُزَكِّيهِم بِهَا﴾

Take *Sadaqah* (alms) from their wealth in order to purify them
and sanctify them with it, and invoke Allâh for them.[2]

Some Of The Societal Benefits Of *Zakat*

1) The needs of the poor are fulfilled, an especially important
achievement, considering that the poor represent the greater

---

[1] Al-Bukhari and Muslim
[2] (*At-Tawbah* 9:103)

percentage of populations in most countries. Were every rich Muslim to pay *Zakat* as Allâh commands, there would not remain a single poor, needy person among the Muslims.

2) *Zakat* strengthens Muslims as a whole, and it raises their status, which is why *Jihad* in the way of Allâh is one of the categories deserving of *Zakat* – as we shall soon mention, if Allâh wills.

3) Through *Zakat*, rancor and malice leave the hearts of the poor and the weak. When the poor see the extravagant lifestyle of the rich, without seeing any benefit from their wealth at all, they will perhaps feel anger and enmity toward the rich, who did not give them their due right, and did not help them in their needs. But when the rich give a share of their money to the poor on a yearly basis, that anger disappears, being replaced by love and brotherhood.

4) Wealth increases, and not decreases, when charity is given – because of the blessings of charity. The Prophet ﷺ said:

«مَا نَقَصَتْ صَدَقَةٌ مِنْ مَالٍ»

Charity does not cause one's wealth to diminish,

meaning that though, in quantity, one's wealth ostensibly decreases, it does not decrease in blessings and it causes increase in the future; indeed Allâh replaces the wealth one gives in charity and blesses one in the wealth he has.

5) When the rich in society give *Zakat* as they should give it, wealth is distributed to a much larger circle of people, as opposed to wealth remaining among the few who are rich.

The benefits mentioned above show that *Zakat* is necessary to rectify the individual and society – and glory be to Allâh, the All-Knowing, the All-Wise.

Zakat is obligatory in certain kinds of wealth, such as gold and silver, as long as they reach the *Nisab* – the minimum amount one has to have in order for *Zakat* to be obligatory upon him. For gold it is twenty *Mithqals* or, eleven and three-sevenths Saudi or European *Junaih* (monetary pound). For silver it is fifty-six Saudi Riyals of silver or its equivalent in paper money.

The *Zakat* on gold and silver is 2.5%; this applies when the gold or silver are raw, when they are made into jewelry – and more importantly nowadays, to paper currency. Therefore a woman must pay *Zakat* on her gold and silver jewelry if their value reaches the *Nisab*; she must pay *Zakat* on her jewelry regardless of whether she wears the jewelry herself or lends it out to others. *Zakat* applies to jewelry based on the general proofs indicating that it is obligatory to pay *Zakat* on gold and silver: since those proofs don't go into detail, they apply to all kinds of gold and silver. There are even specific proofs that point to *Zakat* being mandatory on jewelry, even if worn, such as the *Hadith* related by 'Abdullah bin 'Amr bin Al-'Aas, may Allâh be pleased with them, in which a woman went to the Prophet ﷺ, and in her daughter's hands were two gold bracelets. The Prophet ﷺ asked:

«أَتُعطِينَ زَكَاةَ هَذَا؟»

Do you give *Zakat* for this?

She said, "No." The Prophet ﷺ said:

«أَيَسُرُّكِ أَنْ يُسَوِّرَكِ الله بِهِمَا سِوَارَيْنِ مِنَ النَّارِ»

Does it please you that because of them Allâh encloses you in two bracelets made of Fire.

She threw them, and said, "They are for Allâh and His Messenger." The author of *Bulugh Al-Maram* said that the three *Sunan* compilers related it, and that its chain is strong.

This is the safer view, and what is safer is more preferable. However, some scholars hold that *Zakat* is not obligatory on jewelry that is used among women.

Another form of wealth upon which *Zakat* is obligatory is anything that is meant for sale – land, cars, cattle, clothing, and so on. It is obligatory to pay 2.5% on this kind of wealth; when the year arrives (from the date it was allotted for sale) the goods are estimated, and 2.5% percent is paid on them. This applies both when the estimated amount for the goods is more than the amount that was originally paid, or less than that amount. But if one has goods that he uses himself or that he rents out, such as land and cars, then there is no *Zakat* on those items, for the Prophet ﷺ said:

«لَيْسَ عَلَى الْمُسْلِمِ فِي عَبْدِهِ وَلَا فَرَسِهِ صَدَقَةٌ»

There is no *Sadaqah* on the slave or horse of a Muslim.[1]
But it is obligatory on the money received as rent when one year
passes and upon gold and silver jewelry, as mentioned.

The Categories Of People Who May Receive *Zakat*

Allâh Almighty clarified the categories of people to whom *Zakat* is
paid when He said:

﴿إِنَّمَا ٱلصَّدَقَٰتُ لِلْفُقَرَآءِ وَٱلْمَسَٰكِينِ وَٱلْعَٰمِلِينَ عَلَيْهَا وَٱلْمُؤَلَّفَةِ قُلُوبُهُمْ وَفِى
ٱلرِّقَابِ وَٱلْغَٰرِمِينَ وَفِى سَبِيلِ ٱللَّهِ وَٱبْنِ ٱلسَّبِيلِ فَرِيضَةً مِّنَ ٱللَّهِ وَٱللَّهُ
عَلِيمٌ حَكِيمٌ﴾

As-Sadaqat (here it means *Zakat*) are only for the *Fuqara'*
(poor), and *Al-Masakin* (the needy) and those employed to
collect (the funds); and to attract the hearts of those who have
been inclined (towards Islam); and to free the captives; and for
those in debt; and for Allâh's cause (i.e., for *Mujahidun* – those
fighting in the holy wars), and for the wayfarer (a traveler who
is cut off from everything); a duty imposed by Allâh. And Allâh
is All-Knower, All-Wise.[2]

They Are Of Eight Categories

1) The poor: they are those who can barely find less than half of what
they need. If a person doesn't find enough to spend on himself and
his family for a period of six months, then he is considered to be a
poor person, and is given what is enough for him and his family for a
period of one year.

2) The needy (a level of poverty above that of the poor): They are
those who can find half or more of what they need, but are not able
to find what they need over a period of an entire year. They are given
a sufficient amount so that their expenditures for the year are
satisfied. If a man doesn't have money, but receives money
continually through his occupation, salary, or investments – that

[1] Agreed upon
[2] (*At-Tawbah* 9:60)

which is enough to sustain him – then he is not given from the *Zakat*, for the Prophet ﷺ said:

$$«لَا حَظَّ فِيهَا لِغَنِيٍّ وَلَا لِقَوِيٍّ مُكْتَسِبٍ»$$

The rich person, and the strong person who earns, they have no share in it.[1]

3) *Zakat* Employees: These are the people the general ruler of the country appoints to collect the *Zakat* from those who must give it, and to distribute it to those who deserve it; and those who are appointed to safeguard the *Zakat* wealth between the period that it is paid and the period it is paid off to its recipients. They are given from *Zakat* money in proportion to their work, even if they are rich.

4) *Zakat* is also for those who are inclined toward Islam, those whose hearts can be further attracted to the true religion. This mainly applies to leaders and chiefs whose level of faith is weak; they are given wealth to strengthen their faith, so that they can be good examples for others and so that they may call others to Islam. But what if one's faith is weak, and rather than being a chief or leader in the community, he is an average member thereof – is *Zakat* paid to him to attract his heart to Islam?

Some scholars are of the opinion that he is given from the *Zakat* because the benefits of religion are greater than that of the body, meaning that if he is poor, we give him money to maintain his body, so because his faith and religion is weak, he should be given *Zakat* to maintain or strengthen his religion - and the benefit of doing so is greater than the benefit of maintaining the body. However, other scholars are of the view that the common man is not given from the *Zakat* if his faith is weak, simply because the benefits of giving him are constricted to him as an individual, as opposed to a leader or chief: the benefits of giving them are not limited because they are more able to influence others when calling them to Islam.

5) Slaves and captives: *Zakat* money can be used to buy a slave and free him, to complete the payments for those slaves who have a contract with their owners to give certain amounts of payments until they free themselves. *Zakat* money can also be used to ransom

---

[1] Agreed upon

Muslim prisoners.

6) Those in debt: If one in debt doesn't have enough to pay off his debt, he may receive *Zakat* money to do so; he may be given *Zakat* money regardless of whether his debt is small or great. Even if one is rich in the sense that he has a salary that allows him to feed himself and his family, he may receive *Zakat* money to pay off a debt that he cannot pay off himself. If one's intention is to give *Zakat* to a poor person he owes money to, his debt stands: he still must pay it off. If one owes money to his father or son, he too may receive *Zakat* money to pay off his debts – according to the correct view from among the different views of the scholars in this issue. If the one who pays *Zakat* knows that someone owes someone else money without being able to pay it off, he may go directly to the one owed and pay the debt for him, even if the one in debt does not know what he did.

7) And for Allâh's cause: Those fighting for the cause of Allâh are given that amount which is enough for them in their *Jihad*. So from the *Zakat* money, weapons for *Jihad* may be purchased. "For Allâh's cause" here includes those who are seeking Islamic knowledge, so the student of Islamic knowledge is given an amount that is sufficient for him to pursue his studies – books and whatever else he needs, unless he has enough money himself to pursue his studies.

8) The wayfarer: If a traveler is cut off from the means of continuing his travel to his destination, he may be given enough so that he can reach his country.

These are the categories of *Zakat* that Allâh Almighty mentioned in His Book, and He informed us that it is an obligation which He ordered us to perform, based on His Complete Knowledge and Wisdom, for He is All-Knowing, All-Wise. *Zakat* wealth, then, can be used for no other purpose: it cannot be used to build *Masjids* or to fix roads. Allâh Almighty mentioned the categories of *Zakat* in such a way as to limit the *Zakat* to them.

If one reflects on the categories of *Zakat*, he should find that *Zakat* is paid to those who need it for their own selves, or to those whom the Muslims need. Hence one realizes the wisdom in the legislation of *Zakat*: building a good and strong society in which its individuals complement and complete each other as much as possible. Islam, a complete way of life, did not neglect legislation in regard to wealth and in regard to the benefits that can be derived from wealth; furthermore, Islam does not give freedom to those souls that are greedy or miserly to follow their desires, greed, or miserliness. Islam guides mankind completely to that which is good, and all praise is for Allâh, the Lord of all that exists.

Note: *Zakatul-Fitr* is discussed under the topic of fasting due to its close relationship to it.

Categories Of Wealth In Which
Zakat Is Obligatory

The kind of *Zakat*	The *Nisab*	Amount of *Zakat*	Notes
Gold and silver	1) Gold: 20 *Mithqals* or more 2) Silver: 100 *Dirhams* or more	For both: 2.5% every year	Its amount is eleven Saudi pounds and $^3/_1$ of a pound. The *Nisab* is equal to 56 Saudi riyals or about 16 dollars (15.175 dollars)
Goods meant for selling or buying	The same as gold and silver	2.5% every year	Properties, buildings, cars, and tools – all these are included if they are meant for sale
What grows out of the earth from crops	60 *Sa's*	One-tenth for what is watered by rains and One-twentieth for what is watered through toil	This applies to fruits, such as dates and raisins, and to vegetables as well. *Zakat* is according to their value when the year ends. (One *Sa'* is equal to four handfuls of a man of average built – his hands should be full)
Livestock: sheep and cows	40 sheep,	For sheep: 1 sheep every year.	If there are more than 40 then there is no more due until there are 121 sheep, in which case the *Zakat* is 2 sheep. The next level is 201 sheep, in which case the *Zakat* is 3 sheep. Then if there are 301 sheep, there is one sheep that is given for *Zakat*, for every 100 sheep.
	30 cows	For cows: a cow that is five years of age.	If there are more than 30 cows then there is no other *Zakat* until there reaches 40 cows, in which the *Zakat* is a cow 2 years of age. And so on, for every 30 the *Zakat* is a cow 5 years of age, and for every 40 the *Zakat* is a cow 2 years of age.

The *Zakat* Of Camels

The *Nisab*	The Amount Of *Zakat* That Must Be Paid
From To 5 - 9	1 Sheep
10 - 14	2 Sheep
15 - 19	3 Sheep
20 - 24	4 Sheep
25 - 35	One female camel that has completed her first year and has entered upon her second one
36 - 45	One female camel that has completed her second year and has entered upon her third one
46 - 60	One female camel that has completed her third year and has entered upon her fourth one
61 - 75	One female camel that has completed her fourth year and has entered upon her fifth one
76 - 90	Two female camels that have completed their second year and have entered upon their third one
91 - 120	Two female camels that have completed their third year and have entered upon their fourth one
More than 120	For every fifty, one that is in her fourth year, and for every forty, one that is in her third year

The Fourth Pillar: Fasting[1]

1) Fasting means for one to abstain – for a set period – from food, drink, and sex, seeking closeness to Allâh thereby.

2) The time of the fast: From the beginning of dawn until the sun sets.

3) Fasting the month of Ramadhan is obligatory and is the fourth Pillar of Islam.

4) Fasting Ramadhan is obligatory upon every sane Muslim adult who is able to perform the fast – this applies to both men and women.

5) There are four conditions that, if fulfilled, make the fast obligatory:

i) Islam: The fast is not obligatory upon the disbeliever until he accepts Islam.

ii) Sanity: Therefore an insane person does not have to fast, at least not until he is cured.

iii) Adulthood, meaning that one has reached puberty. The young person who has not reached puberty does not have to fast; however, when a child is able to fast, he should be ordered to do so, so that he may become used to it.

iv) The ability to fast: the one who is unable to fast – such as the very old person or the one who is so sick that hope is lost for his cure – can instead feed a sick person for each day of fasting that he misses.

6) There are six conditions for one's fast to be correct:

i) Islam: Fasting is not acceptable from a disbeliever until he accepts Islam.

ii) Sanity: Fasting is not accepted from the insane person until he becomes sane.

iii) *Tamyeez* (discernment): Fasting is not accepted from someone who is so young that he lacks discernment (the

---

[1] From the book *Khulasatul-Kalam fee Ahkamis-Siyam* by 'Abdullah Al-Jarullah, p. 2 and what follows.

conditions for discernment are mentioned in books of *Fiqh*).

iv) That menstrual blood ceases to come out: Therefore fasting is not accepted from a menstruating woman until her blood ceases to flow.

v) That postnatal bleeding stops: Therefore fasting is not accepted from a woman who is experiencing postnatal bleeding, not until she is purified.

vi) Making intention in the night for the next day of fasting – for all of the days of fasting: and this is compulsory. Fasting is not accepted without intention, and intention is made in the heart. The exception here is voluntary fasting, for it doesn't require intention from the night before.

7) The Sunnah Elements Of Fasting Are Six:

a) Delaying the late-night (*Sahur*) meal until the last part of the night, as long as one does not fear that the time of dawn will arrive.

b) Hastening to break the fast when one is sure that the sun has set.

c) Increasing in good deeds, voluntary prayers, charity, recitation of the Qur'ân, remembrance, supplication, and the seeking of forgiveness from Allâh Almighty.

d) If someone curses the fasting person, rather than curse him back, he should simply say, "Indeed I am fasting." He should reciprocate the evil done to him with a good deed, so as to achieve a reward and remain safe from sinning.

e) Just before breaking fast, one should invoke Allâh Almighty with those invocations that he wishes to make, such as the following one:

»اللَّهُمَّ لَكَ صُمْتُ وَعَلَى رِزْقِكَ أَفْطَرْتُ فَتَقَبَّلْ مِنِّي إِنَّكَ أَنْتَ السَّمِيعُ الْعَلِيمُ«

O Allâh, for You I have fasted, with Your sustenance did I break my fast, and so accept from me; indeed, You are All-Hearing, All-Knowing.

f) Breaking fast with ripe dates; if they are not available, then with dry ones; and if they are not available, then with water.

8) The rulings of those who do not have to fast in Ramadhan

There are four kinds of people who do not have to fast during Ramadhan:

i) The sick person who is harmed by fasting and the traveler who is permitted to shorten his prayer – not fasting is better for these two groups, but they have to make up for their fasts at a later date. And if they fast, then their fast is correct and sufficient.

ii) Menstruating women and women who are experiencing postnatal bleeding; they shouldn't fast, and they have to make up for those fasts that they miss; however, in their case, if they do fast, their fast is not correct and not sufficient.

iii) The pregnant and breast-feeding mother: if they fear that fasting will have negative repercussions on their child, then they may break their fast and make up for it later, but they must also feed a poor person for every day they missed. And if they fast, then that is sufficient and correct; however, if their fears are not related to their child, but to their own selves, then they may still break their fast and make up for it later, but they do not have to feed a poor person for every day they missed.

iv) One who is not able to fast may also break his fast – such as one who has reached the age of decrepitude or one whose sickness is so severe that doctors have lost hope for his cure. Such people may break their fast and must feed a poor person for each day that they missed. The amount of food they must give is approximately a kilo and a half of a staple food in one's country.

The Recommended Fasts

1) Any six days in the month of Shawwal (the month after Ramadhan): if one fasts those days as well as the month of Ramadhan, then one has completed his rewards so that they are equal to fasting for a year.

2) Fasting Monday and Thursday, for those are the two days that one's deeds are displayed before Allâh.

3) Fasting three days from every month: when one does this his reward is equal to fasting for a year. This is because a good deed is

multiplied ten times. Regarding these three days, it is preferred that one fasts what are known as the "white days" – the 13th, 14th, and 15th – of every (lunar) month.

4) Fasting the first nine days of Thul-Hijjah, the most emphasized of which is the 9th, the day of *'Arafah* for one who is not making the pilgrimage.

5) Fasting the month of Muharram, and the most emphasized days for fasting in that month are the ninth and the tenth, which is the day of *'Ashura*.

When Is It Prohibited To Fast?

1) Fasting the day of doubt, which is the 30th day of Sha'ban (it is the day before the month of fasting, Ramadhan, begins).

2) Fasting on the two days of *'Eid* – *'Eidul-Adha* and *'Eidul-Fitr*.

3) Fasting the days of *Tashreeq*, which are the 11th, 12th, and 13th of Thul-Hijjah, the exceptions are for those performing *Hajj At-Tamattu'* and for the one performing *Qiran*, but is not able to find the *Hady* (sacrifice).

4) It is disliked to single out Friday for fasting, unless one fasts on Thursday or Saturday as well, in which case there is no harm.

5) A woman performing a voluntary fast without the permission of her husband.

Some Additional Points Related To Fasting

1) One must fast Ramadhan, having faith and seeking his reward with Allâh, and for no other reason.

2) It may happen that as one is fasting, he involuntarily has a nosebleed or an injury; he also might vomit or drink water or anything else unintentionally – all of the above do not spoil one's fast as long as they are not done on purpose.

3) While one is sexually impure, he may intend to fast, and then perform *Ghusl* after the beginning of dawn. As for the menstruating woman and the woman experiencing post-natal bleeding, if they become purified before dawn, they must perform *Ghusl*, perform *Maghrib* and *'Isha'* prayers and then fast.

4) If a woman experiencing postnatal bleeding becomes purified

before the completion of 40 days, she should perform *Ghusl*, after which she may pray and fast, and furthermore, she becomes lawful to her husband.

5) A fasting person may clean his teeth, using *Siwak* (a stick from the *Arak* tree used for cleaning teeth), at the beginning and end of the day. It is Sunnah for the fasting person to use *Siwak* just as it is Sunnah to do so for the one who is not fasting.

6) The fasting person, as well as others, must perform all compulsory acts of worship, while abstaining from all that is forbidden – obeying orders and staying away from prohibited matters, so that one may be among those who are successful and whose deeds are accepted.

7) One should take advantage of the blessed hours in Ramadhan to perform good deeds – prayer, charity, recitation of Qur'ân, remembrance of Allâh, supplication, the seeking of forgiveness from Allâh, and the performance of *'Umrah*. Time in Ramadhan, more so than any other time, is like a planting-ground for Allâh's worshippers to be used to purify their hearts from falsehood.

8) A fasting person, as well as others, must protect their limbs from sins, in terms of false speech, the forbidden look, listening to that which is forbidden, eating or drinking that which is forbidden, walking toward that which is forbidden, or doing anything that is forbidden. One avoids such matters so that his fast may be accepted, and so that he deserves forgiveness and deserves being saved from the Hellfire.

9) If one is permitted to break his fast in Ramadhan because he is sick or a traveler, he is not permitted to fast that day for someone else, such as one who fasts for someone who is deceased because that deceased person made a vow to fast but did not perform it before dying.

10) If one travels so that he doesn't have to fast, then it is forbidden for him to travel and to break his fast; in this case, he must fast.

11) If fasting is obligatory on someone who is about to eat due to forgetfulness or ignorance, then it becomes the obligation of one who sees him to notify and remind him of his duty, for that is from helping one another to goodness and righteousness.

12) One's fast is not rendered void if a fly or dust or smoke goes down his throat by accident (i.e., not on purpose), because these are matters that are not possible to avoid.

13) Whoever eats, thinking that dawn has not begun or that the sun has set and later on realizes that he was wrong, his fast is correct because he was ignorant regarding the time.[1]

14) Following in the way of the Prophet ﷺ and seeking Allâh's reward, one should be especially generous in the month of Ramadhan and one should recite as much Qur'ân as one is able to.

15) From the ways of achieving forgiveness in the month of Ramadhan is to fast it, stand late during its nights to pray, stand on the night of *Qadr* to pray, recite the Qur'ân, remember Allâh, supplicate to Him, seek His forgiveness, repent to Him, feed those who are breaking their fast, and give charity.

16) The best charity is that which is given in Ramadhan.

17) When making up for fasts that one missed during Ramadhan, it is recommended to fast on continuous days, but it is not obligatory. It is also recommended to hasten to make up for those fasts.

18) If one missed fasts in Ramadhan on long hot days, it is permissible to make up for those fasts in the winter on days that are short, and vice versa.

19) If one is excused from fasting on a certain day, he may fast it anyway, as long as doing so is not burdensome, for Allâh says:

$$﴿ وَأَن تَصُومُوا۟ خَيْرٌ لَّكُمْ ﴾$$

And that you fast, it is better for you.[2]

20) Fasting is a spiritual school, in which one trains his soul to be patient.

21) From the special qualities of the last ten days of Ramadhan, it is recommended to do the following during them:

---

[1] This is the opinion of Shaikh Ibn 'Uthaimin; the opposing view, however, is held by the majority of the people of knowledge. Shaikh Ibn Baz, for example, holds that though such a person is not sinning, he must make up for that fast.

[2] (*Al-Baqarah* 2:184)

i) Staying awake during the night praying and worshipping.

ii) Waking up one's family to pray.

iii) Staying away from women and applying oneself to worship.

22) Fasting is also like a hospital for many kinds of sicknesses; in a *Hadith*, the Prophet ﷺ said,

«صُومُوا تَصِحُّوا»

Fast, and you will be in good health.

It was recorded by Ibn As-Sunni and Abu Nu'aym. As-Suyuti graded it as *Hasan*.

23) During the night of *'Eidul-Fitr*, and until the *'Eid* Prayer, Muslims are recommended to say the *Takbir* and to say it in *Masjids*, homes, and marketplaces, for Allâh says:

﴿ وَلِتُكْمِلُوا الْعِدَّةَ وَلِتُكَبِّرُوا اللَّهَ عَلَىٰ مَا هَدَىٰكُمْ وَلَعَلَّكُمْ تَشْكُرُونَ ﴾

(He wants that you) must complete the same number (of days), and that you must magnify Allâh [i.e., to say *Takbir* (*Allâhu Akbar*; Allâh is the Most Great) on seeing the crescent of the months of Ramadhan and Shawwal] for having guided you so that you may be grateful to Him[1]

The special way of saying the *Takbir* on this occasion is to say, "*Allâhu Akbar, Allâhu Akbar. Laa Ilaha Illallâh, Wallâhu Akbar, Allâhu Akbar, wa Lillahil-Hamd* (Allâh is the Most Great, Allâh is the Most Great; none has the right to be worshipped but Allâh, and Allâh is the Most Great. Allâh is the Most Great, and to Him belongs all praise).

The Special Qualities Of Ramadhan

1) Fasting Ramadhan is the fourth pillar of Islam.

2) There are special night prayers that one should perform during Ramadhan, praying them with faith and seeking reward from Allâh — the *Tarawih* prayer, along with the late-night (*Tahajjud*) prayers in the last ten days.

3) The Qur'ân was revealed in the month of Ramadhan:

---

[1] (*Al-Baqarah* 2:185)

> ﴿شَهْرُ رَمَضَانَ ٱلَّذِىٓ أُنزِلَ فِيهِ ٱلۡقُرۡءَانُ هُدٗى لِّلنَّاسِ وَبَيِّنَٰتٖ مِّنَ ٱلۡهُدَىٰ وَٱلۡفُرۡقَانِۚ﴾

The month of Ramadhan in which was revealed the Qur'ân, a guidance for mankind and clear proofs for the guidance and the criterion (between right and wrong).[1]

4) During Ramadhan, there is a night called the Night of *Qadr*, which is better than one thousand months, meaning that it is better than eighty-three years and four months.

5) The greater Battle of Badr took place in Ramadhan, a battle in which Allâh made clear for us on its morning the distinction between truth and falsehood. Islam and its adherents defeated *Shirk* and its adherents.

6) Makkah was conquered during Ramadhan, and that was a great help from Allâh for His Messenger ﷺ, because people entered Allâh's religion in flocks.

7) The doors of Paradise and mercy are opened in Ramadhan, while the doors of the Hellfire are closed, and the devils are shackled therein.

8) The smell that emanates from the fasting person's mouth is better and purer to Allâh than the smell of musk.

9) The angels ask forgiveness for those who are fasting until they break their fast.

10) In a *Hadith*, it is related that a voluntary act in Ramadhan is equal to a compulsory one, and that a compulsory act during Ramadhan is equal to seventy compulsory acts that are performed outside of Ramadhan. Ibn Khuzaimah, Al-Baihaqi, and others relate this.

11) During Ramadhan, mercy descends, sins are discharged, and supplications are answered.

12) The beginning of Ramadhan is mercy, its middle is forgiveness, and its end is freedom from the Hellfire.

13) It is a month of patience, and the reward for patience is Paradise.

---

[1] (*Al-Baqarah* 2:185)

14) Those who fast are forgiven in the last night of Ramadhan; that is because a worker takes his wages as soon as he finishes his work. There are many blessings and rewards that are attached to Ramadhan; therefore one must take advantage of its many opportunities by repenting to Allâh and performing good deeds, in the hope that one will be among the successful ones whose deeds are accepted.

Additional Advice You Should Heed Regarding The Fast

1) You should fast the month of Ramadhan out of faith while seeking the reward from Allâh Almighty, so that Allâh will forgive your past sins.

2) Beware, brother Muslim, from breaking any of the fasts of Ramadhan without a valid excuse. But if you do perpetrate that sin, then make up for the day you missed and repent sincerely to Allâh.

3) Stand – may Allâh have mercy on you – and pray the *Tarawih* and *Tahajjud* prayers during Ramadhan, especially on the Night of *Qadr*, but do so with faith while seeking the reward from Allâh, so that He forgives you your past sins.

4) Make sure that your food, drink, and clothing are not only lawful, but are also lawfully derived, so that your deeds and supplications may be accepted. Beware of fasting from what is lawful and breaking your fast with what is unlawful.

5) When the time arrives for breaking the fast, feed others who are fasting as well, so that you may achieve a reward similar to their reward.

6) Be steadfast in performing the five obligatory prayers on time and in congregation, to achieve their rewards, and so that Allâh protects you through them.

7) Give much charity because the best charity is that which is given during Ramadhan.

8) Beware of wasting your time without doing good deeds, for you will be asked and held accountable regarding lost time; furthermore, you will be recompensed for the deeds you may have perpetrated during that lost time.

9) Perform '*Umrah* during Ramadhan, for '*Umrah* during Ramadhan is equal to *Hajj* in reward.

10) In order to help facilitate your fast during the day, partake of a meal in the last part of the night, as long as you do not fear that dawn has begun.

11) To achieve Allâh's love for you, hasten to break your fast when you are sure that the sun has set.

12) Before the time of *Fajr*, perfom *Ghusl* from sexual impurity if you need to take it, so that you can perform worship in its time.

13) Take advantage of the fact that you are alive in Ramadhan by occupying yourself with the best that has descended during that month: recitation of the Noble Qur'ân, contemplation of its meanings, so that it may be a proof for you with your Lord and an intercessor for you on the Day of Judgement.

14) Protect your tongue from lying, cursing, backbiting, or spreading false rumors, because all of these take away from your reward for fasting.

15) Do not allow fasting to get to your head, making you feel that you are so righteous that you have the right, for example, to show anger to others; rather, fasting should be a means of making your soul feel humble and tranquil and at rest.

16) Come out of your fast with fear of Allâh, knowing that when you do deeds, He sees all of your deeds, whether you perform them in open or in secret. Demonstrate your gratitude for His many favors and because He has guided you to righteousness, by applying all of His commands and staying away from all of His prohibitions.

17) At all times, and especially during Ramadhan remember Allâh, seek His forgiveness, ask for Paradise, and seek protection from the Hellfire. You should especially perform these deeds when you are fasting, at the time of *Sahur* and the time when you are breaking your fast; doing good deeds on those occasions will help bring about forgiveness.

18) Supplicate as often as you can, for yourself, your parents, your children, and for all Muslims. Allâh Almighty ordered us to supplicate while guaranteeing the answer Himself.

19) At all times, repent to Allâh sincerely, by:

  i) Abandoning the sin you committed.

  ii) Feeling remorse and regret for that sin

  iii) Resolving to never return to that sin in the future.

Indeed Allâh forgives the one who repents.

20) Fast six days from Shawwal, for whoever fasts Ramadhan, following it up with six days from Shawwal, then it is as if he has fasted the entire year.[1]

21) Fast the day of 'Arafah, which is the 9th of Thul-Hijjah, which may remove the sins of the previous year, as well as the following year. But if you are performing *Hajj* and are standing at 'Arafat, then do not fast on that day, because the Prophet ﷺ stood at 'Arafat without fasting.

22) Fast the day of 'Ashura – the 10th of Muharram – along with the 9th as well, so that you may achieve expiation for a year's sins.

23) Continue to be righteous and to perform good deeds and to have faith after the month of Ramadhan, and until you die:

﴿وَٱعْبُدْ رَبَّكَ حَتَّىٰ يَأْتِيَكَ ٱلْيَقِينُ﴾

And worship your Lord until there comes to you the certainty (i.e., death).[2]

24) Allow for the effects of worship – such as prayer, fasting, *Zakat*, *Hajj* – to appear in your character, by sincerely repenting to Allâh and by leaving those habits that are contrary to the *Shari'ah*.

25) Send many blessings and salutations upon the Messenger of Allâh ﷺ – O Allâh, send blessings and salutations upon Muhammad, his family, his Companions, and his followers until the Day of Judgement. O Allâh, make us, and all the Muslims among those who fast Ramadhan, and stand in prayer during its nights, having faith and seeking our reward from You. O Allâh, forgive our past and future sins.

And know – may Allâh have mercy on you – for a fact that the

---

[1] Muslim, in a *Hadith* related by Abu Qatadah.

[2] (*Al-Hijr* 15:99)

Muslims agree that fasting Ramadhan is obligatory. Whoever denies that fasting Ramadhan is obligatory is an apostate, a disbeliever who is asked to repent. If he repents and acknowledges that fasting is obligatory, then that is well; if not, then he is killed as a disbeliever.[1]

Fasting was legislated in the second year after *Hijrah* (The Prophet's migration to Al-Madinah), so the Prophet ﷺ fasted Ramadhan for nine years.

Fasting is compulsory upon every sane adult Muslim. Therefore it is not obligatory upon the disbeliever, nor is it accepted from him were he to perform it, until he accepts Islam. Fasting is also not obligatory upon the child who has not reached adulthood. Adulthood in Islam means the completion of fifteen years or the time when pubic hairs begin to grow, or the discharge of semen during a wet dream, and there are other signs as well; for a female, there is an additional sign of adulthood, and that is menstruation. So when one of the above signs appear, the child then becomes an adult, and fasting becomes compulsory upon him.

As for the child, he should be ordered to fast when it is deemed that he can handle the fast and will not be harmed thereby, so that he can get used to fasting. Fasting is also not obligatory upon one who has lost his mind and has gone insane. Therefore if a person in old age begins to speak nonsense and loses the ability to distinguish between different matters, as normal people are able to do, neither fasting nor feeding the poor is obligatory upon him.

Some Of The Benefits And Wisdom Behind The Legislation Of Fasting:

Al-Hakeem is one of Allâh's Names, and Al-Hakeem is One Who is described as having wisdom. *Hikmah* – wisdom – means perfecting matters and placing them where they belong. One of the implications of this name is this: everything that Allâh created and legislated is for a far-reaching wisdom – of which some have knowledge and others do not.

---

[1] From a dissertation on Fasting written by Shaikh Muhammad bin Salih Al-'Uthaimin

There is tremendous wisdom behind fasting, which Allâh has legislated and made obligatory upon his worshippers, and it also has special benefits; here are some of them:

1) Fasting is a form of worship through which the worshipper attains closeness to his Lord; he leaves those things that he loves, things he is innately made to love – in terms of food, drink, and sexual intercourse – so that he may achieve the pleasure of his Lord and success in the next life. So through the fast, what becomes manifest is one's love for those matters his Lord loves over those matters he loves himself, and one's preference for the Hereafter over this world.

2) Fasting leads to righteousness and a fear of Allâh, but only if the one fasting does what is required of him during his fast. Allâh Almighty says:

$$ ﴿ يَٰٓأَيُّهَا ٱلَّذِينَ ءَامَنُوا۟ كُتِبَ عَلَيْكُمُ ٱلصِّيَامُ كَمَا كُتِبَ عَلَى ٱلَّذِينَ مِن قَبْلِكُمْ لَعَلَّكُمْ تَنفَقُونَ ﴾ $$

O you who believe! Fasting is prescribed for you as it was prescribed for those before you, that you may be pious.[1]

The fasting person is ordered to have *Taqwa* (piety) which means to apply Allâh's Commands and to stay away from His prohibitions, an achievement which is the main purpose behind fasting. Torturing the one fasting by making him stay away from food, drink, and sexual intercourse, is not the intent of the fast, for the Prophet ﷺ said:

«مَنْ لَمْ يَدَعْ قَوْلَ الزُّورِ وَالْعَمَلَ بِهِ وَالْجَهْلَ فَلَيْسَ لِلهِ حَاجَةٌ فِي أَنْ يَدَعَ طَعَامَهُ وَشَرَابَهُ»

Whoever does not leave false speech, acting according to false speech, and ignorance, then Allâh has no need for him to leave his food and drink.[2]

What false speech is referring to in this *Hadith* is all speech that is forbidden – including lying, backbiting, cursing, and even forbidden deeds. Applying false speech means all forbidden actions – such as attacking others using means of treachery, cheating, physically

---

[1] (*Al-Baqarah* 2:183)
[2] Related by Al-Bukhari

striking, usurping wealth, and so on. This also embraces listening to music, which is forbidden. Ignorance means foolishness, and here it means staying far away from right guidance in both speech and action. If the one who is fasting acts according to his knowledge of the above-mentioned verse and *Hadith*, then his fasting will help him grow as a person, solidifying his character and manners. Such a person will come out of Ramadhan greatly changed, with changes that will appear in his self, his manners, and his dealings.

3) The rich person, through fasting, gains an appreciation of Allâh's great favors upon him. Allâh made it easy for him to get food, drink, and a wife (or wives) – all things which Allâh made permissible in His *Shari'ah* and made possible for such a person by His Divine Decree. Therefore one should thank his Lord for His many favors and remember his poor brother who cannot have the things he has, and show generosity, giving charity and help to his poor brother.

4) Through fasting, one learns self-control thus keeping his desires in check, so that one develops the ability to lead his self to all that is good for it, in terms of happiness in this world and the next. In this way, one stays away from the characteristics of men who act as beasts do – those who are not able to control their desires and lusts.

5) There are many health benefits that are related to the fast: one learns to take smaller portions of food; one gives a break to his digestion system for a certain period of time, allowing for certain harmful waste matter to leave his body.

The Sick Person And The Traveler: Should They Fast?

Allâh Almighty says:

$$﴿وَمَن كَانَ مَرِيضًا أَوْ عَلَى سَفَرٍ فَعِدَّةٌ مِّنْ أَيَّامٍ أُخَرَ يُرِيدُ اللَّهُ بِكُمُ الْيُسْرَ وَلَا يُرِيدُ بِكُمُ الْعُسْرَ﴾$$

And whoever is ill or on a journey, the same number [of days which one did not observe *Sawm* (fasts) must be made up for] from other days. Allâh intends for you ease, and He does not want to make things difficult for you.[1]

---

[1] (*Al-Baqarah* 2:185)

In regards to fasting, there are two kinds of sick people:

1) One whose sickness stays with him continuously, with no hope of it leaving, such as cancer. Such a person does not have to fast, for in his case, it is not generally hoped that he will later on be able to perform it. Rather, he must feed a poor person for each day that he misses; he can either gather a number of poor people corresponding to the number of days he missed, and then feed them lunch or dinner, which is what Anas bin Malik used to do when he reached old age. The other option is for one to divide food for poor people according to the number of days he missed; each poor person gets approximately a kilo and a half of a staple food in his country - such as dates, rice, and so on.

2) One whose sickness is sudden, and temporary, such as a fever. There are three situations for a sick person in this category:

i) Fasting is not difficult for him, nor does it harm him; in this case, he must fast because he has no excuse not to.

ii) Fasting is difficult for him, but does not harm him. It is disliked for such a person to fast, for by fasting in this situation, one deviates from Allâh's exception and allowance, while also deviating from showing compassion to his own self.

iii) Fasting harms him, in which case it is forbidden for him to fast, because he is bringing harm upon himself. Allâh Almighty says:

﴿وَلَا تَقْتُلُوٓاْ أَنفُسَكُمْ إِنَّ ٱللَّهَ كَانَ بِكُمْ رَحِيمًا﴾

And do not kill yourselves (nor kill one another). Surely, Allâh is Most Merciful to you.[1]

And:

﴿وَلَا تُلْقُواْ بِأَيْدِيكُمْ إِلَى ٱلتَّهْلُكَةِ﴾

And do not throw yourselves into destruction.[2]

And in a *Hadith* related from the Prophet ﷺ, he ﷺ said:

---

[1] (*An-Nisa'* 4:29)

[2] (*Al-Baqarah* 2:195)

«لَا ضَرَرَ وَلَا ضِرَارَ»

There is no harm to one's own self and no harm to others.[1]

How does one know whether fasting will harm a sick person? One knows either because the sick person himself feels that he is being harmed or because a trusted doctor informs him that in his situation, fasting is bad for him. A sick person from this category who misses fasts must make up for the days he missed when he gets well, and if he dies before getting well, then he is absolved from the days he missed because his obligation is to fast a number of other days, and he never reached those other days.

The Categories For The Traveler

1) One whose intention behind traveling is to avoid having to fast. It is forbidden for this person to break his fast because trickery in one's obligatory Islamic duties does not absolve one from having to perform them.

2) One who doesn't have the said intention; there are three situations for this person:

i) Fasting is extremely difficult for him, in which case it is forbidden for him to fast. When the Prophet ﷺ was fasting during the conquest of Makkah, he learned that people were finding it extremely difficult to fast and were only waiting to see what he did. After 'Asr, he ﷺ called for a container of water and he ﷺ drank from it, while the people observed him. It was later said to him, "Some of the people have fasted," and he said:

«أُولَئِكَ الْعُصَاةُ أُولَئِكَ الْعُصَاةُ»

They are indeed the disobedient ones; they are indeed the disobedient ones.[2]

ii) Fasting is not extremely difficult for him, but is nonetheless difficult. It is disliked for him to fast, for by fasting, he deviates from Allâh's exception and licence and he deviates from showing compassion to his own self.

---

[1] Ibn Majah and Al-Hakim. An-Nawawi said, "It has different chains, each one strengthens the other."

[2] Related by Muslim

iii) Fasting is not difficult for him at all, in which case one does what is easier for him in terms of fasting or not fasting, for Allâh Almighty says:

﴿يُرِيدُ ٱللَّهُ بِكُمُ ٱلۡيُسۡرَ وَلَا يُرِيدُ بِكُمُ ٱلۡعُسۡرَ﴾

Allâh intends for you ease, and He does not want to make things difficult for you.[1]

In this verse, "intends" carries the meaning of "loves." If the two choices carry equal weight, then fasting is better, for that is the practice of the Prophet ﷺ.

In *Sahih Muslim* it is recorded that Abu Ad-Darda' said, "We went out during Ramadhan on a very hot day with the Prophet ﷺ, so severe was the heat that one of us would put his hand on his head. The only ones who were fasting among us were the Messenger of Allâh ﷺ and 'Abdullah bin Rawahah.''

One is considered to be a traveler as soon as one leaves his country and remains so as long as he doesn't return to it. Even if one stays in a city for a certain period during his travel, he is still considered to be a traveler as long as his intention is to not stay there after he is finished with his mission for traveling there in the first place. Hence he has licence to do what the traveler does, even if he is staying in a specific place for a long period of time.[2] No specific period for traveling after which one is no longer considered to be a traveler has been related from the Prophet ﷺ, and as such, travel and its rulings apply until proof is given to cancel it out or to cancel out its rulings.

The licences of the travel apply to all kinds of travelers – those who are traveling to perform *Hajj* or *'Umrah*, those who are visiting relatives, those that are traveling for business, and so on, and also those who are continuously traveling, such as the long-distance taxi drivers: as soon as they leave their country, they are travelers, and they are like all other travelers, in that they may miss days of

---

[1] (*Al-Baqarah* 2:185)

[2] This is the opinion held by some scholars; others hold that if he stays in a city for a period of four days or less, he is considered to be traveler, but if he stays in a city for more than four days, he is considered to be a dweller, in terms of Islamic rulings.

Ramadhan (those days that they are in travel), shorten four-unit prayers to two units, and combine between prayers when there is a need – between *Zuhr* and *'Asr* and between *Maghrib* and *'Isha'*. Missing a fast in their case is better for them than fasting when it is easier for them, for instance, because they can make up for those days in the winter. Such drivers and others like them have a city that is theirs, and so they are considered as dwellers when they are in that city, and they take on all of the rulings of dwellers. And when they are outside of that city, they are travelers and take on all of the rulings of travelers.

There Are Seven Matters That Spoil One's Fast, Rendering It Void

1) Sexual intercourse – inserting the male private part into the female private part, so whenever a fasting person has sexual intercourse, his fast is null. If one engages in sexual intercourse during day in Ramadhan – when fasting is compulsory – then, because of the enormity of his action, the harsh expiation applies to him. This means that he must free a slave; if he is not able to do so, then he must fast two continuous months; and if he is not able to do that, then he must feed sixty poor people. But if one engages in sexual intercourse during the day of Ramadhan when fasting is not obligatory upon him, for instance, when he is traveling, then he has to make up for the fast without having to make any atonement.

2) The discharge of semen due to kissing, hugging, and so on. But if one kisses without semen discharging, then there is nothing upon him.

3) Eating and drinking, which means that food reaches one's inside. So based on this definition, eating and drinking include food entering through the mouth or through the nose – whatever the kind of food or drink. The fasting person is not allowed to breath in the smoke of incense, so that it reaches his inside, because smoke is considered to have mass. As for smelling things that exude pleasant fragrances, there is no harm in that.

4) That which carries the meaning of eating or drinking, such as nourishing injections that replace food and drink. But if the contents of an injection are not nourishing, then one's fast is not

affected in any way, regardless of whether it enters a vein or a muscle.

5) Blood exiting because of cupping – and bloodletting of any kind that has a similar effect to cupping – carries the same ruling. But if one gives a small amount of blood for testing, then one's fast is not affected in any way, because the body is not weakened when a small amount of blood is withdrawn as opposed to cupping and the like.

6) Vomiting on purpose.

7) Blood discharging from a woman whose menstrual cycle is beginning and a woman experiencing postnatal bleeding.

These matters that nullify one's fast only nullify it when three conditions are fulfilled:

1) One is knowledgeable of the ruling, and knowledgeable of the time.

2) One remembers.

3) One has a choice.

So if one is cupped, thinking that it does not affect his fast, then his fast is correct, because he is ignorant of the correct ruling. Indeed Allâh Almighty says:

﴿وَلَيْسَ عَلَيْكُمْ جُنَاحٌ فِيمَآ أَخْطَأْتُم بِهِۦ وَلَٰكِن مَّا تَعَمَّدَتْ قُلُوبُكُمْ﴾

And there is no sin on you if you make a mistake therein, except in regard to what your hearts deliberately intend.[1]

And:

﴿رَبَّنَا لَا تُؤَاخِذْنَآ إِن نَّسِينَآ أَوْ أَخْطَأْنَا﴾

"Our Lord! Punish us not if we forget or fall into error."[2]

In answer to the supplication of this last verse, Allâh said, "Indeed, I have done so (forgiven)."

In the Two *Sahihs*, it is recorded that 'Adi bin Hatim said he put two strings, one black and the other white – underneath his pillow. He began to eat and look at them, and when one of them would appear

---

[1] (*Al-Ahzab* 33:5)
[2] (*Al-Baqarah* 2:286)

distinct from the other, he would stop eating, thinking that he was applying this verse:

$$﴿ حَتَّىٰ يَتَبَيَّنَ لَكُمُ ٱلۡخَيۡطُ ٱلۡأَبۡيَضُ مِنَ ٱلۡخَيۡطِ ٱلۡأَسۡوَدِ مِنَ ٱلۡفَجۡرِ ﴾$$

until the white thread (light) of dawn appears to you distinct from the black thread (darkness of night).[1]

He then informed the Prophet ﷺ of what he did, and the Prophet ﷺ said:

$$« إِنَّمَا ذَلِكَ بَيَاضُ النَّهَارِ وَسَوَادُ اللَّيْلِ »$$

Indeed that is the whiteness of the day and the blackness of the night.

Yet the Prophet ﷺ did not order him to repeat his fast. So, if one eats, wrongly thinking that dawn has not yet begun, his fast is still correct. Similarly, if one eats at night, thinking that the sun has set, but later finding out that he was wrong, his fast is correct, because he is ignorant regarding the time.[2]

In *Sahih Al-Bukhari*, it is recorded that Asma' bint Abu Bakr, may Allâh be pleased with her, said, "During the life of the Prophet ﷺ, we continued to eat on a cloudy day and then the sun rose." If making up for the missed day were obligatory in this case, the Prophet ﷺ would have pointed that out. Allâh has completed this religion, and so if the Prophet ﷺ clarified this issue, his Companions would have transmitted that information, because Allâh Almighty guaranteed to preserve this religion. Since the Companions related nothing in this regard, we know that the Prophet ﷺ said nothing about this issue. If he didn't say anything, then we know that it is not compulsory. And because it is an important matter to transmit to future generations, it is not possible that the Companions forgot to relate it. If one forgets that he is fasting during Ramadhan and consequently eats something, his fast is not affected in any way, for the Prophet ﷺ said:

---

[1] (*Al-Baqarah* 2:187)

[2] This is the opinion held by Shaikh Ibn 'Uthaimin; the second opinion, which is held b the majority of the people of knowledge – including Shaikh Ibn Baz – states that although there is no sin upon such a person, he must make up for the missed day. And this opinion is safer.

«مَنْ نَسِيَ وَهُوَ صَائِمٌ فَأَكَلَ أَوْ شَرِبَ فَلْيُتِمَّ صَوْمَهُ فَإِنَّمَا أَطْعَمَهُ اللهُ وَسَقَاهُ»

Whoever forgets while he is fasting, and then eats or drinks, then let him complete his fast, for indeed it was Allâh Who fed him and gave him drink. (Agreed upon)

When one is forced or compelled to eat or drink; to gargle, when the water reaches his stomach; to take eye drops, and the nourishment thereof reaches one's insides; or when one has a wet dream and his semen discharges – in all of the above situations one's fast is correct, because they all happened without one having a choice.

When one cleans his teeth using *Siwak*, his fast is not nullified, because using the *Siwak* is Sunnah, both for one who is fasting and one who is not fasting, and at all times, including the daytime as well. The fasting person is also allowed to reduce the effects of extreme heat by cooling himself down with water. The Prophet ﷺ "used to pour water over his head when he was fasting, because of thirst." And when Ibn 'Umar, may Allâh be pleased with him, was fasting, he dampened a garment and then threw it over himself. This is from the mercy that Allâh has for us – and all praise belongs to Allâh, for His blessings and making it easy to follow legislation.

At-Tarawih (Ramadhan Night Prayers)[1]

At-Tarawih are those units of prayer that are performed in congregation during Ramadhan; the time for this prayer is anytime between '*Isha*' prayer and dawn. The Prophet ﷺ encouraged us to stand up for prayer at night during Ramadhan, saying:

«مَنْ قَامَ رَمَضَانَ إِيمَاناً وَاحْتِسَاباً غُفِرَ لَهُ مَا تَقَدَّمَ مِنْ ذَنْبِهِ»

Whoever stands (for prayer) in Ramadhan, with faith, and seeking his reward from Allâh, he is forgiven for his previous sins.

In *Sahih Al-Bukhari* it is recorded that 'Aishah, may Allâh be pleased with her, said, "During one night, the Prophet ﷺ stood in the *Masjid* (to pray), and people followed him in his prayer. Then he prayed the

---

[1] This section is taken from a work written by Shaikh Ibn Al-'Uthaimin.

next night, and many people attended. Then the people gathered on the third and fourth night, but the Prophet ﷺ did not come out to them. When the morning came, he ﷺ said:

«قَدْ رَأَيْتُ الَّذِي صَنَعْتُمْ فَلَمْ يَمْنَعْنِي مِنَ الْخُرُوجِ إِلَيْكُمْ إِلَّا أَنَّنِي خَشِيتُ أَنْ تُفْرَضَ عَلَيْكُمْ»

I indeed saw what you did, and nothing prevented me from coming out to you except that I feared it would be made obligatory upon you.

This happened during Ramadhan.

The Sunnah is to limit this prayer to eleven units, making *Taslim* after every two units. When 'Aishah, may Allâh be pleased with her, was asked about how the Prophet ﷺ would pray during Ramadhan, she said, "Neither in Ramadhan nor at any other time would he perform more than eleven units." (Agreed upon).

In *Al-Muwatta* it is reported from Muhammad bin Yusuf (who is trustworthy with a sound memory for transmitting *Hadith*) from Sa'ib bin Yazid, may Allâh be pleased with him, (who was a Companion), that 'Umar bin Al-Khattab, my Allâh be pleased with him, ordered Ubai bin Ka'b and Tamim Ad-Dari to lead the people in eleven units of prayer.

One doesn't do wrong, however, by praying more than eleven units, because when the Prophet ﷺ was asked about standing in the night to pray, he ﷺ said:

«مَثْنَى مَثْنَى إِذَا خَشِيَ أَحَدُكُمُ الصُّبْحَ صَلَّى رَكْعَةً وَاحِدَةً تُوتِرُ لَهُ مَا قَدْ صَلَّى»

Two (units) at a time, and if one of you fears the arrival of dawn, let him pray one unit, making odd that which he prayed. (It was recorded in the Two *Sahihs*)

Yet praying that number of units which is related in the Sunnah while performing them slowly – as long as doing so is not difficult upon the people – is better and more complete.

Some people go against what is legislated when they recite in a quick and hasty manner, and if such hastiness leads to leaving out a compulsory element of prayer or a pillar of prayer, then one's prayer is nullified.

Many of the *Imams* in different *Masjids* do not take their time when leading the *Tarawih* prayer, and this is a mistake on their part, because an *Imam* is not praying for himself only; rather, he is praying for himself and for others. He is like a governor whose responsibility is to do that which is best for his people. The people of knowledge have said that it is hated for the *Imam* to recite in such a quick fashion that his followers are prevented from what is obligatory upon them.

Muslims should establish the *Tarawih* prayer – without wasting the *Tarawih* prayer by going from *Masjid* to *Masjid* in one night. For whoever stands with the *Imam* until he leaves, the reward for standing the entire night is written for him even if he then goes to sleep.

Women may also attend the *Tarawih* prayer as long as no temptation is caused by their presence. They should leave the place of prayer in a modest way, and not in a way to attract others by adorning themselves, or by wearing makeup and perfume.

Zakatul-Fitr[1]

1) It is a compulsory form of *Zakat* that is legislated because of the breaking of the fast after Ramadhan.

2) It is compulsory upon every Muslim, for himself and for each person that it is obligatory for him to spend upon.

3) Its amount: One *Sa'* (a measurement, which is further explained below) from the most prevalent kind of food in the country. One must give this charity if he has enough of the given food for himself and his family for the day of *'Eid* and its night.

4) One *Sa'* is equal to four *Mudds*. One *Mudd* is what can be placed in two average-sized hands. A *Sa'*, then, is equal to approximately three kilograms.

5) If one can only find a portion of a *Sa'*, then he should give it – and fear Allâh as much as you are able to.

6) It is recommended to give this *Zakat* on behalf of a child in his mother's womb; however, doing so is not obligatory.

7) It is best to give that kind of food that is most beneficial to the poor.

8) One must give this *Zakat* before the *'Eid* prayer, and it is permissible to give it a day or two in advance. It is forbidden, though, to delay it until after the *'Eid* prayer without a legitimate Islamic excuse. If one delays giving it until after the prayer without an excuse, then it is not accepted from him; instead, it is considered to be a regular kind of charity. But if one delays it with an excuse, then there is no harm, such as one who is in a secluded area when *'Eid* arrives: he neither finds the necessary food for *Zakatul-Fitr* nor someone who would accept it from him.

9) You give *Zakatul-Fitr* in the area where you live.

10) It is not permissible to give the money value of the food, because doing so goes against the Sunnah.

11) It becomes compulsory to give *Zakatul-Fitr* when the sun sets

---

[1] *Khulasatul-Kalam* by Shaikh Al-Jarullah, pp. 16-17. We previously discussed *Zakatul-Fitr* briefly, and it is mentioned again here because of its relationship to fasting.

on the night before *'Eid*. Therefore if one accepts Islam after that time, one doesn't have to give *Zakatul-Fitr*. If one marries after the sun sets on that night or has a child, one doesn't have to give it on behalf of his wife, and in the second situation, on behalf of his child. But if any of the above occurs for someone before the sun sets on the night before *'Eid*, then he must give it on their behalf as well.

12) It is permissible for a group of people to give their *Zakatul-Fitr* to a single person, just as it is permissible for a single person to give his *Zakatul-Fitr* to a group of people.

13) The people who may receive *Zakatul-Fitr* are the same eight categories that may receive the normal *Zakat*; those who take precedence, however, are the poor, the needy, and those in debt.

14) It is obligatory that the *Zakat* should to reach the one who deserves it or his representative on time.

The Fifth Pillar: *Hajj*
(First, The *'Umrah*)

Before discussing *Hajj*, we must first introduce the reader to a brief outline of the rites of *'Umrah*.[1]

1) When the one who wishes to make *'Umrah* reaches the *Miqat*, it is recommended for him to perform *Ghusl* and to clean himself. The same applies to a woman, even if she is menstruating or experiencing postnatal bleeding; the only exception is that she does not perfrom *Tawaf* around the Ka'bah until she becomes purified and performs *Ghusl*. While preparing to enter into *Ihram* (the sacred state of a pilgrim), a man should apply perfume to his body, but not on the clothes he will be wearing for *Ihram*. In case that one cannot perform *Ghusl* at the *Miqat*, there is no harm in that, but if possible, it is recommended to take a shower when one reaches Makkah and before one performs *Tawaf*.

2) A man should remove all stitched clothing from his body; all he should wear is an *Izar* (lower wrap) and a *Rida'* (upper wrap). It is recommended for these garments to be both white and clean. One's head (for the man) must remain uncovered. As for a woman, she may wear her regular clothes, clothes that are not meant for adornment or fame.

3) Next, one makes intention in his heart that he is entering upon the rites of *'Umrah*, and with his tongue, he says, *Labbaik Bi 'Umrah* or *Allâhumma Labbaik Bi 'Umrah* [Here I am, O Allâh (in response to Your call), for *'Umrah*]. If, because one is sick or is afraid of an enemy or something similar, and fears that he will not be able to complete the rites, one may stipulate, saying, "If I am prevented by some obstruction, then my place is where You have confined me." In the *Hadith* of Dhuba'ah bint Az-Zubair, may Allâh be pleased with her, she said, "O Messenger of Allâh, indeed I wish to make *Hajj*, yet I am sick." He ﷺ said:

$$\text{«حُجِّي وَاشْتَرِطِي أَنَّ مُحِلِّي حَيْثُ حَبَسْتَنِي»}$$

---

[1] Taken from *Sifatul-'Umrah*, by Shaikh 'Abdul-'Aziz bin 'Abdullah bin Baz

Perform *Hajj* and stipulate "My place is where You have prevented me." (Agreed upon).

Then one should begin to utter the *Talbiyyah* of the Prophet ﷺ:

«لَبَّيْكَ اللَّهُمَّ لَبَّيْكَ، لَبَّيْكَ لَا شَرِيكَ لَكَ لَبَّيْكَ، إِنَّ الْحَمْدَ وَالنِّعْمَةَ لَكَ وَالْمُلْكَ، لَا شَرِيكَ لَكَ»

Here I am, O Allâh (in response to Your call), here I am. Here I am, You have no partner, here I am. Verily all praise, grace, and sovereignty belong to You. You have no partner.

One should repeat this *Talbiyyah* often and occupy himself with supplication and the remembrance of Allâh Almighty. When the pilgrim reaches Allâh's House (the Ka'bah), he should enter it with his right foot first, saying:

«بِسْمِ اللهِ، وَالصَّلَاةُ وَالسَّلَامُ عَلَى رَسُولِ اللهِ، أَعُوذُ بِاللهِ الْعَظِيمِ وَبِوَجْهِهِ الْكَرِيمِ وَسُلْطَانِهِ الْقَدِيمِ مِنَ الشَّيْطَانِ الرَّجِيمِ، اللَّهُمَّ افْتَحْ لِي أَبْوَابَ رَحْمَتِكَ»

In the Name of Allâh, and blessings and salutations on the Messenger of Allâh. I seek refuge in Allâh, the Supreme, with His Noble Face, and with His eternal authority from the accursed *Shaitan*. O Allâh, open for me the gates of Your mercy.

One says this supplication just as he does when he enters any *Masjid*. Next, one occupies himself with the *Talbiyyah* until he reaches the Ka'bah.

4) When he reaches the Ka'bah, he stops the *Talbiyyah*, and heads toward the Black Stone, facing it, touching it with his right hand, and kissing it if that is possible. Yet one should not harm others by crowding around the stone. When acknowledging and facing the Stone, he says, "*Bismillah, wa Allâhu Akbar* (In the Name of Allâh, and Allâh is the Most Great)," or he may simply say, "*Allâhu Akbar* (Allâh is the Most Great)." If kissing the stone is difficult, one may touch it with his right hand or with a stick or something similar, and then kiss the object that touched the Stone. If even touching it with an object is difficult, he may gesture toward the stone, saying,

"*Allâhu Akbar* (Allâh is the Most Great)," but one doesn't kiss the object that he gestures with. One of the conditions of the *Tawaf* being correct is for one to be pure from major and minor impurities, because the *Tawaf* is like the prayer, except that talking is allowed during the former.

5) One stands so that the Ka'bah is to his left, and then he makes seven circuits around it. When one is parallel to the Yamani corner, one touches it with his right hand if he can, saying, "*Bismillâh wa Allâhu Akbar* (In the Name of Allâh, and Allâh is the Most Great)." However, he should not kiss it. If it is difficult to touch it, he should leave it and continue in his *Tawaf*, in which case he should neither gesture nor make *Takbir* (saying, "*Allâhu Akbar*": Allâh is the Most Great), because neither of the two are related from the Prophet ﷺ. As for the Black Stone, every time one passes it in his *Tawaf*, he should touch it, kiss it, and make *Takbir* – as we have mentioned – or otherwise gesture toward it and make *Takbir*. It is recommended to take very quick short steps in the first three circuits for *Tawaful-Qudum* (the *Tawaf* of arrival), and this is specific to men, if they are able to do so. During *Tawaful-Qudum*, it is also recommended for a man to place the middle of his *Rida'* (upper garment) under his right armpit, with the two sides on his left shoulder. During all circuits, one should remember Allâh Almighty and invoke Him as much as possible, yet there is not any specific supplication or invocation for *Tawaf*; rather, one may choose the supplications and invocations he makes. Between the Yamani corner and the Black Stone, during each circuit, one should recite:

$$﴿رَبَّنَآ ءَاتِنَا فِي ٱلدُّنْيَا حَسَنَةً وَفِي ٱلْأَخِرَةِ حَسَنَةً وَقِنَا عَذَابَ ٱلنَّارِ﴾$$

Our Lord! Give us in this world that which is good and in the Hereafter that which is good, and save us from the torment of the Fire![1]

This practice is established in the Sunnah of the Prophet ﷺ; one should complete the seventh circuit by touching the Black Stone – and kissing it if possible – or by gesturing to it, while making *Takbir* – based on the principles mentioned earlier. After finishing the

---

[1] (*Al-Baqarah* 2:201)

circuits, he may wear his *Rida'*, placing it on his shoulders, with the two sides on his chest.

6) Next, the pilgrim prays two units behind the *Maqam*, if he is able to do so; if not, then he may pray them anywhere in the *Masjid*. After reciting *Al-Fatihah*, he should recite *Surat Al-Kafirun* in the first unit and *Al-Ikhlas* in the second one. That is best, yet it is allowed for one to recite other chapters of the Qur'ân. After praying these two units, one heads toward the Black Stone again, touching it with his right hand if possible.

7) Next, one goes to As-Safa, climbing it or standing at its bottom, though climbing is better if one can do so. Here, one will be pacing between As-Safa and Al-Marwah. Before embarking upon the first phase, one recites:

$$﴿إِنَّ ٱلصَّفَا وَٱلْمَرْوَةَ مِن شَعَآئِرِ ٱللَّهِ﴾$$

Verily! As-Safa and Al-Marwah are of the Symbols of Allâh.[1]

It is recommended to face the *Qiblah* when standing at As-Safa, praising Allâh and declaring His greatness, saying:

«لَا إِلَهَ إِلَّا اللهُ، وَاللهُ أَكْبَرُ، لَا إِلَهَ إِلَّا اللهُ وَحْدَهُ لَا شَرِيكَ لَهُ، لَهُ الْمُلْكُ وَلَهُ الْحَمْدُ وَهُوَ عَلَى كُلِّ شَيْءٍ قَدِيرٌ. لَا إِلَهَ إِلَّا اللهُ وَحْدَهُ، أَنْجَزَ وَعْدَهُ، وَنَصَرَ عَبْدَهُ، وَهَزَمَ الأَحْزَابَ وَحْدَهُ»

None has the right to be worshipped but Allâh, and Allâh is the Most Great. None has the right to be worshipped except Allâh, alone, without partner. To Him belong all sovereignty and praise and He has power over all things. None has the right to be worshipped except Allâh alone. He fulfilled His promise, aided His servant, and He Alone defeated the allies.

Then one supplicates according to what is easy, raising one's hands. One repeats the above-mentioned invocation along with the additional supplication three times. Then one walks toward Al-Marwah; on the way to Al-Marwah, there are two green lights; starting from the first light, a man should walk very fast until he

---

[1] (*Al-Baqarah* 2:158)

reaches the second one. Because a woman has much more of her body to cover and is to be protected from being seen, it is not legislated for her to walk this distance at a fast pace. When one reaches Al-Marwah, one may stand by it or climb it, though climbing it is better if one can do so. One should say and do at Al-Marwah just as one said and did at As-Safa, except for the recitation of the verse, for that is legislated when one climbs As-Safa for the first phase only, because that is the practice of the Prophet ﷺ. Then one descends, returning to As-Safa, walking most of the way, but walking fast between the two signs (green lights). In this fashion, one makes seven phases; going one way to Al-Marwa is considered to be one phase and returning to As-Safa is considered to be one phase. If one performs this pacing, riding a means of conveyance, there is no harm, especially when there is a need. During these phases it is recommended to remember Allâh Almighty and supplicate to Him as much as possible. Though one's pacing is correct if one is not in a complete state of purity, it is recommended that one should be purified from both the minor and major states of impurity.

8) After completing these phases, a man shaves his head or shortens the length of his hair; though both are permissible, shaving is better. Yet if one's entry into Makkah is close to the time of *Hajj*, then merely shortening the length of one's hair is better – in this instance only, so that he can shave the rest of his head during *Hajj*. As for a woman, her hair is gathered, and the length of a fingertip – or less – is taken from her hair. If the *Muhrim* (one who is in *Ihram*) does all of the above, his *'Umrah* is now complete – and all praise is for Allâh! All that was forbidden upon him specifically because of the *Ihram* now becomes permissible.

(Second, The *Hajj*)

The Manners Of *Hajj* And Its Sunnah Actions[1]

Hajj is one of the greatest forms of worship, for combined within it are many different kinds of worship that are not found together in anywhere else. It is a worship of body, wealth, and movement.

---

[1] From *Aadabul-Hajj waz-Ziyarah* by Shaikh 'Abdul-'Aziz bin 'Abdullah bin Hasan Aal Ash-Shaikh.

Therefore, the pilgrim should have a sense of the greatness of this worship, seeking to spend the most purely derived wealth he has on it, for indeed Allâh Almighty is pure and good, and only accepts that which is pure and good. Similarly, the pilgrim should make sure to abstain from any saying, deed, or intention that might nullify his *Hajj* or decrease from his rewards. His intention – for both *Hajj* and *'Umrah* – should be obedience to Allâh Almighty, by following His Orders, and that is achieved by sincerely intending all of one's worship for Allâh. One supplicates only to Allâh, calls out to Him only, seeks help or a cure from Him only, and seeks for a lost one to be returned from Him only. One seeks help from Him and no other, and one relies upon Him and no other. If one seeks any of the above from other than Allâh, then he has indeed intended and directed his worship to other than Allâh; and whoever intends his worship for other than Allâh is a *Mushrik* (polytheist, one who associates partners with Allâh in worship). And whoever associates partners with Allâh in worship, then his deeds are rendered void, and in the Hereafter he is one of the losers – regardless of whether he knew what he was doing was unlawful or not.

A pilgrim should learn those matters that will benefit him, matters that will help to make his *Hajj* accepted. At the same time, he should avoid all forbidden deeds, especially those that stain his belief in *Tawhid*, such as swearing by other than Allâh – by another person's life, by the Prophet ﷺ, by the Ka'bah, and so on. All of that is forbidden whether the pilgrim knows it or not. There is no excuse for the pilgrim, for it is a matter that he must learn and know. A Muslim is required to know his religion and to seek out that knowledge. The pilgrim must also avoid evil speech, harming others, or adding what Allâh and His Messenger ﷺ have not legislated to the religion. Examples of such innovations are praying in a graveyard, supplicating in front of the graves of the righteous, of the Companions, of the Prophet's family; other innovations include seeking blessings from historical places, such as the cave at Hira', the Thawr Mountain, and other similar places. These actions are the most likely of means that lead to a hateful end – that which is the unlawful. The means hold the same rulings as the ends. These deeds were not practiced during the lifetime of the best of people and those among them who strove most in worship – the time of the

Companions, may Allâh be pleased with them, and the early generations.

All that has been legislated for us in Islam is enough and sufficient. Therefore, especially when we are in the sacred area of Makkah, we should renew our covenant with our Lord, asking for help, guidance, and success from Him.

The Obligation to Repent And Its Conditions

When one of us intends to travel for *Hajj*:

1) It is compulsory upon him to repent sincerely from all sins, especially those sins that negate *Tawhid*. In any case, repentance is always required from us at all times, but when one intends to perform any form of worship, the necessity to repent takes on a stronger emphasis. Here are the conditions of a sincere repentance:

2) That one completely desists from the sin he was perpetrating.

3) That one sincerely feels remorse for having perpetrated that sin.

4) That one resolves to never return to that sin in the future.

5) And if the sin involves the right of another person – in terms of wealth, a life, or wealth – that one returns that right to its proper owner or at least seeks absolution from him before traveling.

The Deeds Of *Hajj*

The *Ihram*

The pilgrim arrives at the *Miqat*, where he will make his intention.

If he is coming from Al-Madinah and what is before it, his *Miqat* will be a place known as Thul-Hulaifah. Today, this *Miqat* is known as *Abyar 'Ali* (the Wells of 'Ali).

If he is coming from Ash-Sham (the areas of Syria, Lebanon, and so on) or its surrounding areas, then his *Miqat* is Al-Juhfah. Al-Juhfah is a village that is next to Rabigh.

If he is coming from Najd, then his *Miqat* is Qarn Al-Manazil.

If he is coming from the direction of Yemen, his *Miqat* is Yalamlam.

And if he is coming from Iraq or its surrounding areas, his *Miqat* is

That-'Irq.

When one passes by one of these *Miqats* – whether he is traveling by land, sea, or air – with the intention of *Hajj* or *'Umrah*, he must begin *Ihram* at the *Miqat* or from a place that is parallel to it. If one puts on the clothing of *Ihram* in preparation before actually reaching the *Miqat*, then in that there is no harm, because he then makes the actual intention of *Hajj* or *'Umrah* at the *Miqat*.

If the pilgrim lives within the boundaries of the *Miqat*, such as one who lives in Jeddah or Shara'a', it is not legislated for him to go back to the *Miqat* that is near him; rather, the place where he lives is his *Miqat*, and he makes *Ihram* from there.

Ihram For The Male Pilgrim

The pilgrim, in general, does the following when he reaches the *Miqat*:

1) He removes any stitched clothing.

2) It is recommended for him to take a complete *Ghusl*,

3) And to apply perfume.

4) It is also recommended for him to trim his moustache and, as he normally does, to remove his pubic hair, so that he doesn't have to do so after entering into the state of *Ihram*.

5) As mentioned earlier, the male wears an *Izar* (lower wrap) and a *Rida'* (upper wrap).

6) It is recommended for the two cloths to be white and clean.

7) It is also recommended for one to wear sandals when entering into the state of *Ihram*, for this practice is related from the Prophet ﷺ. For one who does not find sandals, he wears *Khuffs*.

The *Ihram* Of The Woman And What She Must Do

If the pilgrim is a woman, she does the following:

1) It is recommended for her to perform *Ghusl* for *Ihram*, even though she may be menstruating or experiencing postnatal bleeding; she does everything a pilgrim does except for *Tawaf* around the Ka'bah, which she must perform after purifying herself from menstruation or post-natal bleeding.

2) There is no specific kind of garment that is recommended for her.

3) It is permitted for her to use any garment for *Ibram*, be it black, green, or any other color.

4) She must not, however, imitate men in the way she dresses.

5) Her clothing should cover her properly.

6) She must not display her *'Awrab* or her beauty to strangers.

* After the above events occur, both the male and female pilgrims make intention to enter upon the rites one wishes to perform – either *Hajj* or *'Umrab* or both combined.

* At this point, it is legislated for the pilgrim to begin *Talbiyyah*, saying – "*Labbaik Bi 'Umrab*: O Allâh, I am here (answering Your call), (intending to make) *'Umrab*," if one is intending to make *'Umrab*; or: "*Labbaik Bi Hajjah*: O Allâh, I am here (answering Your call), (intending to make) *Hajj*," if one intends to make *Hajj*; and "*Labbaik 'Umratan wa-Hajjan*: O Allâh, I am here (answering Your call), (intending to make) *Hajj* and *'Umrab*," if one intends to perform both. Next, one continues to recite the *Talbiyyah* (which we mentioned in its entirety above).

What Does One in *Ihram* Do When Reaching Makkah?

Upon reaching Makkah, the pilgrim should:

1) Stop uttering the *Talbiyyah*, and commence by making seven circuits around the Ka'bah.

2) Pray two units behind the *Maqam*.

3) Go out to As-Safa and pace seven times between As-Safa and Al-Marwah.

4) Then shave his head or shorten the length of his hair, at which point his *'Umrah* is complete and all things are permissible to him that were previously forbidden specifically due to the *Ibram*. All of this has been explained in the discussion on *'Umrah*.

If one enters the *Miqat* during the months of *Hajj*, one must choose to adhere to one of the three rites (*'Umrah* alone, *Hajj* alone, or both combined), and make *Ibram* accordingly.

1) The three rites just referred to are *Hajj* by itself, *'Umrah* by itself, or both combined.

2) Whoever makes *Ibram* for *Hajj* alone or for *Hajj* combined with *'Umrab* and he doesn't have the sacrifice, then he shouldn't stay

in his *Ihram*; rather, the Sunnah in his case is to make his *Ihram* for *'Umrah*.

3) This means that he should make circuits around the Ka'bah and then pacing between As-Safa and Al-Marwah, after which he shortens the length of his hair and exits the state of *Ihram*.

4) However, if because one arrived late, he fears that he will miss *Hajj*, he may remain in *Ihram*.

5) The diligent believer who desires his actions to be correct should stick to what has been mentioned, performing as much worship that is legislated as possible, such as reciting the Qur'ân and praying in congregation.

6) Afterwards, one should not occupy his time in matters that are of no benefit to him, matters that are not legislated for him.

7) Examples of such matters are searching out for the graves of specific Companions, of the Prophet's wives, of the place where the Prophet ﷺ was born, of the place where revelation came down to him; people think that such places are places specifically meant for worship, that their supplications will be answered if they invoke Allâh in those places, and that such places will bring them blessings, when in reality, none of the above is true.

This Is How The Messenger Of Allâh ﷺ Performed *Hajj*[1]

To my Muslim brothers who are performing *Hajj* to Allâh's Sacred House,

I ask Allâh Almighty to guide us all, to guide us to that which pleases Him and to that which keeps us safe from deviations and trials. I also ask Him to make you all successful in performing your rites, meaning that you perform them in a way that pleases Him. I pray to Allâh that he accepts this worship from you and that he returns you to your lands, safe and guided. Indeed He is the best of those who are asked.

O Muslims:

1) My advice to all is to fear Allâh in all situations and to be upright upon His religion, while staying away from those matters that bring about His anger.

2) The greatest duty upon you is to uphold *Tawhid* of Allâh and to have sincerity to Allâh in all forms of worship. At the same time, you must be steadfast in following the Messenger of Allâh ﷺ, both in sayings and in deeds.

3) Perform the rites of *Hajj* and all other forms of worship in the way that Allâh has legislated for His worshippers, legislated upon the tongue of His Messenger, His *Khalil*, His choice from His creation: our Prophet, Imam, and Leader, Muhammad bin 'Abdullah ﷺ.

4) The greatest evil and crime known to man is associating partners with Allâh, directing an act of worship or part of an act of worship to other than Allâh, for He Almighty says:

$$﴿ إِنَّ اللَّهَ لَا يَغْفِرُ أَن يُشْرَكَ بِهِۦ وَيَغْفِرُ مَا دُونَ ذَٰلِكَ لِمَن يَشَآءُۚ وَمَن يُشْرِكْ بِٱللَّهِ فَقَدِ ٱفْتَرَىٰٓ إِثْمًا عَظِيمًا ﴾$$

Verily, Allâh forgives not that partners should be set up with

---

[1] *Hakatha Hajjar-Rasul* ﷺ, written by Shaikh 'Abdul-'Aziz bin Baz, the previous *Mufti* of the Kingdom of Saudi Arabia – may Allâh have mercy upon him.

him in worship, but He forgives except that (anything else) to whom He wills, and whoever sets up partners with Allâh in worship, he has indeed invented a tremendous sin.[1]

Addressing His Prophet, Muhammad ﷺ, Allâh Almighty said:

﴿وَلَقَدْ أُوحِيَ إِلَيْكَ وَإِلَى ٱلَّذِينَ مِن قَبْلِكَ لَئِنْ أَشْرَكْتَ لَيَحْبَطَنَّ عَمَلُكَ وَلَتَكُونَنَّ مِنَ ٱلْخَاسِرِينَ﴾

And indeed it has been revealed to you (O Muhammad ﷺ), as it was to those (Allâh's Messengers) before you: "If you join others in worship with Allâh, (then) surely (all) your deeds will be in vain, and you will certainly be among the losers."[2]

Those Who Are Performing *Hajj* To Allâh's Sacred House

5) Indeed, our Prophet ﷺ performed one *Hajj* only after his migration to Al-Madinah, and that was at the end of his life; it is known as the Farewell Pilgrimage.

6) In that *Hajj*, the Prophet ﷺ taught people their rites, with his speech and action, and he ﷺ said to them:

«خُذُوا عَنِّي مَنَاسِكَكُمْ»

Take from me your rites.

It Is Compulsory To Follow The Prophet ﷺ

7) It is incumbent upon Muslims to follow the Prophet ﷺ in their rites.

8) They must perform the rites in the manner that has been legislated for them, because the Prophet ﷺ is our teacher and guide; indeed, Allâh Almighty sent him as a mercy to mankind and jinn, and as a proof upon all worshippers, which is why Allâh ordered His creatures to obey him. Allâh informed us that obeying him is a means of entering Paradise and being saved from the Fire. It is also a proof, indicating the worshipper's sincere love for his Lord, and also indicating Allâh's love for His worshippers, as Allâh Almighty says:

﴿وَمَا ءَاتَىٰكُمُ ٱلرَّسُولُ فَخُذُوهُ وَمَا نَهَىٰكُمْ عَنْهُ فَٱنتَهُوا﴾

---

[1] (*An-Nisa'* 4:48)
[2] (*Az-Zumar* 39:65)

And whatsoever the Messenger (Muhammad ﷺ) gives you, take it, and whatsoever he forbids you, abstain (from it).[1]

And:

﴿وَأَقِيمُواْ ٱلصَّلَوٰةَ وَءَاتُواْ ٱلزَّكَوٰةَ وَأَطِيعُواْ ٱلرَّسُولَ لَعَلَّكُمْ تُرْحَمُونَ﴾

And perform *As-Salat*, and give *Zakat* and obey the Messenger (Muhammad ﷺ) that you may receive mercy (from Allâh). [2]

﴿مَّن يُطِعِ ٱلرَّسُولَ فَقَدْ أَطَاعَ ٱللَّهَ﴾

He who obeys the Messenger (Muhammad ﷺ), has indeed obeyed Allâh.[3]

And:

﴿لَّقَدْ كَانَ لَكُمْ فِي رَسُولِ ٱللَّهِ أُسْوَةٌ حَسَنَةٌ لِّمَن كَانَ يَرْجُواْ ٱللَّهَ وَٱلْيَوْمَ ٱلْأَخِرَ وَذَكَرَ ٱللَّهَ كَثِيرًا﴾

Indeed in the Messenger of Allâh (Muhammad ﷺ) you have a good example to follow for him who hopes in (the Meeting with) Allâh and the Last Day and remembers Allâh much.[4]

And:

﴿وَمَن يُطِعِ ٱللَّهَ وَرَسُولَهُ يُدْخِلْهُ جَنَّٰتٍ تَجْرِى مِن تَحْتِهَا ٱلْأَنْهَٰرُ خَٰلِدِينَ فِيهَا وَذَٰلِكَ ٱلْفَوْزُ ٱلْعَظِيمُ ١٣ وَمَن يَعْصِ ٱللَّهَ وَرَسُولَهُ وَيَتَعَدَّ حُدُودَهُ يُدْخِلْهُ نَارًا خَٰلِدًا فِيهَا وَلَهُ عَذَابٌ مُّهِينٌ﴾

And whosoever obeys Allâh and His Messenger (Muhammad ﷺ) will be admitted to Gardens under which rivers flow (in Paradise), to abide therein, and that will be the great success. And whosoever disobeys Allâh and His Messenger (Muham-mad ﷺ), and transgresses His (set) limits, He will cast him into the Fire, to abide therein; and he shall have a disgraceful

---

[1] (*Al-Hashr* 59:7)
[2] (*An-Nur* 24:56)
[3] (*An-Nisa'* 4:80)
[4] (*Al-Ahzab* 33:21)

torment.[1]

And:

$$﴿قُلْ يَٰٓأَيُّهَا ٱلنَّاسُ إِنِّى رَسُولُ ٱللَّهِ إِلَيْكُمْ جَمِيعًا ٱلَّذِى لَهُۥ مُلْكُ ٱلسَّمَٰوَٰتِ وَٱلْأَرْضِ لَآ إِلَٰهَ إِلَّا هُوَ يُحْىِۦ وَيُمِيتُ فَـَٔامِنُوا۟ بِٱللَّهِ وَرَسُولِهِ ٱلنَّبِىِّ ٱلْأُمِّىِّ ٱلَّذِى يُؤْمِنُ بِٱللَّهِ وَكَلِمَٰتِهِۦ وَٱتَّبِعُوهُ لَعَلَّكُمْ تَهْتَدُونَ﴾$$

Say (O Muhammad ﷺ): "O mankind! Verily, I am sent to you all as the Messenger of Allâh – to Whom belongs the dominion of the heavens and the earth. *Laa Ilaha Illa Huwa* (none has the right to be worshipped but He); It is He Who gives life and causes death. So believe in Allâh and His Messenger (Muhammad ﷺ), the Prophet who can neither read nor write (i.e., Muhammad ﷺ) who believes in Allâh and His Words [(this Qur'ân), the Tawrah and the Injil and also Allâh's Word: "Be!" – and he was, i.e. 'Iesa son of Maryam], and follow him so that you may be guided."[2]

And:

$$قُلْ إِن كُنتُمْ تُحِبُّونَ ٱللَّهَ فَٱتَّبِعُونِى يُحْبِبْكُمُ ٱللَّهُ وَيَغْفِرْ لَكُمْ ذُنُوبَكُمْ وَٱللَّهُ غَفُورٌ رَّحِيمٌ﴾$$

Say (O Muhammad ﷺ to mankind): "If you (really) love Allâh then follow me, Allâh will love you and forgive you of your sins. And Allâh is Oft-Forgiving, Most Merciful."[3]

And there are many other verses as well that carry a similar meaning.

9) My advice then to you all, as well as to myself, is to fear Allâh in all circumstances and to be sincere in following the Prophet ﷺ, following his sayings and actions, so that you may achieve happiness and safety, both in this world and in the Hereafter.

What The Pilgrim Should Do On The Eighth Day Of Thul-Hijjah

Brother pilgrims to Allâh's Sacred House, on the eight of Thul-Hijjah, our Prophet, Muhammad ﷺ,

---

[1] (*An-Nisa'* 4:13,14)

[2] (*Al-A'raf* 7:158)

[3] (*Aal 'Imran* 3:31)

10) Set out from Makkah to Mina, uttering the *Talbiyyah*.

11) Ordered his companions, may Allâh be pleased with them, to begin the *Talbiyyah* for *Hajj* from where they were staying and head out for Mina.

12) Didn't order his Companions to perform the Farewell *Tawaf* before going to Mina. This shows that the Sunnah for all pilgrims – those living in Makkah, those who have finished their *'Umrah*, and all other pilgrims – is to head to Mina on the eight day, making *Talbiyyah* for *Hajj*. They do not have to first go the Ka'bah for a Farewell *Tawaf*.

What It Is Recommended For The Pilgrim To Do When Entering Into *Ihram*

13) When the pilgrim is entering into the state of *Ihram* – meaning the time he makes *Ihram* for *Hajj*, because after he performed *'Umrah*, he exited from the state of *Ihram*, waiting for the *Hajj* – he should take a shower, apply perfume, and clean himself, just as he did at the *Miqat*. That is what the Prophet ﷺ ordered 'Aishah, may Allâh be pleased with her, to do; originally, she made *Ihram* for *'Umrah*, but she began to menstruate when she entered Makkah, making it impossible for her to perform *Tawaf* before heading out to Mina, so the Prophet ﷺ ordered her to perform *Ghusl* and to begin *Ihram* for *Hajj*. That is what she did, so she was one of those who performed the *Qiran* form of *Hajj* and *'Umrah*.

14) While in Mina, the Prophet ﷺ and his Companions shortened their four-unit prayers to two units, without combining between any of the prayers, so that is the Sunnah of the Prophet ﷺ in this regard.

15) During this trip, it is Sunnah for the pilgrim to occupy his time by saying the *Talbiyyah*, by remembering Allâh, by reciting the Qur'ân, and by doing other acts of obedience to Allâh, such as calling others to the way of Allâh, ordering others to do good, forbidding others from perpetrating evil, and helping the poor.

What The Muslim Should Do On The Day Of *'Arafah*

16) When the sun had risen on the day of *'Arafah*, the Prophet ﷺ and his Companions headed toward 'Arafat – some were uttering the *Talbiyyah* while others were uttering the *Takbir*.

17) When he reached 'Arafat, he halted at Nimarah in western 'Arafat where a camel-hair tent was erected for him, under which he was shaded. This proves that it is permissible for pilgrims to take shade in tents, under trees, and so on.

18) At midday, the Prophet ﷺ climbed his mount and gave a sermon to the people, reminding them and teaching them the rites of their *Hajj*. He warned them not to deal in usury and not to perform deeds of ignorance. Their blood, wealth, and honor – he informed them that all of these are inviolable, and he ordered them to hold fast to Allâh's Book and to His Messenger's Sunnah. He then told them that they wouldn't go astray so as long as they adhered to Allâh's Book and His Messenger's Sunnah.

19) It is incumbent upon all Muslims, no matter where they may be, to cling to this advice and to apply it.

20) All Muslim rulers must adhere to Allâh's Book and His Prophet's Sunnah; they must apply the rulings found in those two sources in all of their affairs, forcing their citizens to apply them as well. This is the way to honor, happiness, and safety in this world and in the Hereafter – may Allâh grant success to us all.

21) Then the Prophet ﷺ shortened the *Zuhr* and *'Asr* prayers, combining between them in the time of *Zuhr*, with one *Athan* and two *Iqamahs*.

22) Then the Prophet ﷺ, while on his mount, moved a little further, faced the *Qiblah*, then remembered Allâh and supplicated to Him with his hands raised, until the sun had set. Because he wasn't fasting on that day, we learn that it is legislated for all pilgrims to do as he did at 'Arafat, in terms of not fasting, and in terms of remembering Allâh, supplicating – with their hands raised, and uttering the *Talbiyyah* until the sun sets. In an authentic *Hadith*, the Prophet ﷺ said:

«مَا مِنْ يَوْمٍ أَكْثَرَ عِتْقاً مِنَ النَّارِ مِنْ يَوْمِ عَرَفَةَ، وَإِنَّهُ سُبْحَانَهُ لَيَدْنُو فَيُبَاهِي بِهِمْ مَلَائِكَتَهُ»

There is no day wherein more people are liberated from the Fire than on the day of *'Arafah*. Indeed, He (Allâh) comes close and boasts about them to His angels.

It has also been related from the Prophet ﷺ that Allâh says to His angels on the day of *'Arafah*:

«انْظُرُوا إِلَى عِبَادِي! أَتَوْنِي شُعْثاً غُبْرًا يَرْجُونَ رَحْمَتِي أُشْهِدُكُمْ أَنِّي قَدْ غَفَرْتُ لَهُمْ»

Look at My worshippers! They have come to Me, disheveled and dust-covered, hoping for my mercy. I make you bear witness that I indeed forgive them..

In another authentic *Hadith*, the Prophet ﷺ said:

«وَقَفْتُ هَاهُنَا وَعَرَفَةُ كُلُّهَا مَوْقِفٌ»

I have stood here, yet all of 'Arafat is a place for standing.

What A Pilgrim Does In Muzdalifah

23) The Prophet ﷺ prayed combined *Maghrib* and *'Isha'*, praying three units for the former and two for the latter – and making the prayers with one *Athan* and two *Iqamahs*.[1]

24) Then he ﷺ spent the night in Mina, praying *Fajr* and the Sunnah of *Fajr*, with the *Athan* and the *Iqamah*.

25) Then the Prophet ﷺ went to the *Al-Mash'ar*, he remembered Allâh there and uttered the *Takbir* and *Laa Ilaha Illallah*, supplicated with his hands raised and said:

«وَقَفْتُ هَاهُنَا وَجَمْعٌ كُلُّهَا مَوْقِفٌ»

I have stood here, yet all of it is a place for standing:

This shows that Muzdalifah in its entirety is a stopping place for pilgrims – each pilgrim spends the night in his place, remembering Allâh Almighty and asking His forgiveness, without the need of going to the spot where the Prophet ﷺ stood.

---

[1] Some people occupy themselves on the night of Muzdalifah by gathering pebbles for the stoning, mistakenly thinking that the pebbles may be taken from Muzdalifah only. So rather than spending their time in prayer, they gather pebbles. This is a mistake, and the Sunnah is to pick up seven pebbles for the *Jamratul-'Aqabah* on the day of *Nahr*, following the Sunnah of the Prophet ﷺ. So one gathers the stones while going to Mina, after having prayed *Fajr*.

26) The Prophet ﷺ allowed the weak to go to Mina during the night of Muzdalifah.

27) This means that the weak – including women, the sick, the old, and those like them – can leave Muzdalifah to go to Mina in the last half of the night, using the license they have, fearing the hardship of crowds.

28) It is also permissible for those who are weak to Stone the *Jamarat* (pebbles), as is established from Umm Salamah and Asma' bint Abu Bakr, may Allâh be pleased with them.

29) Asma' bint Abu Bakr, may Allâh be pleased with her, related that the Prophet ﷺ permitted women to throw the pebbles at night.

30) When the sun began to really shine, the Prophet ﷺ headed to Mina, uttering the *Talbiyyah*.

What The Pilgrim Does On The Day Of *Nahr*

31) After the sun had risen, the Prophet ﷺ went to *Jamaratul-'Aqabah* and stoned it with seven pebbles, uttering the *Takbir* (i.e., saying, "*Allâhu Akbar*") with the throwing of each pebble.

32) Then the Prophet ﷺ slaughtered the sacrifice.

33) Then he ﷺ shaved his head.

34) Next, 'Aishah, may Allâh be pleased with her, applied perfume on him.

35) Then he ﷺ went to Ka'bah and performed *Tawaf*.

The Ruling For Changing The Order Of The Rites

36) On the Day of *Nahr*, the Prophet ﷺ was asked about one who slaughtered the sacrifice before throwing the stones, or who shaved before slaughtering, or who went to the Ka'bah before stoning, and he ﷺ said:

«لَا حَرَجَ»

There is no harm.

The narrator of this *Hadith* said, "On that day, in all of the matters regarding putting before or putting after that the Prophet ﷺ was asked about, he said, 'Do so, there is no harm.'"A man asked the Prophet ﷺ, 'I made *Sa'y* (pacing between As-Safa and Al-Marwah) before making *Tawaf*, and the Prophet ﷺ said:

«لَا حَرَجَ»

'There is no harm.' "

37) From the above, we learn that the Sunnah for pilgrims is to begin by stoning on the day of *'Eid*, following that by slaughtering – if they have a sacrifice, then shaving their head or shortening the length of their hair – though shaving is better, for the Prophet ﷺ supplicated for forgiveness and mercy three times for those who shave, and only once for those who shorten the length of their hair.

38) At this point, the pilgrim is released from the *Ihram* for the first of two times,

39) Which means that he may now wear stitched clothing and apply perfume.

40) It also means that he may do all that was forbidden upon him by *Ihram*, except for sexual intercourse and the things that lead to it.

41) Then he goes to the Ka'bah, performing *Tawaf* on the day of *'Eid* or the day after *'Eid*.

42) If he is making the *Tamattu'* form of *Hajj*, he then makes seven phases between As-Safa and Al-Marwah; after he completes these phases, he completely exits from the state of *Ihram*, which means that he may also engage in lawful sexual intercourse.

43) As for one who is making *Hajj* by itself or one performing the *Qiran* form of *Hajj*, then the first *Sa'y* he made with the *Tawaf* of arrival is enough for him.

44) However, if he wasn't able to make *Sa'y* with the *Tawaf* of arrival, he must make it with *Tawaful-Ifadhah* (i.e., the *Tawaf* for returning).

The Deeds Of The Pilgrim After The Day Of *Nahr*

45) He then returns to Mina, staying there for the rest of the day of *'Eid*, along with the 11th, 12th, and 13th.

46) On each of the days of *Tashriq* – the 11th, 12th, and 13th – he stones the *Jamarat* after midday, throwing seven pebbles at each *Jamrah*, and uttering the *Takbir* with each stone he throws. He

should supplicate, raising his hands after finishing the first and second *Jamrat*, placing the first one on his left when supplicating after throwing the pebbles there, and placing the second one on his right when supplicating after throwing pebbles there, and without standing to supplicate at the third *Jamrah*.

47) On the 13th day, after having stoned the *Jamarat*, the Prophet ﷺ stayed in Abtah, praying *Zuhr*, *'Asr*, *Maghrib*, and *'Isha'* there.

The Farewell *Tawaf*

48) At the end of that night, one goes and stays in Makkah. On the day of the 14th, the Prophet ﷺ led the people in *Fajr* prayer.

49) He ﷺ performed the Farewell *Tawaf* before *Fajr* prayer.

50) After the *Fajr* prayer, the Prophet ﷺ set out toward Al-Madinah – O Allâh, send prayers and salutations upon him.

51) From the above, we learn what it is Sunnah for the pilgrim to do during the days of Mina.

52) On each of the three days, he stones all three *Jamarat* after midday. At each *Jamrah*, he throws seven pebbles, uttering the *Takbir* with each throwing.

53) After stoning the first *Jamrah*, it is legislated for the pilgrim to raise his hands, face the *Qiblah*, and invoke Allâh, placing the *Jamrah* to his left.

54) He does the same at the second *Jamrah* after stoning it, except that he places the *Jamrah* to his right.

55) Supplicating thus is recommended, and not compulsory.

56) He should not stand and supplicate after the third *Jamrah*; if it is not possible for one to throw the stones after midday and before the setting of the sun, he may throw them in the night until the last part of the night, to make up for that day. This is the correct view from the different scholars in this issue, and it is a ruling in which one appreciates Allâh's mercy for His worshippers.

57) If one wishes to go early, leaving on the 12th day after throwing the pebbles, then there is no harm in that.

58) But it is better to stay for the stoning of the 13th day, for that is in accordance to the practice of the Prophet ﷺ.

59) It is Sunnah for the pilgrim to spend the night in Mina on the nights before the 11th and 12th.

60) Spending these two nights in Mina is considered to be obligatory by many scholars.

61) To be considered to have spent the night in Mina, one should have spent at least most of the night there – if that is possible.

62) Whoever has a legitimate Islamic excuse – such as those with important responsibilities elsewhere – he does not have to spend the night in Mina.

63) For those who leave Mina early on the 12th – meaning they leave it before the sun has set – then they do not have to spend the night in Mina.

64) But as for those who are still in Mina after sunset, then they should spend the night in Mina and throw pebbles at the three *Jamarat* on the following day (the 13th), after midday, just as they threw pebbles at them on the 11th and 12th. After that, they may leave.

65) No one should throw pebbles after the 13th, even if they are still staying in Mina.

66) When the pilgrim is about to leave for his land, he must perform the Farewell *Tawaf*, for the Prophet ﷺ said,

«لَا يَنْفِرُ أَحَدٌ مِنْكُمْ حَتَّى يَكُونَ آخِرُ عَهْدِهِ بِالْبَيْتِ»

Let not one of you depart until it is his last duty at the House.

67) The exceptions are menstruating women and women experiencing postnatal bleeding, for they do not have to perform the Farewell *Tawaf*. It is confimred that Ibn 'Abbas, may Allâh be pleased with them, said: "He ordered them to make it their last action in the House – except that he relieved the menstruating woman."

68) Whoever delays the *Tawaful-Ifadhah* until he is about to travel, and then performs *Tawaf*, that one *Tawaf* is sufficient for the Farewell *Tawaf* as well – based on the two general proofs given above.

The Sacrifice And The *Fidyah*[1]

If the pilgrim is performing the *Tamattu'* form of *Hajj*, or the *Qiran* form, and if he is not a resident of Makkah, he is responsible for the sacrifice of either a sheep, one-seventh of a camel, or one-seventh of a cow, from a pure and lawfully derived income, for Allâh Almighty is good and pure and He accepts only that which is good and pure. If someone from the said categories of pilgrims cannot make the above-mentioned sacrifice, then he must fast three days during *Hajj*, regardless of whether those days are before the day of *Nahr* or after it, during the days of *Tashriq* (the 11th, 12th, and 13th). Then he must fast seven extra days when he returns to his home; he has the option of fasting seven days in a row or one at a time, skipping days.

Visiting The Prophet's *Masjid* In Al-Madinah

Visiting the Prophet's *Masjid* immediately before or after the *Hajj* is Sunnah, or even in other months, though there is no connection between visiting it and the *Hajj*. Visiting the Prophet's *Masjid* is neither a pillar of *Hajj* nor is it one of its compulsory elements. Nevertheless, one prayer in that *Masjid* – at any time – is better than prayer in any other *Masjid*, except for the Sacred *Masjid* (in Makkah). This fact is established in an authentic *Hadith* related by Al-Bukhari and Muslim.

How To Enter The *Masjid* of Allâh's Messenger ﷺ

Generally speaking, the manners one must adhere to in the Prophet's *Masjid* are the same as those manners that one must adhere to in any *Masjid* established for prayer on the earth. It is recommended for one who enters the *Masjid* to enter with his right foot first, supplicating with the invocation for entering the *Masjid*, which is related from the Prophet ﷺ. Similarly, when one is leaving the *Masjid*, one should make the supplication for leaving a *Masjid*, which is also related from the Prophet ﷺ. However, there is no specific supplication that pertains to the Prophet's *Masjid*. Next, the visitor prays two units in any part of the *Masjid*, two units that are called *Tahiyyatul-Masjid* (Greeting the *Masjid*). If one prays them in the honored *Rawdhah* (an area in the front of the Prophet's *Masjid*),

---

[1] From *Aadabul-Hajj wal-'Umrah waz-Ziyarah Ash-Shari'ah* by Shaikh 'Abdul-'Aziz bin 'Abdullah bin Hasan Aal Ash-Shaikh.

then that is better.

Visiting The Grave Of The Messenger Of Allâh ﷺ

Because the visiting Muslim is in near proximity to the Prophet's grave, it is good for him to visit it, along with the graves of his two Companions, Abu Bakr and 'Umar, may Allâh be pleased with them (both of which are adjacent to the Prophet's grave). One should visit it in a respectful manner, in a manner that conforms to the *Shari'ah*, showing good manners and lowering one's voice, saying, "*As-Salaamu 'Alaikum Yaa Rasoolallâh wa Rahmatullahi wa Barakaatuhu* (May the peace, mercy, and blessings of Allâh be upon you, O Messenger of Allâh)." To mention his noble qualities, to bear witness that he ﷺ fulfilled the duties of his mission, and to bear witness that the Prophet ﷺ performed *Jihad* in the way of Allâh in the truest sense – to do all of these is permissible. Next, one greets Abu Bakr and 'Umar, may Allâh be pleased with them, supplicating for them and invoking Allâh to be pleased with them. What has just been described is the legislated visitation that is known from the Companions and those who came after them from our pious predecessors. After that, one should leave; but if one wishes to remain and supplicate, he should turn around, face the *Qiblah*, and then invoke Allâh with those invocations that he wishes to make.

Visiting Graves Is Limited To Men Only

Because of the general prohibition on women visiting graves, visiting the Prophet's grave is legislated for men only. Indeed, the Messenger of Allâh ﷺ cursed women who visit graves. The pilgrim must consider this and beware of perpetrating any sin that may nullify his good deeds – sins that include wiping the enclosure (thinking that doing so will bring him benefit) or the bars surrounding it, or to make *Tawaf* around the enclosure as opposed to the Ka'bah, for all of these actions are forbidden. It is also strictly forbidden to ask the Messenger of Allâh ﷺ to fulfill one's needs, to divert hardship, to cure the sick, to enrich the poor, or to intercede for him on the Day of Judgement. All of these matters are unlawful; none can answer such requests except Allâh, and to ask from other than Allâh regarding such matters is *Shirk* in worship.

$$ ﴿إِنَّ اللَّهَ لَا يَغْفِرُ أَن يُشْرَكَ بِهِۦ﴾ $$

Verily, Allâh forgives not that partners should be set up with him in worship.[1]

However, you may invoke Allâh for the Prophet ﷺ – or righteous people – to intercede for you.

Whoever lives far from Al-Madinah, he should not make a journey to it for the purpose of visiting the Prophet's grave; one's intention (based on the Sunnah) should be to visit the Prophet's *Masjid*. Visiting his grave is secondary to visiting the *Masjid*.

When one visits Al-Madinah, it is also recommended for him to visit the *Quba Masjid* and to pray in it, for the Prophet ﷺ used to visit the *Quba Masjid*, riding to reach there or walking, and then he would pray two units of prayer.

These are some of the manners of *Hajj* and visitation that we wished to mention, as well as those matters that a Muslim must beware of (from the traps of the *Shaitan*) when he is performing this great act of worship, an act of worship which contains many different forms of worship. And success lies with Allâh.

General Points To Consider

First, while making *Tawaf*, one should supplicate, saying those invocations that he wishes to make, without limiting oneself to a book of supplication. If one finds it difficult to supplicate the entire time, one should recite the Qur'ân, remember Allâh, and glorify Him. One should make *Tawaf* and *Sa'y* without a guide leading him.

Second, during the days of *Hajj*, one should supplicate as often as possible and perform many acts of obedience, while avoiding forbidden deeds. One should especially beware of missing prayer or staying behind from congregational prayer, or wasting one's time in general or in listening to music.

Third, it is forbidden for the Muslim woman to beautify herself or to display her natural beauty in any way; it is also forbidden for her to crowd with men – so as not to be in physical contact with them – during the rites of *Hajj* and in the marketplace.

Fourth, many people make a grave mistake when they venerate a

[1] (*An-Nisa'* 4:48)

Shaikh of an order, by glorifying him and fearing him. This gravely affects and negates one's belief in *Tawhid* – because such acts of worship are only for Allâh, for He alone knows what is hidden in souls. If one venerates a *Shaikh* to such a high level, then that is *Shirk*, no doubt. It is also forbidden to recite invocations as the Sufis do during *Hajj* or on any other occasion, for the recitation of such invocations is an innovation – the introduction of a new matter in the religion. It is also forbidden to recite invocations that are not authentically related from the Messenger of Allâh ﷺ, that he didn't teach to his Companions, or that were not uttered by the pious early generation of Muslims – worshipping Allâh by such invocations is not allowed.

A Benefit

As we discussed *Hajj* and the sacrifice, it is appropriate here to discuss certain matters related to the *Udhhiyyah* (sacrifice) and the *'Aqeeqah*.[1]

Al-Udhhiyyah

Its Definition: It is the sheep that is slaughtered on the morning of *'Eid* day, seeking closeness to Allâh thereby.

Its Ruling: It is Sunnah for the inhabitants of every Muslim household – if they are able – to perform the *Udhhiyyah*, for Allâh Almighty says:

$$﴿ فَصَلِّ لِرَبِّكَ وَٱنْحَرْ ﴾$$

Therefore turn in prayer to your Lord and sacrifice (to Him only).[2]

The Messenger of Allâh ﷺ said:

$$«مَنْ كَانَ ذَبَحَ قَبْلَ الصَّلَاةِ فَلْيُعِدْ»$$

Whoever slaughtered before the prayer, then let him repeat it.[3]

Abu Ayyub Al-Ansari said, "During the life of the Prophet ﷺ, a man used to sacrifice a lamb on his behalf and on behalf of the inhabitants of his house."[4]

Its Virtues: To appreciate the great virtues of the *Udhhiyyah*, one should ponder this saying of the Messenger of Allâh ﷺ:

$$«مَا عَمِلَ ابْنُ آدَمَ يَوْمَ النَّحْرِ عَمَلاً أَحَبَّ إِلَى اللهِ مِنْ إِرَاقَةِ دَمٍ، وَإِنَّهَا$$
$$لَتَأْتِي يَوْمَ الْقِيَامَةِ بِقُرُونِهَا وَأَظْلَافِهَا وَأَشْعَارِهَا، وَإِنَّ الدَّمَ لَيَقَعُ مِنَ$$
$$اللهِ عَزَّ وَجَلَّ بِمَكَانٍ قَبْلَ أَنْ يَقَعَ عَلَى الْأَرْضِ فَطِيبُوا بِهَا نَفْسًا»$$

On the day of *Nahr*, no worshipper performed a deed more

---

[1] From *Minhajul-Muslim*, by Al-Jaza'iri.
[2] (*Al-Kawthar* 108:2)
[3] Agreed upon
[4] At-Tirmithi, who declared it to be authentic.

beloved than spilling blood (sacrifice of the sheep). Indeed, it (the sacrifice) will come on the Day of Judgement with its horns, hooves, and hair. Indeed the blood falls before Allâh Almighty before it hits the ground. So let your selves be pleased with it.[1]

In another *Hadith*, the Companions asked, "What is this sacrifice?" He ﷺ said:

«سُنَّةُ أَبِيكُمْ إِبْرَاهِيمَ»

"The Sunnah of your father, Ibrahim."

They said, "And what do we get for it." He ﷺ said:

«بِكُلِّ شَعَرَةٍ حَسَنَةٌ»

"For every hair a good deed."

They said, "And what about its wool." He ﷺ said,

«بِكُلِّ شَعَرَةٍ مِنَ الصُّوفِ حَسَنَةٌ»

"For every hair of its wool a good deed."[2]

The Wisdom Behind It Being Legislated: From the wisdom of *Udhhiyyah* is the following:

1) One performs the *Udhhiyyah* to achieve closeness to Allâh, for He Almighty says:

﴿فَصَلِّ لِرَبِّكَ وَٱنْحَرْ﴾

Therefore turn in prayer to your Lord and sacrifice (to Him only).[3]

And:

﴿قُلْ إِنَّ صَلَاتِي وَنُسُكِي وَمَحْيَايَ وَمَمَاتِي لِلَّهِ رَبِّ ٱلْعَٰلَمِينَ ۝ لَا شَرِيكَ لَهُۥ﴾

Say (O Muhammad ﷺ): "Verily, my *Salat* (prayer), my sacrifice, my living, and my dying are for Allâh, the Lord of

---

[1] Ibn Majah and At-Tirmithi, who ruled it to be *Hasan* even though he declared it *Gharib*.
[2] Ibn Majah and At-Tirmithi; it is *Hasan*
[3] (Al-Kawthar 108:2)

the *'Alamin* (mankind, jinn and all that exists)." He has no partner.[1]

The word *Nusuk*, which generally means rites of pilgrimage, is used in this verse, and it specifically refers to the sacrifice that one performs on the day of *Nahr*, seeking closeness to Allâh.

2) By applying this Sunnah, one revives the Sunnah of the Imam of those who believe in *Tawhid*, Ibrahim Al-Khalil, peace be upon him, Allâh inspired him to slaughter his son, Isma'il, peace be upon him. Then Allâh Almighty ransomed him with a ram, and Ibrahim, peace be upon him, slaughtered the ram instead of Isma'il. Allâh Almighty says:

$$﴿ وَفَدَيْنَٰهُ بِذِبْحٍ عَظِيمٍ ﴾$$

And We ransomed him with a great sacrifice (i.e., a ram);[2]

3) On the day of *'Eid*, one should especially be generous to one's family, and one should spread mercy to the poor and needy.

4) Especially on the occasion of *Udhhiyyah*, all Muslims should be grateful to Allâh for putting livestock at their disposal:

$$﴿ فَكُلُوا۟ مِنْهَا وَأَطْعِمُوا۟ ٱلْقَانِعَ وَٱلْمُعْتَرَّ كَذَٰلِكَ سَخَّرْنَٰهَا لَكُمْ لَعَلَّكُمْ تَشْكُرُونَ ٣٦ لَن يَنَالَ ٱللَّهَ لُحُومُهَا وَلَا دِمَآؤُهَا وَلَٰكِن يَنَالُهُ ٱلتَّقْوَىٰ مِنكُمْ ﴾$$

Then, when they are down on their sides (after slaughter), eat thereof, and feed the beggar who does not ask (men), and the beggar who asks (men). Thus have We made them subject to you that you may be grateful. It is neither their meat nor their blood that reaches Allâh, but it is piety from you that reaches Him.[3]

The Rulings Of The *Udhhiyyah*

1) **Its Age**: The *Udhiyyah* is not accepted if the sheep is less than a *Jatha'ah* – a sheep that has lived for six months and is entering into its seventh month. If one is slaughtering a goat, the slaughter is not correct unless it has lived for at least one complete year and is

---

[1] (*Al-An'am* 6:162,163)

[2] (*As-Saffat* 37:107)

[3] (*Al-Hajj* 22:36,37)

entering into its second. If one is slaughtering a camel, it must have lived for at least four years and is entering into its fifth year. And if one is slaughtering a cow, it must have lived for at least two years and is entering into its third year. The Prophet ﷺ said:

«لَا تَذْبَحُوا إِلَّا مُسِنَّةً، إِلَّا أَنْ يَعْسُرَ عَلَيْكُمْ فَتَذْبَحُوا جَذَعَةً مِنَ الضَّأْنِ وَالْمَسِنَّةِ مِنَ الْأَنْعَامِ هِيَ الثَّنِيَّةُ»

Do not slaughter other than a *Musinnah*, unless that is not possible for you, then slaughter a *Jatha'ah* sheep. And a *Musinnah* among the cattle is the *Thaniyah*.[1]

2) Its Health: The only animal that is accepted for the *Udhhiyyah* is one that is free from all defects in its body structure. Therefore the one-eyed or lame animal is not acceptable; nor is one whose horns are broken from their roots or whose ear is cut from its base; nor is a sick animal accepted or the emaciated one who lacks marrow. This is because the Prophet ﷺ said:

«أَرْبَعٌ لَا تَجُوزُ فِي الْأَضَاحِي: الْعَوْرَاءُ الْبَيِّنُ عَوَرُهَا، وَالْمَرِيضَةُ الْبَيِّنُ مَرَضُهَا، وَالْعَرْجَاءُ الْبَيِّنُ ضَلَعُهَا، وَالْكَبِيرَةُ الَّتِي لَا تُنْقِي – يَعْنِي لَا نَقْيَ فِيهَا – أَيْ لَا مُخَّ فِي عِظَامِهَا وَهِيَ الْهَازِلُ الْعَجْفَاءُ»

Four are not allowed in the *Udhhiyyah*: the one that is clearly one-eyed, the one that is clearly sick, the one that is clearly limping, and the one that is very thin such that it does not have marrow in its bones.

3) The Best *Udhhiyyah*: The best *Udhhiyyah* is the horned, white, male ram, which is partly black around its eyes and in its legs, because this is the description that the Messenger of Allâh ﷺ chose and slaughtered. 'Aishah, may Allâh be pleased with her, said, "Indeed the Prophet ﷺ slaughtered a horned ram, one that would stamp with black (i.e., black hooves), walk with black (i.e., black legs), and see with black (i.e., around its eye is blackness)."[2]

4) The Time Of The Slaughter: The time to perform the *Udhhiyyah* is the morning of 'Eid day, after the 'Eid Prayer. It is not considered

---

[1] Muslim.
[2] At-Tirmithi, who declared it to be authentic.

Udhhiyyah if one slaughters before the prayer, for the Prophet ﷺ said:

«مَنْ ذَبَحَ قَبْلَ الصَّلَاةِ فَإِنَّمَا يَذْبَحُ لِنَفْسِهِ، وَمَنْ ذَبَحَ بَعْدَ الصَّلَاةِ فَقَدْ تَمَّ نُسُكُهُ وَأَصَابَ سُنَّةَ الْمُسْلِمِينَ»

Whoever slaughters before the prayer, then he is indeed slaughtering for himself, and whoever slaughters after the prayer, then his sacrifice is complete and he has fulfilled the Sunnah of the Muslims.[1]

As for after 'Eid day, one may delay the slaughter to the second or third day after 'Eid, for it has been related that:

«كُلُّ أَيَّامِ التَّشْرِيقِ ذَبْحٌ»

Every day of *Tashriq* is (a day of) slaughter.[2]

5) During The Slaughter: When slaughtering the sacrifice, it is recommended to make it face the *Qiblah*; then, one should say, "Indeed I have directed my face to the One Who has created the heavens and the earth *Hanifan* (As one who worships Allâh alone without associating any partner with Him in worship) and I am not of the polytheists. Indeed my prayer, my slaughter, my life, and my death are for Allâh, Lord of all that exists, and He has no partner. Upon that I have been commanded, and I am the first of the Muslims." Upon performing the sacrifice, one should say, "*Bismillâh* (In the Name of Allâh)."[3]

6) Assigning An Agent To Perform It On One's Behalf: It is recommended for the Muslim to perform the *Udhhiyyah* himself, but if he appoints another to do it for him, then that is permissible,

---

[1] Al-Bukhari

[2] Related by Ahmad, but the chain has been criticized; however, there are sayings of 'Ali, Ibn 'Abbas, and other Companions, may Allâh be pleased with them, that attest to the meaning of this *Hadith*. "Do not delay the *Udhhiyyah* after the third day of 'Eid": Malik and Abu Hanifah made this statement and it is also related from 'Umar and his son, may Allâh be pleased with them.

[3] Based on this verse in the Qur'ân, saying "*Bismillah*" here is compulsory:

﴿وَلَا تَأْكُلُوا مِمَّا لَمْ يُذْكَرِ اسْمُ اللَّهِ عَلَيْهِ﴾

Eat not of that on which Allâh's Name has not been pronounced. (*Al-An'am* 6:121)

and regarding its permissibility there is no disagreement among the people of knowledge.

7) The Recommended Distribution Of The Slaughter: It is recommended to divide the *Udhhiyyah* into three parts: his family eats a third, he gives a third in charity, and he gives the last third as a gift to friends, for the Prophet ﷺ said,

«كُلُوا وَادَّخِرُوا وَتَصَدَّقُوا»

Eat, preserve, and give in charity.

Giving all of the meat in charity is permissible. It is also permissible not to give any of it as a gift.

8) The Butcher's Payment For slaughtering The *Udhhiyyah*: The butcher receives no payment from the *Udhhiyyah* itself. 'Ali said, "The Messenger of Allâh ﷺ ordered me to take care of the slaughter of his camel; and that I should give its meat, skin, and bones to charity; and that I should not give the butcher anything from it." And he ﷺ said:

«نَحْنُ نَعْطِيهِ مِنْ عِنْدِنَا»

We will give him from us (ourselves).[1]

9) Is Slaughtering A Sheep Sufficient For One's Entire House-hold?: Slaughtering a sheep is enough for an entire household even if that household consists of many members. Abu Ayyub, may Allâh be pleased with him, said, "During the life of the Messenger of Allâh ﷺ, a man used to perform *Udhhiyyah* with a sheep on his own behalf and on behalf of the members of his household."[2]

10) What The One Who Intends To Perform The *Udhhiyyah* Should Avoid: When the month of Thul-Hijjah begins, it is extremely disliked for one who intends to perform *Udhhiyyah* to take anything from his hair or nails until after performing the *Udhhiyyah*, for the Prophet ﷺ said:

«إِذَا رَأَيْتُمْ هِلَالَ ذِي الْحِجَّةِ وَأَرَادَ أَحَدُكُمْ أَنْ يُضَحِّيَ فَلْيُمْسِكْ عَنْ شَعْرِهِ، وَأَظْفَارِهِ حَتَّى يُضَحِّيَ»

---

[1] Agreed upon.

[2] At-Tirmithi, who declared it to be authentic.

When you see the crescent for *Thul-Hijjah* and you intend to perform the *Udhhiyyah*, then abstain from (cutting) your hair and nails until you perform the *Udhhiyyah*.[1]

11) The *Udhhiyyah* of the Messenger of Allâh ﷺ On Behalf Of His Entire Nation: A Muslim who is unable to perform the *Udhhiyyah* receives the reward of those who perform it, because when the Prophet ﷺ was slaughtering one of two rams, he ﷺ said:

«اللَّهُمَّ هَذَا عَنِّي وَعَمَّنْ لَمْ يُضَحِّ مِنْ أُمَّتِي»

O Allâh, this is from me and from those who did not perform the *Udhhiyyah* from my nation.[2]

The 'Aqeeqah

1) Its Definition: The 'Aqeeqah is the sheep that is slaughtered for the newborn seven days after he is born – or the 14th day or the 21st day; such is the Sunnah, and after that, the sheep can be slaughtered on any day.

2) Its Ruling: The 'Aqeeqah is an emphasized Sunnah for anyone who is able to perform it from the guardians of the newborn. That is because the Prophet ﷺ said:

«كُلُّ غُلَامٍ رَهِينَةٌ بِعَقِيقَتِهِ تُذْبَحُ عَنْهُ يَوْمَ سَابِعِهِ، وَيُسَمَّى وَيُحْلَقُ رَأْسُهُ»

Each young boy is hostage to his 'Aqeeqah, which is slaughtered on his behalf on his seventh day, which is when he is named and his head is shaved.[3]

3) Its Wisdom: One wisdom behind the 'Aqeeqah is that people should show their gratitude to Allâh for the blessing of a child; it is also a means through which one asks Allâh to protect and take care of his child.

Some Of Its Rulings

1) The Health And Age Of The Sheep: In terms of age and being free from defects, the same applies to the 'Aqeeqah as applies to the

---

[1] Muslim

[2] Ahmad, Abu Dawud, and At-Tirmithi

[3] Abu Dawud and An-Nasa'i; more than one scholar from the people of knowledge has judged it to be authentic.

Udhhiyyah; whatever isn't sufficient for the *Udhhiyyah*, then, is insufficient for the *'Aqeeqah*.

2) Eating Its Meat And Feeding Others From It: It is recommended to divide the meat as one divides it for the *Udhhiyyah*: the household members eat from it, part of it is given in charity, and the rest is given as a gift to friends.

3) What Is Recommended To Do On The Day Of 'Aqeeqah: For the male newborn, it is recommended to slaughter two sheep, "For the Messenger of Allâh ﷺ slaughtered two rams on behalf of Al-Hasan."[1] It is also recommended to name the newborn on the seventh day, choosing one of the best for names. One should also shave the head of the baby, giving gold or silver equal to the weight of his hair in charity, or the amount of money that is equivalent. The Prophet ﷺ said:

«كُلُّ غُلَامٍ رَهِينَةٌ بِعَقِيقَتِهِ تُذْبَحُ عَنْهُ يَوْمَ سَابِعِهِ، وَيُسَمَّى وَيُحْلَقُ رَأْسُهُ»

Each young boy is hostage to his *'Aqeeqah*, which is slaughtered on his behalf on his seventh day, which is when he is named and his head is shaved.[2]

4) The *Athan* And The *Iqamah* In The Ears Of The Newborn: For when the newborn is delivered, the people of knowledge recommend that the *Athan* should be called in his right ear, while the *Iqamah* is performed in his left one, in the hope that he is protected from *Ummus-Sibyan* (the follower of jinn). The following has been related:

«مَنْ وُلِدَ لَهُ مَوْلُودٌ فَأَذَّنَ فِي أُذُنِهِ الْيُمْنَى، وَأَقَامَ فِي أُذُنِهِ الْيُسْرَى لَمْ تَضُرَّهُ أُمُّ الصِّبْيَانِ»

To whoever is born a child, he should make *Athan* in his child's right ear and the *Iqamah* in his left one, and *Ummus-Sibyan* will not hurt him.[3]

---

[1] At-Tirmithi, who graded it authentic.

[2] It is recommended to shave the head of the male baby as opposed to the female one, for it is disliked to do so in her case.

[3] Ibn As-Sunni related it as a *Hadith* from the Prophet ﷺ. The author of *At-Talkhis* related it and said nothing against it.

The Noble Qur'ân

The Qur'ân: It is Allâh's Speech and a miracle. It was revealed to Muhammad ﷺ, it is written in the *Mus-hafs* (books in which only the Qur'ân is written), it has been passed down through so many different sources that there is no doubt surrounding its authenticity, and its recitation is a form of worship.

The Qur'ân has been given a number of different names, each of which conveys a similar meaning:

1) *Al-Furqan* (The Criterion): In the sense that it is speech, it acts as the criterion, separating truth and falsehood - Allâh Almighty says:

$$﴿تَبَارَكَ ٱلَّذِى نَزَّلَ ٱلْفُرْقَانَ عَلَىٰ عَبْدِهِۦ لِيَكُونَ لِلْعَٰلَمِينَ نَذِيرًا﴾$$

Blessed be He Who sent down the Criterion (of right and wrong, i.e., this Qur'ân) to His slave that he may be a warner to the *'Alamin* (mankind and jinn).[1]

2) *Al-Kitab* (The Book): It is Allâh's Speech, written between the two covers of the *Mus-haf*; Allâh Almighty says:

$$﴿الٓمٓ ۝ ذَٰلِكَ ٱلْكِتَٰبُ لَا رَيْبَ ۛ فِيهِ ۛ هُدًى لِّلْمُتَّقِينَ﴾$$

Alif-Lam-Mim. [These letters are one of the miracles of the Qur'ân and none but Allâh (Alone) knows their meanings]. This is the Book (the Qur'ân), whereof there is no doubt, a guidance to those who are *Al-Muttaqun* [the pious and righteous persons who fear Allâh much (abstain from all kinds of sins and evil deeds which He has forbidden) and love Allâh much (perform all kinds of good deeds which He has ordained)]. [2]

3) *Ath-Thikr* (The Remembrance): This name refers to its honor and exaltedness:

$$﴿وَهَٰذَا ذِكْرٌ مُّبَارَكٌ أَنزَلْنَٰهُ﴾$$

And this is a blessed Reminder (the Qur'ân) which We have

---

[1] (*Al-Furqan* 25:1)
[2] (*Al-Baqarah* 2:1,2)

sent down.[1]

4) *At-Tanzil* (The Revelation): i.e., Allâh Almighty revealed it, sections at a time, each section appropriate to the circumstances at the time of revelation. Allâh Almighty says:

$$﴿تَنزِيلٌ مِّنْ حَكِيمٍ حَمِيدٍ﴾$$

Sent down by the All-Wise, Worthy of all praise (Allâh).[2]

There are also other names for the Qur'ân.

In the Qur'ân, Allâh has given us the basis for the knowledge of all matters. Rulings, laws, stories, parables, wisdom, admonitions, the ways that govern souls and the universe alike, man, life, and an all-embracing glimpse of the universe – all of these are contained in the Qur'ân. Allâh Almighty says:

$$﴿وَنَزَّلْنَا عَلَيْكَ ٱلْكِتَٰبَ تِبْيَٰنًا لِّكُلِّ شَىْءٍ وَهُدًى وَرَحْمَةً وَبُشْرَىٰ لِلْمُسْلِمِينَ﴾$$

And We have sent down to you the Book (the Qur'ân) as an exposition of every thing, a guidance, a mercy, and glad tidings for those who have submitted themselves (to Allâh as Muslims).[3]

It is the Final Prophetic Book revealed to a Prophet, and it is the only revealed book that remains and will remain intact; it is the final divine message:

$$﴿وَأَنزَلْنَآ إِلَيْكَ ٱلذِّكْرَ لِتُبَيِّنَ لِلنَّاسِ مَا نُزِّلَ إِلَيْهِمْ وَلَعَلَّهُمْ يَتَفَكَّرُونَ﴾$$

And We have also sent down unto you (O Muhammad ﷺ) the reminder and the advice (the Qur'ân), that you may explain clearly to men what is sent down to them, and that they may give thought.[4]

There are a great many of verses and *Hadiths* that extol the virtues of reciting the Qur'ân and adhering to its precepts. In one such verse,

---

[1] (*Al-Anbiya'* 21:50)

[2] (*Fussilat* 41:42)

[3] (*An-Nahl* 16:89)

[4] (*An-Nahl* 16:44)

Allâh Almighty says:

﴿إِنَّ ٱلَّذِينَ يَتْلُونَ كِتَٰبَ ٱللَّهِ وَأَقَامُوا۟ ٱلصَّلَوٰةَ وَأَنفَقُوا۟ مِمَّا رَزَقْنَٰهُمْ سِرًّا وَعَلَانِيَةً يَرْجُونَ تِجَٰرَةً لَّن تَبُورَ﴾

Verily, those who recite the Book of Allâh, and perform As-*Salat*, and spend out of what We have provided for them, secretly and openly, hope for a (sure) trade-gain that will never perish.[1]

In a *Hadith* related by 'Uthman bin 'Affan, may Allâh be pleased with him, the Messenger of Allâh ﷺ said:

«خَيْرُكُمْ مَنْ تَعَلَّمَ الْقُرْآنَ وَعَلَّمَهُ»

The best of you is he who learns the Qur'ān and teaches it.[2]

The Messenger of Allâh ﷺ also said:

«مَنْ قَامَ بِعَشْرِ آيَاتٍ، لَمْ يُكْتَبْ مِنَ الْغَافِلِينَ، وَمَنْ قَامَ بِمِائَةِ آيَةٍ، كُتِبَ مِنَ الْقَانِتِينَ، وَمَنْ قَامَ بِأَلْفِ آيَةٍ، كُتِبَ مِنَ الْمُقَنْطِرِينَ»

Whoever stands (praying) with ten verses will not be written from the heedless ones; whoever stands with one-hundred verses will be written from the obedient; and whoever stands with one thousand verses will be written from the *Muqantireen* (those who spend huge amounts in the way of Allâh).[3]

'Abdullah bin 'Amr bin Al-'Aas, may Allâh be pleased with them, related that the Messenger of Allâh ﷺ said:

«يُقَالُ لِصَاحِبِ الْقُرْآنِ: اقْرَأْ، وَارْتَقِ، وَرَتِّلْ كَمَا كُنْتَ تُرَتِّلُ فِي الدُّنْيَا، فَإِنَّ مَنْزِلَتَكَ عِنْدَ آخِرِ آيَةٍ تَقْرَؤُهَا»

It will be said to the one who knows the Qur'ân, read and climb (in ranking); and recite distinctly as you used to recite distinctly in the world, for indeed your rank is at the last verse

---

[1] (*Fatir* 35:29)

[2] Recorded by Al-Bukhari

[3] Recorded by Abu Dawud, and the wording here is his; Ibn Khuzaimah, Ibn Hibban, and Ibn As-Sunni also relate it; and the *Hadith* has other narrations that attest to it.

that you recite.[1]

In yet another *Hadith*, 'Aishah, may Allâh be pleased with her, related that the Messenger of Allâh ﷺ said:

«الَّذِي يَقْرَأُ الْقُرْآنَ، وَهُوَ مَاهِرٌ بِهِ، مَعَ السَّفَرَةِ الْكِرَامِ الْبَرَرَةِ، وَالَّذِي يَقْرَأُ الْقُرْآنَ وَيَتَتَعْتَعُ فِيهِ، وَهُوَ عَلَيْهِ شَاقٌّ، لَهُ أَجْرَانِ»

The person who is proficient in the Qur'ân is levelled with the obedient close angels. As for the person who reads the Qur'ân, though it is difficult for him and though he stutters, he has two rewards.[2]

From the greatest of Allâh's blessings for the Muslims is that He chose them to inherit the Book (the Qur'ân), for Allâh says:

﴿ثُمَّ أَوْرَثْنَا ٱلْكِتَٰبَ ٱلَّذِينَ ٱصْطَفَيْنَا مِنْ عِبَادِنَا﴾

Then we gave the Book (the Qur'ân) for inheritance to such of Our worshippers whom We chose (the followers of Muhammad ﷺ).[3]

The Muslims have the honor of having the divine and uncorrupted words of their Lord, transmitted from generation to generation by so many people that its authenticity is a certain and established fact: Muslims recite the Qur'ân today just as the first generation of Muslims recited it. Indeed it is Allâh Almighty Who has protected and preserved the Qur'ân:

﴿إِنَّا نَحْنُ نَزَّلْنَا ٱلذِّكْرَ وَإِنَّا لَهُ لَحَٰفِظُونَ﴾

Verily, We: It is We who have sent down the *Thikr* (i.e., the Qur'ân) and surely, We will guard it (from corruption).[4]

Perhaps more is demanded from Muslims today, in light of present-day advancements, than at any other time in the past – in terms of preserving and memorizing the Qur'ân, printing it, distributing it, translating its meanings into all languages – not to mention having

---

[1] Abu Dawud, and the wording is his; and At-Tirmithi, who said, "A *Hasan Hadith*."

[2] Agreed upon.

[3] (*Fatir* 35:32)

[4] (*Al-Hijr* 15:9)

an understanding of the Qur'ân and applying its precepts based on the example of the Messenger of Allâh's Companions.

'Uthman, 'Abdullah bin Mas'ud, and 'Ubai related that the Messenger of Allâh ﷺ used to teach them ten verses; they wouldn't go beyond them to the next ten until they first learned what is in them in terms of action, and so they gained both knowledge and action.[1]

Memorizing the Qur'ân, understanding its meanings and laws, applying and adhering to it – these comprise the way to honor for the Muslim nation, the way to its success and advancement. Allâh Almighty says:

$$ ﴿لَقَدْ أَنزَلْنَا إِلَيْكُمْ كِتَٰبًا فِيهِ ذِكْرُكُمْ أَفَلَا تَعْقِلُونَ﴾ $$

Indeed We have sent down to you (O mankind) a Book, (the Qur'ân) in which there is *Thikrukum*, (your reminder or an honor for you i.e., the honor for the one who follows the teaching of Qur'ân and acts on its orders). Will you not then understand? [2]

Manners When Dealing With The Qur'ân For The Youth[3]

There are many manners that I must adhere to when dealing with the Qur'ân:

1) I must honor and venerate the Qur'ān.

2) I do not place the Qur'ân behind me, intending to belittle it, nor do I neglect it. I do not enter the toilet with it, nor do I use its words in an inappropriate manner.

3) I do not physically lean on the Qur'ân, or on anything in which is a copy of the Qur'ân – such as a schoolbag.

4) I do not extend my feet, pointing with them to the Qur'ân.

5) I do not put the Qur'ân in filthy places.

6) I do not place the Qur'ân alongside filthy things – such as placing it on a shelf that contains shoes, magazines that contain

---

[1] *Sahih Sunan Abu Dawud*
[2] (*Al-Anbiya'* 21:10)
[3] *As-Suluk wat-Tahtheeb* for the second primary level. A curriculum prepared by *Wazaratul-Ma'arif* p. 9 and what follows it.

pictures, dirty clothes, or instruments of entertainment.

7) I do not tear pages from the Qur'ân, nor do I write in it.

8) While the Qur'ân is being recited or when I am reciting the Qur'ân, I do not occupy my mind with other matters.

9) When reciting the Qur'ân or when the Qur'ân is being recited, I do not play or laugh.

10) I place the Qur'ân always on top of other books.

11) I always place the Qur'ân in its special place.

12) When I want to touch the Qur'ân, I first make ablution.

13) When reciting the Qur'ân, I sit in a correct and decent position.

14) I treat the Qur'ân with respect and veneration; I neither fold it nor hold it from one end - I abstain from the former to prevent pages of the Qur'ân from falling out.

15) If I wish to recite any part of the Qur'ân at any time, I first recite, "*A'oothu Billâhi Minash-Shaitaanir-Rajeem* (I take protection in Allâh from the accursed *Shaitan*)."

16) As I am about to recite the beginning of a chapter of the Qur'ân, I first say, "*Bismillâhir-Rahmaanir-Raheem* (In the Name of Allâh, the Most Beneficent, the Most Merciful)."

The *Tafsir* (Explanation) Of
Certain Chapters Of The Qur'ân[1]

Surat Al-Fatihah

In the Name of Allâh, the Most Beneficent, the Most Merciful. All the praises and thanks be to Allâh, the Lord of the *'Alamin* (mankind, jinn and all that exists). The Most Beneficent and the Most Merciful. The only Owner (and the Only Ruling judge) of the Day of Recompense (i.e., the Day of Resurrection). You (Alone) we worship and you (Alone) we ask for help (for each and everything). Guide us to the Straight Way. The Way of those on whom You have bestowed Your Grace, not (the way) of those who earned Your anger nor of those who went astray.[2]

In the Name of Allâh

I begin by all of Allâh's Names, so this embraces all of Allâh's Beautiful Names.

Allâh

He is the True God, Who, because of His divine and perfect Qualities, alone deserves to be worshipped.

$$﴿ٱلرَّحۡمَٰنِ ٱلرَّحِيمِ﴾$$

---

[1] *Daleelul-Muslim Al-Mubtadi'*, p. 16 and what follows it.
[2] (*Al-Fatihah* 1:1-7)

The Most Beneficent, the Most Merciful

These are two of Allâh's Names, both of which indicate His vast mercy, the first of which embraces all things and everyone alive; the second of which is specific to the Hereafter, to the righteous followers of Allâh's Messengers.

All the praises and thanks be to Allâh

Because Allâh Almighty has perfect and complete Attributes, He alone deserves all praise.

The Lord of the *'Alamin*

The Lord Who takes care of and causes the growth of all that exists, through His many favors – by creating them, providing for them, and guiding them to what is best for them in this world and in the Hereafter. The reality of this phrase means guiding to success in all that is good and keeping one away from all that is evil. "The Lord of all that exists," meaning that He is the sole Creator and Planner of the universe. All blessings are from Him, while He doesn't need anyone. From every viewpoint, all that is created is in need of Allâh. *'Alamin"* in this verse means all other than Allâh, which means all of His creation – such as the world of man, of jinn, of angels, and so on.

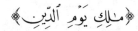

The only Owner (and the Only Ruling Judge) of the Day of Recompense (i.e., the Day of Resurrection)

The only Owner and King is He Who has complete sovereignty, which means that He orders, forbids, rewards, punishes – and has total control over the entire dominion. The dominion here is ascribed to the Day of Recompense, the Day of Resurrection, the Day in which people will be dealt with according to their deeds, whether good and bad.

$$﴿إِيَّاكَ نَعْبُدُ وَإِيَّاكَ نَسْتَعِينُ﴾$$

You (Alone) we worship and you (Alone) we ask for help (for

each and everything)

We single You out alone for our worship and for when we seek help: we worship none but You and we seek help from none but from You. *'Ibadah* (worship) is a comprehensive term for all that Allâh loves and is pleased with, in terms of sayings and deeds, both apparent and hidden. *Al-Isti'anah* (seeking help) means to rely upon Allâh for bringing benefits and for keeping away harm. *'Ibadah* and *Al-Isti'anah* are the means to eternal happiness and the means to being saved from all evil. But we must keep in mind that *'Ibadah* is only *'Ibadah* when it is taken from the Messenger of Allâh ﷺ and when one intends by it Allâh's Face.

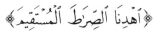

Guide us to the Straight Way

Show us, guide us, and help us to the Straight Path, which is the knowledge of truth and its application, and the way that leads to Allâh Almighty and His Paradise. This supplication is one of the most beneficial, and one of the most embracing of supplications for the worshipper of Allâh - and we are all His worshippers, and that is why we must invoke Allâh with it during our prayer.

The way of those on whom You have bestowed Your Grace

They are the Prophets, the truthful ones, the martyrs, and the righteous ones.

Not (the way) of those who earned Your anger

They are the Jews – and those of their like – who knew the truth yet abandoned it.

Nor of those who went astray

They are the Christians – and those of their like – the people of ignorance and misguidance.

Even though this Chapter is so brief, it contains that which no other chapter of the Qur'ân contains. First, it covers the three categories of *Tawhid*:

1) *Ar-Rububiyyah* (Lordship), which is taken from this verse:

﴿رَبِّ ٱلْعَـٰلَمِينَ﴾

The Lord of the *'Alamin*

2) *Al-Uluhiyyah* (singling out Allâh for worship), which is taken from,

﴿اللّه﴾

Allâh

and,

﴿إِيَّاكَ نَعْبُدُ وَإِيَّاكَ نَسْتَعِينُ﴾

You (Alone) we worship and you (Alone) we ask for help (for each and everything)

3) *Al-Asma' was-Sifat* (Names and Attributes): This category of *Tawhid* means to affirm for Allâh all those perfect Qualities that He affirmed for Himself or that His Messenger affirmed for Him, without distorting, negating, comparing, or likening them to the qualities of creation – and without saying "how". This category is indicated by the verse:

﴿ٱلْحَمْدُ لِلَّهِ﴾

All the praises and thanks be to Allâh

Prophethood is established in this verse:

﴿ٱهْدِنَا ٱلصِّرَٰطَ ٱلْمُسْتَقِيمَ﴾

Guide us to the Straight Way

That we will be rewarded for our deeds is established in this verse:

﴿مَـٰلِكِ يَوْمِ ٱلدِّينِ﴾

The only Owner (and the Only Ruling Judge) of the Day of Recompense (i.e., the Day of Resurrection)

While it establishes Divine Preordainment, the following verse also refutes the people of innovation and misguidance:

$$﴿ اهْدِنَا الصِّرَاطَ الْمُسْتَقِيمَ ﴾$$

Guide us to the Straight Way

It also states that there is a truth that must be followed. In the following verse, sincerity in worshipping Allâh alone is established:

$$﴿ إِيَّاكَ نَعْبُدُ وَإِيَّاكَ نَسْتَعِينُ ﴾$$

You (Alone) we worship and you (Alone) we ask for help (for each and everything).

Surat An-Nas

﴿بِسْمِ ٱللَّهِ ٱلرَّحْمَٰنِ ٱلرَّحِيمِ﴾

﴿قُلْ أَعُوذُ بِرَبِّ ٱلنَّاسِ ١ مَلِكِ ٱلنَّاسِ ٢ إِلَٰهِ ٱلنَّاسِ ٣ مِن شَرِّ ٱلْوَسْوَاسِ ٱلْخَنَّاسِ ٤ ٱلَّذِى يُوَسْوِسُ فِى صُدُورِ ٱلنَّاسِ ٥ مِنَ ٱلْجِنَّةِ وَٱلنَّاسِ﴾

In the Name of Allâh, the Most Beneficent, the Most Merciful.
Say: "I seek refuge with (Allâh) the Lord of mankind. The King of mankind. The *Illah* (God) of mankind. From the evil of the whisperer (devil who whisper in the hearts of men) who withdraws (from his whispering in one's heart after one remembers Allâh). Who whispers in the breasts of mankind. Of jinn and men."[1]

When reciting this chapter, one seeks protection and refuge in the Lord, King, and God of mankind, from the *Shaitan*, who is the root of all evil, and whose activities include whispering into the hearts of men, beautifying evil to them, and giving it a handsome shape. At the same time, the *Shaitan* takes man away from all that is good, showing it to them in a form other than its true form. Then, when one remembers his Lord and takes refuge in Him from the accursed *Shaitan*, *Shaitan* recoils and draws back. This is why man should seek help, protection, and aid with Allâh's Lordship over all of mankind, and with His Godhood (by which He alone deserves worship), the reason for which he created them (i.e., to worship Him alone, without associating partners with Him). The whispering referred to in this *Surah* may emanate from jinn and may emanate from man as well:

﴿مِنَ ٱلْجِنَّةِ وَٱلنَّاسِ﴾

Of jinn and men.

---

[1] (*An-Nas* 114:1-6)

Surat Al-Falaq

﴿بِسْمِ ٱللَّهِ ٱلرَّحْمَٰنِ ٱلرَّحِيمِ﴾

﴿قُلْ أَعُوذُ بِرَبِّ ٱلْفَلَقِ ① مِن شَرِّ مَا خَلَقَ ② وَمِن شَرِّ غَاسِقٍ إِذَا وَقَبَ ③ وَمِن شَرِّ ٱلنَّفَّٰثَٰتِ فِى ٱلْعُقَدِ ④ وَمِن شَرِّ حَاسِدٍ إِذَا حَسَدَ﴾

In the Name of Allâh, the Most Beneficent, the Most Merciful.
Say: "I seek refuge with (Allâh) the Lord of *Al-Falaq*. From the evil of what He has created. And from the evil of the darkening (night) as it comes with its darkness; (or the moon as it sets or goes away). And from the evils of those who practice witchcraft when they blow in the knots. And from the evil of the envier when he envies."[1]

﴿قُلْ أَعُوذُ﴾

Say: "I seek refuge"
I seek refuge, protection, and shelter with Allâh.

﴿بِرَبِّ ٱلْفَلَقِ﴾

With (Allâh) the Lord of *Al-Falaq*
Who causes the seed-grain and the fruit-stone (like date-stone, etc.) to split and sprout.

﴿مِن شَرِّ مَا خَلَقَ﴾

From the evil of what He has created
This includes the evil of all that He created – man, jinn, animals, etc. One seeks refuge with their creator from the evil inside of them.

﴿وَمِن شَرِّ غَاسِقٍ إِذَا وَقَبَ﴾

And from the evil of the darkening (night) as it comes with its darkness.
From the evil that occurs in the night, for during the night, evil spirits and harmful animals spread throughout the land.

---

[1] (*Al-Falaq* 113:1-5)

﴿وَمِن شَرِّ ٱلنَّفَّٰثَٰتِ فِى ٱلْعُقَدِ﴾

And from the evils of those who practice witchcraft when they blow in the knots.

From magicians who practice their sorcery by blowing into knots.

﴿وَمِن شَرِّ حَاسِدٍ إِذَا حَسَدَ﴾

And from the evil of the envier when he envies

The envier is one who loves for blessings to be removed from the one whom he is jealous of; therefore one needs to seek protection in Allâh from his evil, so that by the Will of Allâh, his plots are foiled.

Surat Al-Ikhlas

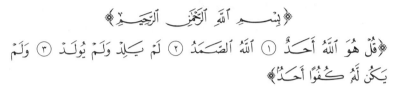

﴿قُلْ هُوَ ٱللَّهُ أَحَدٌ ① ٱللَّهُ ٱلصَّمَدُ ② لَمْ يَلِدْ وَلَمْ يُولَدْ ③ وَلَمْ يَكُن لَّهُ كُفُوًا أَحَدٌ﴾

In the Name of Allâh, the Most Beneficent, the Most Merciful.
Say: "He is Allâh, (the) One. *Allâhus-Samad* (Allah – the Self-Sufficient Master, Whom all creatures need, He neither eats nor drinks). He begets not, nor was He begotten. And there is none coequal or comparable unto Him."[1]

﴿قُلْ هُوَ ٱللَّهُ أَحَدٌ﴾

Say: "He is Allâh, (the) One"

Say, believing it with certainty and knowing its meaning, that indeed Allâh is the One; He alone has the most beautiful Names and the most elevated Attributes; there is none equal or comparable to Him.

﴿ٱللَّهُ ٱلصَّمَدُ﴾

Allâhus-Samad (Allâh – the Self-Sufficient Master, Whom all creatures need, He neither eats nor drinks)

The One Whose help is sought and needed in all matters; all worshippers ask for their need from none but Him; they desire aid in their tasks and projects from none but Him – and that is because He is complete and perfect in His Qualities: therefore He is the All-Knowing, the One Whose Knowledge is complete; completely attentive of His creatures, He is the Most Merciful, Whose mercy embraces everyone in the heavens and in the earth.

﴿لَمْ يَلِدْ وَلَمْ يُولَدْ﴾

He begets not, nor was He begotten

That is because He is the complete Self-Sufficient Master.

---

[1] (*Al-Ikhlas* 112:1-4)

﴿وَلَمْ يَكُن لَّهُ كُفُوًا أَحَدُ﴾

And there is none coequal or comparable unto Him

Not in His Names, not in His Attributes, and not in His actions. This *Surah* deals with the third category of *Tawhid*, *Al-Asma' was-Sifat*.

Surat An-Nasr

﴿بِسْمِ ٱللَّهِ ٱلرَّحْمَٰنِ ٱلرَّحِيمِ﴾

﴿إِذَا جَاءَ نَصْرُ ٱللَّهِ وَٱلْفَتْحُ ① وَرَأَيْتَ ٱلنَّاسَ يَدْخُلُونَ فِى دِينِ ٱللَّهِ أَفْوَاجًا ② فَسَبِّحْ بِحَمْدِ رَبِّكَ وَٱسْتَغْفِرْهُ إِنَّهُ كَانَ تَوَّابًا﴾

In the Name of Allâh, the Most Beneficent, the Most Merciful.
When there comes the help of Allâh and the Conquest. And
you see that people enter in Allâh's religion in crowds. So
glorify the praises of your Lord, and ask for His forgiveness.
Verily, He is the One who accepts the repentance and
forgives.[1]

This *Surah* consists of three matters:

- Glad tidings for the Messenger of Allâh ﷺ.
- Orders for him ﷺ.
- And a hint as to the results of those glad tidings.

The glad tidings are of Allâh's help for His Messenger ﷺ, of the
Conquest of Makkah, and of people entering into Allâh's religion in
flocks; hence many people became from the followers and
supporters of Islam, people who at one point used to be its enemies.

Allâh Almighty orders the Messenger of Allâh ﷺ to do the following
after all of the above occur: to thank Him for those blessings, to
glorify Him, to praise Him, and to seek His forgiveness.

In this *Surah*, Allâh Almighty hints to the continuation of victory and
of the growth of Islam as long as the Prophet ﷺ glorifies Him, praises
Him, and seeks His forgiveness. Allâh Almighty says:

﴿لَئِن شَكَرْتُمْ لَأَزِيدَنَّكُمْ﴾

If you give thanks, I will give you more (of My blessings)[2]

At the time of its revelation, this *Surah* also hinted to the death of the
Messenger of Allâh ﷺ: that it was near at hand.

---

[1] (*An-Nasr* 110:1-3)
[2] (*Ibrahim* 14:7)

Surat Al-Kafirun

﴿بِسْمِ ٱللَّهِ ٱلرَّحْمَٰنِ ٱلرَّحِيمِ﴾

﴿قُلْ يَٰٓأَيُّهَا ٱلْكَٰفِرُونَ ١ لَآ أَعْبُدُ مَا تَعْبُدُونَ ٢ وَلَآ أَنتُمْ عَٰبِدُونَ مَآ أَعْبُدُ ٣ وَلَآ أَنَا۠ عَابِدٌ مَّا عَبَدتُّمْ ٤ وَلَآ أَنتُمْ عَٰبِدُونَ مَآ أَعْبُدُ ٥ لَكُمْ دِينُكُمْ وَلِيَ دِينِ﴾

In the Name of Allâh, the Most Beneficent, the Most Merciful.

Say: "O disbelievers! I worship not that which you worship. Nor will you worship that which I worship. And I shall not worship that which you are worshipping. Nor will you worship that which I worship. To you be your religion, and to me my religion."[1]

Say, O Muhammad, to the disbelievers, openly and clearly:

﴿لَآ أَعْبُدُ مَا تَعْبُدُونَ﴾

I worship not that which you worship

I am innocent of that which you worship other than Allâh – whether you do so openly or secretly.

﴿وَلَآ أَنتُمْ عَٰبِدُونَ مَآ أَعْبُدُ﴾

Nor will you worship that which I worship

And that is because you lack sincerity in your worship of Allâh, because the worship that is joined with *Shirk* (associating partners with Allâh) nullifies one's worship and cancels his rewards for that worship; and in fact, such an act is not even called worship.

﴿لَكُمْ دِينُكُمْ وَلِيَ دِينِ﴾

To you be your religion, and to me my religion.

You are innocent of what I practice and I am innocent of what you practice.

---

[1] (*Al-Kafirun* 109:1-6)

Surat Al-Kawthar

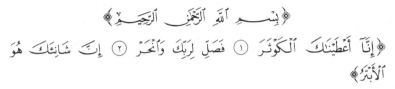

﴿بِسْمِ ٱللَّهِ ٱلرَّحْمَنِ ٱلرَّحِيمِ﴾

﴿إِنَّآ أَعْطَيْنَٰكَ ٱلْكَوْثَرَ ١ فَصَلِّ لِرَبِّكَ وَٱنْحَرْ ٢ إِنَّ شَانِئَكَ هُوَ ٱلْأَبْتَرُ﴾

In the Name of Allâh, the Most Beneficent, the Most Merciful
Verily, We have granted you *Al-Kawthar*. Therefore turn in prayer to your Lord and sacrifice. For he who hates you, he will be cut off.[1]

Allâh says to His Prophet ﷺ:

﴿إِنَّآ أَعْطَيْنَٰكَ ٱلْكَوْثَرَ﴾

Verily, We have granted you *Al-Kawthar*

Favors and blessings in abundance, included in which is the river called *Al-Kawthar* as well as the Basin (*Hawdh*), whose length is one month and whose width is one month; its water is whiter than milk and sweeter than honey; its vessels are as numerous as stars in the sky. Whoever takes a drink from it will never feel thirsty again.

﴿فَصَلِّ لِرَبِّكَ وَٱنْحَرْ﴾

Therefore turn in prayer to your Lord and sacrifice

After Allâh mentioned His favor upon His Messenger ﷺ and that He granted him *Al-Kawthar*, He then orders him to be grateful for His blessings, saying:

﴿فَصَلِّ لِرَبِّكَ وَٱنْحَرْ﴾

Therefore turn in prayer to your Lord and sacrifice.

The two kinds of worship mentioned in this verse are among the best kinds of worship: prayer includes submission and reverence to Allâh, while the sacrifice – such as the *Hady* and the *Udhhiyyah* – is also among the best forms of worship, for it consists of an added element: spending wealth.

---

[1] (*Al-Kawthar* 108:1-3)

﴿ إِنَّ شَانِئَكَ هُوَ ٱلْأَبْتَرُ ﴾

For he who hates you, he will be cut off

The one who hates you, and the one who disparages you, is cut off from all good and from every virtue.

Surat Al-'Asr

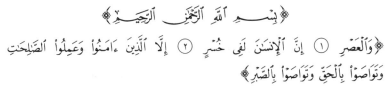

In the Name of Allâh, the Most Beneficent, the Most Merciful.
By *Al-Asr* (the time). Verily! Man is in loss. Except those who
believe and do righteous good deeds, and recommend each
other to the truth, and recommend one another to
patience.[1]

Here, Allâh Almighty swears by *Al-'Asr*, the time, though *Al-'Asr* is
also said to mean the night and day, the time in which the deeds of
man take place. Allâh Almighty can swear by whatever He wishes
from His creation; His worshippers, however, may only swear by
their Lord. Then Allâh informs us that man as a species is in a state of
loss, except for those who are described with four qualities:

1) Faith in whatever Allâh ordered us to have faith in. Faith is not
complete without knowledge.

2) They perform righteous deeds; this includes apparent and
hidden deeds, deeds having to do with Allâh's Rights and deeds
having to do with the rights of His creatures - those deeds that are
obligatory as well as those that are voluntary.

3) They recommend one another to the truth and to good, i.e., to
faith and to righteous deeds.

4) They recommend one another to be patient in their obedience of
Allâh, while avoiding disobedience to Him; they also recommend
one another to be patient at those of His Decrees that may be
painful.

---

[1] (*Al-'Asr* 103:1-3)

Surat Al-Bayyinah

﴿بِسْمِ اللَّهِ الرَّحْمَنِ الرَّحِيمِ﴾

﴿لَمْ يَكُنِ الَّذِينَ كَفَرُوا مِنْ أَهْلِ الْكِتَابِ وَالْمُشْرِكِينَ مُنفَكِّينَ حَتَّى تَأْتِيَهُمُ الْبَيِّنَةُ ۝ رَسُولٌ مِّنَ اللَّهِ يَتْلُوا صُحُفًا مُّطَهَّرَةً ۝ فِيهَا كُتُبٌ قَيِّمَةٌ ۝ وَمَا تَفَرَّقَ الَّذِينَ أُوتُوا الْكِتَابَ إِلَّا مِنْ بَعْدِ مَا جَاءَتْهُمُ الْبَيِّنَةُ ۝ وَمَا أُمِرُوا إِلَّا لِيَعْبُدُوا اللَّهَ مُخْلِصِينَ لَهُ الدِّينَ حُنَفَاءَ وَيُقِيمُوا الصَّلَاةَ وَيُؤْتُوا الزَّكَاةَ وَذَلِكَ دِينُ الْقَيِّمَةِ ۝ إِنَّ الَّذِينَ كَفَرُوا مِنْ أَهْلِ الْكِتَابِ وَالْمُشْرِكِينَ فِي نَارِ جَهَنَّمَ خَالِدِينَ فِيهَا أُولَئِكَ هُمْ شَرُّ الْبَرِيَّةِ ۝ إِنَّ الَّذِينَ ءَامَنُوا وَعَمِلُوا الصَّالِحَاتِ أُولَئِكَ هُمْ خَيْرُ الْبَرِيَّةِ ۝ جَزَاؤُهُمْ عِندَ رَبِّهِمْ جَنَّاتُ عَدْنٍ تَجْرِي مِن تَحْتِهَا الْأَنْهَارُ خَالِدِينَ فِيهَا أَبَدًا رَّضِيَ اللَّهُ عَنْهُمْ وَرَضُوا عَنْهُ ذَلِكَ لِمَنْ خَشِيَ رَبَّهُ﴾

In the Name of Allâh, the Most Beneficent, the Most Merciful.

Those who believe from among the People of Scripture and among the polytheists, were not going to leave (their disbelief) until there came to them clear evidence. A Messenger from Allâh, reciting purified pages containing correct and straight laws from Allâh. And the People of the Scripture differed not until after there came to them clear evidence. And they were commanded not, but that they should worship Allâh, and worship none but Him Alone, and perform *As-Salat* and give *Az-Zakat*; and that is the right religion. Verily, those who disbelieve from among the People of Scripture and the polytheists will abide in the fire of Hell. They are the worst of creatures. Verily, those who believe and do righteous good deeds, they are the best of creatures. Their reward with their Lord is 'Adn (Eden) Paradise (Gardens of Eternity), underneath which rivers flow, they will abide therein forever, Allâh well-pleased with them, and they with Him. That is for Him who fears His Lord.[1]

Allâh Almighty says:

---

[1] (*Al-Bayyinah* 98:1-8)

﴿لَمْ يَكُنِ ٱلَّذِينَ كَفَرُوا۟ مِنْ أَهْلِ ٱلْكِتَـٰبِ﴾

Those who believe from among the People of Scripture
They are the Jews and the Christians.

﴿وَٱلْمُشْرِكِينَ﴾

And among polytheists
The rest of the nations who worship other than Allâh.

﴿مُنفَكِّينَ حَتَّىٰ تَأْتِيَهُمُ ٱلْبَيِّنَةُ﴾

Were not going to leave (their disbelief) until there came to
them clear evidence
A plain and clear proof.

﴿رَسُولٌ مِّنَ ٱللَّهِ﴾

A Messenger from Allâh
Allâh sent him to call people to *Tawhid*, to worshipping Allâh
sincerely and purely. Allâh revealed to him the Qur'ân, which he
recites, teaching people the wisdom. He purifies them and takes
them out of darkness, while bringing them into the light – by the Will
of Allâh, and that is the religion of Islam.

﴿يَتْلُوا۟ صُحُفًا مُّطَهَّرَةً﴾

Reciting purified pages
It is protected from the *Shaitan*; none but the purified touch it, and
they are the angels.

﴿فِيهَا كُتُبٌ قَيِّمَةٌ﴾

Containing correct and straight laws from Allâh
Those purified pages contain truthful news and just orders, orders
that guide to the truth and to the Straight Path. If the people do not
submit and abandon their stubbornness, then that is because they
differed not,

﴿إِلَّا مِنْ بَعْدِ مَا جَاءَتْهُمُ ٱلْبَيِّنَةُ﴾

Until after there came to them clear evidence.

A clear evidence that required them to unite and to agree.

﴿وَمَآ أُمِرُوٓاْ إِلَّا لِيَعۡبُدُواْ ٱللَّهَ مُخۡلِصِينَ لَهُ ٱلدِّينَ حُنَفَآءَ﴾

And they were commanded not, but that they should worship
Allâh, and worship none but Him Alone

Hence they were ordered to worship Allâh alone in all religious
matters and to stay away from worshipping all false deities, because
worshipping them is contrary to pure *Tawhid*.

﴿وَيُقِيمُواْ ٱلصَّلَوٰةَ وَيُؤۡتُواْ ٱلزَّكَوٰةَ وَذَٰلِكَ دِينُ ٱلۡقَيِّمَةِ﴾

And perform *As-Salat* and give *Az-Zakat*; and that is the right
religion

Though both come under the general heading of worship (from the
last verse), prayer and *Zakat* are specifically mentioned because of
their high status in Islam, and because the one who establishes them
necessarily establishes the other principles of the religion.

﴿وَذَٰلِكَ دِينُ ٱلۡقَيِّمَةِ﴾

That is the right religion

Tawhid and sincerity are the right religion. This verse says,
therefore, that those who apply Allâh's Book and the Prophet's
Sunnah are the ones who apply the religion that leads to the
Gardens of Paradise.

﴿إِنَّ ٱلَّذِينَ كَفَرُواْ مِنۡ أَهۡلِ ٱلۡكِتَٰبِ وَٱلۡمُشۡرِكِينَ فِى نَارِ جَهَنَّمَ﴾

Verily, those who disbelieve from among the People of
Scripture and the polytheists will abide in the fire of Hell

Their punishment therein will be most severe.

﴿أُوْلَٰٓئِكَ هُمۡ شَرُّ ٱلۡبَرِيَّةِ﴾

They are the worst of creatures

That is because they knew the truth but abandoned it, losing out on
this world and the Hereafter.

﴿إِنَّ ٱلَّذِينَ ءَامَنُواْ وَعَمِلُواْ ٱلصَّٰلِحَٰتِ أُوْلَٰٓئِكَ هُمۡ خَيۡرُ ٱلۡبَرِيَّةِ﴾

Verily, those who believe and do righteous good deeds, they

are the best of creatures

That is because they knew Allâh and worshipped Him without associating any partners with Him from the creation; hence they gained Gardens in Paradise.

﴿جَزَآؤُهُمْ عِندَ رَبِّهِمْ جَنَّٰتُ عَدْنٍ﴾

Their reward with their Lord is *'Adn* (Eden) Paradise (Gardens of Eternity)

Their reward with their Creator and God is the reward for their sincerity to Allâh in worship and for their faith and good deeds. The Gardens of *'Adn* (Eden) are the best gardens of Paradise.

﴿تَجْرِى مِن تَحْتِهَا ٱلْأَنْهَٰرُ خَٰلِدِينَ فِيهَآ أَبَدًا رَّضِىَ ٱللَّهُ عَنْهُمْ وَرَضُوا۟ عَنْهُ﴾

Underneath which rivers flow, they will abide therein forever, Allâh well-pleased with them, and they with Him.

Meaning the different gardens in Paradise, where they will abide forever; the life of bliss and pleasure they will have therein is an eternal one. Allâh is pleased with them and they with Him for all of the blessings and rewards He prepared for them; He gives them in Paradise that which no eye has seen, no ear has heard (or heard of) – that which has not even occurred to the heart of man.

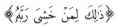

﴿ذَٰلِكَ لِمَنْ خَشِىَ رَبَّهُۥ﴾

That is for Him who fears His Lord

The one who fears Allâh and abstains from disobeying Him, all the while doing what is obligatory upon him, hoping for Allâh's rewards and for eternal bliss in Paradise.

Surat Al-Qadr

﴿بِسْمِ اللَّهِ الرَّحْمَٰنِ الرَّحِيمِ﴾

﴿إِنَّا أَنزَلْنَاهُ فِي لَيْلَةِ الْقَدْرِ ۝ وَمَا أَدْرَاكَ مَا لَيْلَةُ الْقَدْرِ ۝ لَيْلَةُ الْقَدْرِ خَيْرٌ مِّنْ أَلْفِ شَهْرٍ ۝ تَنَزَّلُ الْمَلَائِكَةُ وَالرُّوحُ فِيهَا بِإِذْنِ رَبِّهِم مِّن كُلِّ أَمْرٍ ۝ سَلَامٌ هِيَ حَتَّىٰ مَطْلَعِ الْفَجْرِ﴾

In the Name of Allâh, the Most Beneficent, the Most Merciful.

Verily! We have sent it (this Qur'ân) down in the night of *Al-Qadr* (Decree). And what will make you know what the night of *Al-Qadr* (Decree) is? The night of *Al-Qadr* (Decree) is better then a thousand months. Therein descend the angels and the *Ruh* (Jibril) by Allâh's permission with all Decrees, Peace! Until the appearance of dawn.[1]

On the night of *Al-Qadr*, We have revealed the Qur'ân in its entirety from *Al-Lawh Al-Mahfuz* to the heaven of the world, and then the Qur'ân was revealed sections at a time to the Prophet ﷺ, so a number of verses or a verse was revealed for the circumstances at the time. The period between the first verse of the Qur'ân being revealed to the Prophet ﷺ and the last verse is 23 years.

﴿وَمَا أَدْرَاكَ مَا لَيْلَةُ الْقَدْرِ﴾

And what will make you know what the night of *Al-Qadr* (Decree) is?

For its significance is huge and truly amazing; acts of obedience performed on that night are rewarded for with a tremendous reward.

﴿لَيْلَةُ الْقَدْرِ خَيْرٌ مِّنْ أَلْفِ شَهْرٍ﴾

The night of *Al-Qadr* (Decree) is better then a thousand months.

This means that deeds performed on that night are better than deeds performed in one thousand other months.

---

[1] (*Al-Qadr* 97:1-5)

﴿نَنَزَّلُ ٱلْمَلَـٰٓئِكَةُ وَٱلرُّوحُ فِيهَا بِإِذْنِ رَبِّهِم مِّن كُلِّ أَمْرٍ﴾

Therein descend the angels and the *Ruh* (Jibril) by Allâh's permission with all Decrees

The *Ruh* (Jibril) and the angels descend; Jibril is specifically mentioned because of his nobleness and leadership.

﴿سَلَـٰمٌ هِىَ حَتَّىٰ مَطْلَعِ ٱلْفَجْرِ﴾

Peace! Until the appearance of dawn

The night of *Qadr* is free from every evil and defect, and that blessed period begins at the setting of the sun and ends at dawn.

The Sunnah

In the Arabic language, Sunnah means a way, regardless of whether it is a good or evil way, a meaning that is confirmed in this *Hadith*:

«مَنْ سَنَّ سُنَّةً حَسَنَةً، فَلَهُ أَجْرُهَا وَأَجْرُ مَنْ عَمِلَ بِهَا إِلَي يَوْم الْقِيَامَةِ، وَمَنْ سَنَّ سُنَّةً سَيِّئَةً فَعَلَيْهِ وِزْرُهَا، وَوِزْرُ مَنْ عَمِلَ بِهَا إِلَى يَوْم الْقِيَامَةِ»

Whoever establishes a good Sunnah (way), then he has its reward and the reward of all those who apply it until the Day of Judgement. And whoever establishes an evil Sunnah (way), then upon him is its sin and the sin of all those who apply it until the Day of Judgement.[1]

As a term used by scholars of *Hadith*, Sunnah means, "All that is transmitted from the Prophet ﷺ, in terms of speech, deed, approval, his description – his physical description and a description of his qualities, or his biography, both before the beginning of his mission and after it.''

In one of his legal rulings, Imam Taqi Ad-Deen Ibn Taymiyyah said, "The Prophetic *Hadith* – when mentioned in general – points to what is related from the Prophet's speech, action, and approval, for his Sunnah is established from these three facets. It is compulsory, then, to believe and have faith in the information he told us of. It is incumbent upon us to follow what he ﷺ legislated – commands, prohibitions, and rulings that indicate something is lawful. The verses of the Qur'ân that refer to Prophethood indicate that the Prophets are infallible in what they inform us of regarding Allâh; all of what they tell us is true, and that is the meaning of Prophethood, which implies that Allâh Almighty inspires a Prophet ﷺ. And the *Rasul* (Messenger) is ordered to invite the creation to the messages of his Lord.''

---

[1] Muslim

An Explanation Of The Four *Hadiths* Around Which The Entire Religion Revolves[1]

The First *Hadith*:

«إِنَّمَا الْأَعْمَالُ بِالنِّيَّاتِ وَإِنَّمَا لِكُلِّ امْرِيءٍ مَا نَوَى»

Indeed deeds are based on intentions, and for each person is that which he intended.

Deeds of speech or action, both outward and inner deeds – none are complete without intention (*Niyyah*), a fact that shows the great significance of intention in Islam. When one does a good deed without intention, he benefits nothing from that deed and Allâh Almighty doesn't accept it from him.

«وَإِنَّمَا لِكُلِّ امْرِيءٍ مَا نَوَى»

And for each person is that which he intended

If by his deed, one sincerely worships Allâh, seeking His pleasure alone, then from Allâh he will have a reward; but if he intended some worldly benefit, making his worship a means of achieving that benefit, or if he had a wicked intention, then his is that which he intended, and his accountability is with Allâh.

The Second *Hadith*:

«الْحَلَالُ بَيِّنٌ وَالْحَرَامُ بَيِّنٌ»

The lawful is clear and the unlawful is clear...

In the plain verses of His Book, Allâh clarified this for, and the Messenger of Allâh ﷺ explained it to us in his pure *Shari'ah*. The lawful is clear: it is that which souls find comfort in, matters in which there is no doubt whatsoever; and that the unlawful is clear for one who wishes to stay away from it. Between the lawful and unlawful are matters that are not so clear. If a Muslim stays away from those matters, he will have safeguarded his religion and honor. But whoever hovers around those matters will necessarily fall into what is prohibited. We must fear Allâh in our sayings and deeds, taking the clear path that Allâh and His Messenger ﷺ delineated for us. In a *Hadith*:

«دَعْ مَا يَرِيبُكَ إِلَى مَا لَا يَرِيبُكَ»

---
[1] *Daleel Al-Muslim Al-Mubtadi'*, pp. 28-29.

Leave that which causes you doubt to that which doesn't cause you doubt.

Meaning, leave that which you are not sure about – is it lawful and harmless or not? And instead go to that which you have certain knowledge about – that it is indeed lawful and harmless.

The Third *Hadith*:

«مِنْ حُسْنِ إِسْلَامِ الْمَرْءِ تَرْكُهُ مَا لَا يَعْنِيهِ»

From the goodness of one's Islam is to leave that which does not concern him.

Under Islam come faith and *Ihsan*. This *Hadith* is one of the foundations of the religion. The Muslim is described with one of two qualities: he is either one who is upright, obeying Allâh and His Messenger's commandments, staying away from base and meaningless matters – then he is the true Muslim. Then there is one who follows up on base and meaningless speech and action, not deeming himself to be above rumours and false speech – He has deviated from the true and upright religion. Let us consider the Prophet's saying:

«الْمُسْلِمُ مَنْ سَلِمَ الْمُسْلِمُونَ مِنْ لِسَانِهِ وَيَدَهِ»

The Muslim is he from whom the Muslims are safe, safe from his tongue and his hand.

The Fourth *Hadith*:

«مَنْ أَحْدَثَ فِي أَمْرِنَا هَذَا مَا لَيْسَ مِنْهُ فَهُوَ رَدٌّ»

Whoever introduces into this matter of ours that which is not from it, then it is rejected.

This proves that every innovation introduced in the religion – meaning that it doesn't have a basis in the Qur'ân or Sunnah, regardless of whether it is a saying or a deed, such as those deeds that Allâh didn't legislate and the Prophet ﷺ didn't command us with – then it is rejected for the one who introduced it. This is because his action is not founded on the Qur'ân and Sunnah. Whoever's action is in agreement with Allâh's Book and His Messenger's Sunnah, his action is accepted – by the Will of Allâh.

Selected Invocations For
The Young And Old[1]

How To Supplicate, And The Manners Of Supplication

1) Supplication is worship; not only did Allâh order us to supplicate to Him, but He also promised to answer our supplications:

﴿وَقَالَ رَبُّكُمُ ٱدْعُونِيٓ أَسْتَجِبْ لَكُمْ إِنَّ ٱلَّذِينَ يَسْتَكْبِرُونَ عَنْ عِبَادَتِي سَيَدْخُلُونَ جَهَنَّمَ دَاخِرِينَ﴾

And your Lord said: "Invoke Me, I will respond to you. Verily! Those who scorn My worship they will surely enter Hell in humiliation!"[2]

2) Immediately before and after supplicating, praise Allâh and send prayers upon the Prophet ﷺ.

3) Do not invoke other than Allâh.

4) Show reverence and submission to Allâh as you are supplicating.

5) Be persistent in supplication, but do not be impatient regarding its answer; furthermore, invoke Allâh during those times when you are more likely to be answered.

6) Supplicate for yourself, your parents, your brothers, your relatives, the Muslims, your sick neighbors, those Muslims who are dead, the leaders, the scholars, and those who have done you a favor. Also, invoke Allâh to guide sinners.

7) Never, even when angry, supplicate against yourself, your family, or even your wealth.

8) When you hear others supplicating, say *"Aameen"* (which means, "O Allâh, answer!")

* The Benefits Of Supplication And Remembrance

1) Achieving closeness to Allâh.

2) Supplication is one of the means by which a Muslim achieves his goals and aims.

---

[1] *As-Suluk wat-Tahtheeb* for the third primary level.
[2] (*Ghafir* 40:60)

Supplications And Phrases Of Remembrance For Both The Young And Old[1]

What you say...

Just before entering the toilet:

«بِسْمِ اللهِ اللَّهُمَّ إِنِّي أَعُوذُ بِكَ مِنَ الْخُبُثِ وَالْخَبَائِثِ»

Bismillâh. Allâhumma Innee A'oothu Bika Minal-Khubuthi wal-Khaba'ith.

"In the Name of Allâh. O Allâh, I take refuge with You from all evil and evildoers."

When exiting from the toilet:

«غُفْرَانَكَ»

Ghufraanaka.

"I ask You (Allâh) for forgiveness."

Upon entering the *Masjid*:

«اللَّهُمَّ افْتَحْ لِي أَبْوَابَ رَحْمَتِكَ»

Allâhummaftah lee Abwaaba Rahmatika.

"O Allâh, open the gates of Your mercy for me."

Upon leaving the *Masjid*:

«اللَّهُمَّ إِنِّي أَسْأَلُكَ مِنْ فَضْلِكَ»

Allâhumma Innee As'aluka Min Fadhlika

"O Allâh, I ask You from Your favor."

Before sleeping:

«بِاسْمِكَ اللَّهُمَّ أَحْيَا وَأَمُوتُ»

Bismikallâhumma Ahya wa Amoot.

"In Your Name, O Allâh, I live and die."

---

[1] Curriculum for the second primary level.

Upon waking up from sleep:

«الْحَمْدُ للهِ الَّذِي أَحْيَانَا بَعْدَ مَا أَمَاتَنَا وَإِلَيْهِ النُّشُورُ»

Al-Hamdu lillâhillathee Ahyaanaa Ba'da Maa Amaatanaa wa Ilayhin-Nushoor.

"All praise is for Allâh Who gave us life after having taken it from us and unto Him is the resurrection."

Upon sneezing

«الْحَمْدُ للهِ»

Al-Hamdu lillâh.

"All praise is for Allâh."

Upon hearing somebody sneezing and saying, "All praise is for Allâh": say to him:

«يَرْحَمُكَ اللهُ»

Yarhamukallâh.

"May Allâh have mercy upon you."

If you are the one who sneezed, and heard someone invoking Allâh to have mercy on you, say to that person:

«يَهْدِيكُمُ اللهُ وَيُصْلِحُ بَالَكُمْ»

Yahdeekumullâh, wa Yuslihu Baalakum.

"May Allâh guide you and rectify your condition."

Upon sitting in a car or in (or on) any other means of conveyance:

«سُبْحَانَ الَّذِي سَخَّرَ لَنَا هَذَا وَمَا كُنَّا لَهُ مُقْرِنِينَ وَإِنَّا إِلَى رَبِّنَا لَمُنْقَلِبُونَ»

Subhaanallathee Sakhkhara Lana Hatha, wa Maa Kunnaa Lahu Muqrineena wa Innaa Ilaa Rabbina Lamunqaliboon.

"Gbrified is He Who has subjected this to us, and we could have never had it (by our efforts). And verily, to our Lord we indeed are to return."

When you are in fear: seek refuge in Allâh from the accursed *Shaitan.*

Supplications Of The Muslim During The Day And Night

Supplications For When One Is About To Sleep And When One Wakes Up

* When on his bed and about to sleep, the Muslim should say:

«اللَّهُمَّ أَسْلَمْتُ نَفْسِي إِلَيْكَ، وَوَجَّهْتُ وَجْهِي إِلَيْكَ وَفَوَّضْتُ أَمْرِي إِلَيْكَ وَأَلْجَأْتُ ظَهْرِي إِلَيْكَ رَغْبَةً وَرَهْبَةً إِلَيْكَ لَا مَلْجاً وَلَا مَنْجَى مِنْكَ إِلَّا إِلَيْكَ، آمَنْتُ بِكِتَابِكَ الَّذِي أَنْزَلْتَ، وَبِنَبِيِّكَ الَّذِي أَرْسَلْتَ»

Allâhumma Aslamtu Nafsee Ilayka, wa wajjahtu Wajhee Ilayka, wa Fawwadhtu Amree Ilayka, wa Alja'tu Thahree Ilayka, Raghbatan wa Rahbatan Ilayka, Laa Malja' wa Laa Manjaa Minka Illaa Ilayka, Aamantu Bi Kitaabikallathee Anzalta, wa Binabiyyikallathee Arsalta.

O Allâh, I submit my soul unto You and I entrust my affair unto You, and I turn my face towards You, and I totally rely on You, in hope and fear of You. Verily there is no refuge nor safe haven from You except with You. I believe in Your Book which You have revealed and in Your Prophet whom You have sent.[1]

Before sleeping, recite *Ayatal-Kursi* (Related by Al-Bukhari). Also, join your hands together and blow into them, after which you recite the last three *Surahs* of the Qur'ân. Then wipe your hands on as much of your body as you are able; repeat the above three times (Related by Al-Bukhari and Muslim). You should also recite the last two verses from *Surat Al-Baqarah* (Al-Bukhari and Muslim). Furthermore, say *"Subhaanallâh"* (How perfect Allâh is!) thirty-three times, *"Al-Hamdu lillâh"* (All praise is for Allâh) thirty-three times, and *"Allâhu Akbar"* (Allâh is the Most Great) thirty-three times.

* When turning over in the night, say:

---

[1] Recorded by Al-Bukhari and Muslim.

«لَا إِلَهَ إِلَّا اللهُ الْوَاحِدُ الْقَهَّارُ، رَبُّ السَّمَاوَاتِ وَالْأَرْضِ، وَمَا بَيْنَهُمَا الْعَزِيزُ الْغَفَّارُ»

Laa Ilaha Illallâhul-Waahidul-Qahhaar, Rabbus-Samaawaa-ti wal-Ardh, wa Maa Bainahumal-'Azeezul-Ghaffaar.

"None has the right to be worshipped except Allâh. The One, Al-Qahhar (The One Who Subdues). Lord of the heavens and the earth and all between them. The Exalted in might, the Oft-Forgiving."[1]

* Upon experiencing unrest, fear, worry and the like during sleep, say:

«أَعُوذُ بِكَلِمَاتِ اللهِ التَّامَّاتِ، مِنْ غَضَبِهِ وَعِقَابِهِ، وَشَرِّ عِبَادِهِ وَمِنْ هَمَزَاتِ الشَّيَاطِينِ، وَأَنْ يَحْضُرُونَ»

A'oothu Bikalimatillahit-Taammaati, Min Ghadhabihi wa 'Iqaabihi, wa Sharri 'Ibaadihi, wa Min Hamazaatish-Shayateeni, wa An Yahdhuroon.

"I take refuge in the perfect Words of Allâh from His anger and punishment, and from the evil of His servants, and from the madness and appearance of devils."[2]

* Upon having a bad dream, do the following:

- Spit (lightly) three times to your left.
- Seek refuge in Allâh from the *Shaitan* (and from the evil that you saw).
- Hence the dream will not harm you (Al-Bukhari and Muslim).
- Turn, sleeping on the opposite side of what you were previously sleeping on. (Muslim)
- Do not mention your dream to anyone. (Al-Bukhari and Muslim)

* Upon waking up, say:

«الْحَمْدُ للهِ الَّذِي أَحْيَانَا بَعْدَ مَا أَمَاتَنَا وَإِلَيْهِ النُّشُورُ»

[1] Recorded by Al-Hakim, who declared it to be authentic; Ath-Thahabi agreed.
[2] Recorded by Abu Dawud and At-Tirmithi, to whom belongs the above wording. He said, "It is a *Hasan Gharib Hadith.*"

Al-Hamdu lillâhillathee Ahyaanaa Ba'da Maa Amaatanaa wa Ilayhin-Nushoor

"All praise is for Allâh Who gave us life after having taken it from us and unto Him is the resurrection."[1]

And,

«الْحَمْدُ للهِ الَّذِي عَافَانِي فِي جَسَدِي وَرَدَّ عَلَيَّ رُوحِي وَأَذِنَ لِي بِذِكْرِهِ»

Al-Hamdu lillâhillathee 'Aafaanee Fee Jasadee wa Radda 'Alayya Roohee, wa Athina lee Bithikrih.

"All praise is for Allâh Who restored to me my health and returned my soul and has allowed me to remember Him."[2]

Supplications For The Morning And Evening

*   Say in the morning:

«اللَّهُمَّ بِكَ أَصْبَحْنَا، وَبِكَ أَمْسَيْنَا، وَبِكَ نَحْيَا، وَبِكَ نَمُوتُ، وَإِلَيْكَ النُّشُورُ»

Allâhumma Bika Asbahnaa wa Bika Amsaynaa, wa Bika Nahyaa, wa Bika Namootu, wa Ilaykan-Nushoor.

"O Allâh, by Your leave we have reached the morning and by Your leave we have reached the evening, by Your leave we live and die and unto You is our resurrection."[3]

* In the evening, say:

«اللَّهُمَّ بِكَ أَمْسَيْنَا، وَبِكَ أَصْبَحْنَا وَبِكَ نَحْيَا، وَبِكَ نَمُوتُ، وَإِلَيْكَ الْمَصِيرُ»

Allâhumma Bika Amsaynaa, wa Bika Asbahnaa, wa Bika Nahyaa, wa Bika Namootu, wa Ilaykal-Maseer.

"O Allâh, by Your leave we have reached the evening and by Your leave we have reached the morning, by Your leave we live and die and unto You is our return."[4]

---

[1] Al-Bukhari and Muslim
[2] Recorded by Tirmithi
[3] Recorded by At-Tirmithi
[4] Recorded by At-Tirmithi, who graded it *Hasan*.

Supplications Related To One's Attire

* When wearing a garment, say:

«الْحَمْدُ لله الَّذِي كَسَانِي هَذَا، وَرَزَقَنِيهِ مِنْ غَيْرِ حَوْلٍ مِنِّي وَلَا قُوَّةٍ»

Al-Hamdu lillâhil-lathee Kasaanee Hathaa, wa Razaqaneehi Min Ghairi Hawlin Minnee wa Laa Quwwatin.

"All praise is for Allâh Who has clothed me with this garment and provided it for me, with no power nor might from myself."[1]

* Before undressing, say:

«بِسْم الله»

Bismillâh (In the Name of Allâh).[2]

* Upon wearing a new garment, say:

«اللَّهُمَّ لَكَ الْحَمْدُ أَنْتَ كَسَوْتَنِيهِ، أَسْأَلُكَ مِنْ خَيْرِهِ، وَخَيْرِ مَا صُنِعَ لَهُ، وَأَعُوذُ بِكَ مِنْ شَرِّهِ، وَشَرِّ مَا صُنِعَ لَهُ»

Allâhumma Lakal-Hamdu, Anta Kasawtaneehi, As'aluka min Khairihi wa Khairi Maa Suni'a Lahu, wa A'oothu Bika Min Sharrihi, wa Sharri Maa Suni'a Lahu.

"O Allâh, for You is all praise, You have clothed me with it (i.e., the garment), I ask You for the good of it and the good for which it was made, and I seek refuge with You from the evil of it and the evil for which it was made."[3]

* When you see your brother Muslim wearing new clothing, say to him:

«الْبَسْ جَدِيدًا، وَعِشْ حَمِيدًا، وَمُتْ شَهِيدًا»

Ilbas Jadeedan, wa 'Ish Hameedan, wa Mut Shaheedan.

"Wear anew, live commendably, and die as a martyr."[4]

---

[1] Recorded by Abu Dawud
[2] Recorded by At-Tabarani
[3] Recorded by Abu Dawud, and this wording is his; At-Tirmithi related it as well, and he declared it to be *Hasan*.
[4] Recorded by Ibn Majah

Supplications Related To Food

* As you are about to eat, say:

«بِسْم اللهِ»

Bismillâh (In the Name of Allâh).

And if you forget to say this before eating, say upon remembering:

«بِسْم اللهِ أَوَّلَهُ وَآخِرَهُ»

Bismillâhi Awwalahu wa Aakhirahu.

"In the Name of Allâh in its beginning and end."[1]

* Upon finishing a meal, say:

«الْحَمْدُ للهِ الَّذِي أَطْعَمَنِي هَذَا الطَّعَامَ وَرَزَقَنِيهِ مِنْ غَيْرِ حَوْلٍ مِنِّي وَلَا قُوَّةٍ»

Al-Hamdu lillâhIl-lathee At'amanee Hathat-ta'aama, wa Razaqaneehi Min Ghairi Hawlim-Minnee wa Laa Quwwatin.

All praise is for Allâh Who fed me this food and provided it for me without any might nor power from myself."[2]

* If you are about to break your fast, say:

«ذَهَبَ الظَّمَأُ وَابْتَلَّتِ الْعُرُوقُ وَثَبَتَ الْأَجْرُ إِنْ شَاءَ اللهُ»

Thahabath-Thama'u Wabtallatil-'Urooqu Wa Thabatal-Ajru In Shaa' Allâh.

"The thirst has gone and the veins are quenched, and reward is confirmed, if Allâh wills."[3]

* If one gave you food or drink, say:

«اللَّهُمَّ أَطْعِمْ مَنْ أَطْعَمَنِي وَاسْقِ مَنْ سَقَانِي»

Allâhumma At'im Man At'amanee Wasaqi Man Saqaanee.

"O Allâh, feed him who fed me, and provide drink for him who provided me with drink."[4]

---

[1] Recorded by At-Tirmithi
[2] Recorded by Ahmad
[3] Recorded by Abu Dawud
[4] Recorded by Muslim

* When breaking fast in someone's home, supplicate for him, saying:

«أَفْطَرَ عِنْدَكُمُ الصَّائِمُونَ، وَأَكَلَ طَعَامَكُمُ الْأَبْرَارُ، وَصَلَّتْ عَلَيْكُمُ الْمَلَائِكَةُ»

Aftara 'Indakumus-Saa'imoona wa Akala Ta'amakumul-Abraaru, wa Sallat 'Alaykumul-Malaa'ikatu.

May the fasting break their fast in your home, and may the dutiful and pious eat your food, and may the angels send prayers upon you."[1]

Supplications Related To One's Home

* When you enter the home, remember Allâh (a practice that is related by Muslim). Then give greetings of peace to the members of your household, for Allâh Almighty says:

﴿فَإِذَا دَخَلْتُم بُيُوتًا فَسَلِّمُواْ عَلَىٰٓ أَنفُسِكُمْ﴾

But when you enter the houses, greet one another with a greeting from Allâh (i.e., say: *As-Salamu Alaikum* – peace be on you) blessed and good.[2]

And before you enter the house of your brother, seek his permission first:

﴿يَٰٓأَيُّهَا ٱلَّذِينَ ءَامَنُواْ لَا تَدْخُلُواْ بُيُوتًا غَيْرَ بُيُوتِكُمْ حَتَّىٰ تَسْتَأْنِسُواْ وَتُسَلِّمُواْ عَلَىٰٓ أَهْلِهَا ذَٰلِكُمْ خَيْرٌ لَّكُمْ لَعَلَّكُمْ تَذَكَّرُونَ﴾

O you who believe! Enter not houses other than your own, until you have asked permission and greeted those in them – that is better for you, in order that you may remember. [3]

* When leaving the home:

«بِسْمِ اللهِ، تَوَكَّلْتُ عَلَى اللهِ، لَا حَوْلَ وَلَا قُوَّةَ إِلَّا بِاللهِ»

Bismillâh, Tawakkaltu 'Alallâh, Laa Hawla wa Laa Quwwata Illaa Billâh.

---

[1] Recorded by Abu Dawud
[2] (*An-Nur* 24:61)
[3] (*An-Nur* 24:27)

"In the Name of Allâh, I place my trust in Allâh, and there is neither might nor power except with Allâh."[1]

Supplications Related To the *Wudhu'*

* When starting ablution, say:

«بِسْم اللهِ»

Bismillâh (In the Name of Allâh). (Related by At-Tirmithi)

* Upon completing *Wudhu'*, say:

«أَشْهَدُ أَنْ لَا إِلَهَ إِلَّا اللهُ، وَحْدَهُ لَا شَرِيكَ لَهُ، وَأَشْهَدُ أَنَّ مُحَمَّدًا عَبْدُهُ وَرَسُولُهُ»

Ashhadu An Laa Ilaha Illallâh, Wahdahu Laa Shareeka Lahu, wa Ashhadu Anna Muhammadan 'Abduhu wa Rasooluh.

"I bear witness that none has the right to be worshipped except Allâh, alone, without partner, and I bear witness that Muhammad is His slave and Messenger."[2]

And the following addition is found in the narration of At-Tirmithi:

«اللَّهُمَّ اجْعَلْنِي مِنَ التَّوَّابِينَ، وَاجْعَلْنِي مِنَ الْمُتَطَهِّرِينَ»

Allâhummaj'alnee Minat-Tawwaabeena, Waj'alnee Minal-Mutatahhireen.

"O Allâh, make me of those who return to You often in repentance and make me of those who remain clean and pure."

Supplications Related To The *Masjid*

* When going to the *Masjid*, say:

«اللَّهُمَّ اجْعَلْ فِي قَلْبِي نُورًا، وَفِي لِسَانِي نُورًا، وَاجْعَلْ فِي سَمْعِي نُورًا، وَاجْعَلْ فِي بَصَرِي نُورًا، وَاجْعَلْ مِنْ خَلْفِي نُورًا، وَمِنْ أَمَامِي نُورًا، وَاجْعَلْ مِنْ فَوْقِي نُورًا، وَمِنْ تَحْتِي نُورًا، اللَّهُمَّ اعْطِنِي نُورًا»

Allâhummaj'al Fee Qalbee Nooran, wa Fee Lisaanee Nooran,

---

[1] Recorded by At-Tirmithi
[2] Muslim

Waj'al Fee Sam'ee Nooran, Waj'al Fee Basaree Nooran, Waj'al Min Khalfee Nooran, wa Min Amaamee Nooran, Waj'al Min Fawqee Nooran, wa Min Tahtee Nooran, Allâhumma A'tinee Noora.

"O Allâh, place within my heart light, and upon my tongue light, and within my ears light, and within my eyes light, and place behind me light and in front of me light and above me light and beneath me light. O Allâh, bestow upon me light."[1]

* Upon entering the *Masjid*, say:

«بِسْمِ اللهِ، وَالسَّلَامُ عَلَى رَسُولِ اللهِ، اللَّهُمَّ اغْفِرْ لِي ذُنُوبِي»

Bismillâh, was-Salaamu 'Alaa Rasoolillâh. Allâhummaghfir lee Thunoobee.

In the name of Allâh, and peace be upon the Messenger of Allâh. O Allâh, forgive me my sins."[2]

«اللَّهُمَّ افْتَحْ لِي أَبْوَابَ رَحْمَتِكَ»

Allâhummaftah lee Abwaaba Rahmatik.

"O Allâh, open the gates of Your mercy for me."[3]

* When leaving the *Masjid*, say:

«بِسْمِ اللهِ، وَالسَّلَامُ عَلَى رَسُولِ اللهِ، اللَّهُمَّ اغْفِرْ لِي ذُنُوبِي»

Bismillâh, was-Salaamu 'Alaa Rasoolillâh. Allâhummaghfir lee Thunoobee.

"In the Name of Allâh, and peace be upon the Messenger of Allâh. O Allâh, forgive me my sins."[4]

«اللَّهُمَّ إِنِّي أَسْأَلُكَ مِنْ فَضْلِكَ»

Allâhumma Innee As'aluka Min Fadhlik.

"O Allâh, I ask You from Your favor."[5]

---

[1] Recorded by Muslim
[2] Recorded by Ibn Majah
[3] Recorded by Muslim
[4] Recorded by Ibn Majah
[5] Recorded by Muslim

Supplication For The Expiation Of Sins At The Conclusion Of A Gathering

«سُبْحَانَكَ اللَّهُمَّ وَبِحَمْدِكَ، أَشْهَدُ أَنْ لَا إِلَهَ إِلَّا أَنْتَ، أَسْتَغْفِرُكَ وَأَتُوبُ إِلَيْكَ»

Subhaanakal-laahumma wa Bihamdika Ashhadu An Laa Ilaha Illa Anta, Astaghfiruka wa Atoobu Ilayk.

"How perfect You are, O Allâh, and I praise You. I bear witness that none has the right to be worshipped except You. I seek Your forgiveness and turn to You in repentance."[1]

Visiting The Sick

* When you visit your sick Muslim brother, wipe his right hand three times, saying:

«اللَّهُمَّ رَبَّ النَّاسِ، أَذْهِبِ الْبَأْسَ، اشْفِ أَنْتَ الشَّافِي، لَا شِفَاءَ إِلَّا شِفَاؤُكَ، شِفَاءً لَا يُغَادِرُ سَقَمًا»

Allâhumma Rabban-Naasi, Athhibil-Ba'sa, Ashfi Antash-Shaafee, Laa Shifaa'a Illaa Shifaa'uka, Shifaa'an Laa Yughaadiru Saqama.

"O Allâh, Lord of mankind, remove the pain, and cure, for You are the Curer; there is no cure except Your cure, a cure that leaves behind no sickness."[2]

And say:

«لَا بَأْسَ، طَهُورٌ إِنْ شَاءَ اللهُ»

La Ba'sa Tahoorun In Shaa' Allâh.

"It is no harm, rather it is purification, if Allâh wills."[3]

And:

«أَسْأَلُ اللهَ الْعَظِيمَ، رَبَّ الْعَرْشِ الْعَظِيمِ، أَنْ يَشْفِيَكَ»

As'alullaahal-'Atheem Rabbal-'Arshil-'Atheemi, An Yashfiyak.

---

[1] Recorded by At-Tirmithi
[2] Al-Bukhari and Muslim
[3] Recorded by Al-Bukhari

"I ask Allâh, the Supreme, Lord of the Magnificent Throne to cure you."[1]

* When performing *Ruqyah* (i.e., reciting phrases of remembrance or invocations) over the sick, say:

بِسْمِ اللهِ أَرْقِيكَ، مِنْ كُلِّ شَيْءٍ يُؤْذِيكَ، مِنْ شَرِّ كُلِّ نَفْسٍ، وَعَيْنٍ حَاسِدٍ. بِسْمِ اللهِ أَرْقِيكَ، وَاللهُ يَشْفِيكَ»

Bismillâh Arqeeka, Min Kulli Shay'in Yu'theeka, Min Sharri Kulli Nafsin, wa 'Aynin Haasidin. Bismillâhi Arqeeka, Wallâhu Yashfeek.

"In the Name of Allâh do I make *Ruqyah* for you, from all things that may harm you, from the evil of every soul, from the evil eye of the jealous one. In the Name of Allâh do I make *Ruqyah* for you, and may Allâh cure you."[2]

Supplication For When Afflicted With Hardship

«لَا إِلَهَ إِلَّا اللهُ الْعَظِيمُ الْحَلِيمُ، لَا إِلَهَ إِلَّا اللهُ رَبُّ الْعَرْشِ الْعَظِيمِ، لَا إِلَهَ إِلَّا اللهُ رَبُّ السَّمَاوَاتِ وَرَبُّ الْأَرْضِ رَبُّ الْعَرْشِ الْكَرِيمِ»

Laa Ilaha Illallâhul-'Atheemul-Haleem, Laa Ilaha Illallâhu Rabbul-'Arshil-'Atheem, Laa Ilaha Illallahu Rabbus-Samawaati wa Rabbul-Ardhi Rabbul-'Arshil-'Kareem.

"None has the right to be worshipped except Allâh, the Supreme, the Forbearing. None has the right to be worshipped except Allâh, Lord of the Magnificent Throne. None has the right to be worshipped except Allâh, Lord of the heavens, Lord of the earth and Lord of the Noble Throne."[3]

Supplication For Entering The Marketplace

«لَا إِلَهَ إِلَّا اللهُ وَحْدَهُ لَا شَرِيكَ لَهُ، لَهُ الْمُلْكُ وَلَهُ الْحَمْدُ، يُحْيِي وَيُمِيتُ، وَهُوَ حَيٌّ لَا يَمُوتُ، بِيَدِهِ الْخَيْرُ وَهُوَ عَلَى كُلِّ شَيْءٍ قَدِيرٌ»

Laa Ialaha Illallâhu, Wahdahu Laa Shareeka Lahu, Lahul-

---

[1] Recorded by At-Tirmithi
[2] Recorded by At-Tirmithi
[3] Agreed upon

Mulku wa Lahul-Hamdu, Yuhyee wa Yumeetu, wa Huwa Hayyun Laa Yamootu, Biyadihil-Khairu, wa Huwa 'Ala Kulli Shay'in Qadeer.

"None has the right to be worshipped except Allâh, alone, without partner, to Him belongs all sovereignty and praise. He gives life and causes death, and He is living and does not die. In His Hand is all good and He has power over all things."[1]

Supplication Said To One Who Does You A Favor

«جَزَاكَ اللهُ خَيْرًا»

Jazaakallâhu Khairan.

"May Allâh reward you with goodness."

If one had lent you money, say the following to him when you pay him back:

«بَارَكَ اللهُ لَكَ فِي أَهْلِكَ وَمَالِكَ»

Baarakallâhu Laka Fee Ahlika wa Maalika.

"May Allâh bless you in your family and wealth."[2]

From The Supplications Of Prayer

Abu Bakr As-Siddiq, may Allâh be pleased with him, related that he asked the Messenger of Allâh ﷺ, "Teach me an invocation that I can supplicate with in my prayer." The Prophet ﷺ said:

«اللَّهُمَّ إِنِّي ظَلَمْتُ نَفْسِي ظُلْمًا كَثِيرًا، وَلَا يَغْفِرُ الذُّنُوبَ إِلَّا أَنْتَ، فَاغْفِرْ لِي مَغْفِرَةً مِنْ عِنْدِكَ، وَارْحَمْنِي، إِنَّكَ أَنْتَ الْغَفُورُ الرَّحِيمُ»

Allâhumma Innee Thalamtu Nafsee Thulman Katheeran, wa Laa Yaghfiruth-Thunooba Illa Anta, Faghfir lee Maghfiratan Min 'Indika, Warhamnee, Innaka Antal-Ghafoorur-Raheem.

"O Allâh, I have indeed oppressed my soul excessively, and none can forgive sins except You, so forgive me a forgiveness from Yourself and have mercy upon me. Surely, You are the Most Forgiving, the Most Merciful."[3]

---

[1] Recorded by At-Tirmithi, and the wording is his; it is also related by Al-Hakim.
[2] Recorded by Ibn Majah
[3] Agreed upon

The Prophet's Biography And His Manners[1]

His Birth

The Messenger of Allâh ﷺ was born to a family well known for their honorable manners; Arabs, as a whole, acknowledge his noble lineage; they admit to his family's leadership over the Arabs, to their eloquent speech, to their noble manners, to their bravery and skills of war, and to their compassion for the weak. His is a Hashimi family, from the tribe of Quraish.

His home city is Makkah, in which he ﷺ was born on Monday, the 12th of Rabi' Al-Awwal, 570, the year that is known as the Year of the Elephant.

His Lineage

He is Muhammad bin 'Abdullah bin 'Abdul-Muttalib bin Hashim bin 'Abd-Munaf bin Qusay bin Kilab bin Murrah bin Ka'b bin Lua'iy bin Ghalib bin Fahr bin Malik bin An-Nadhr bin Kinanah bin Khuzaimah bin Mudrikah bin Ilyas bin Mudar bin Nizar bin Ma'd bin 'Adnan.

The Prophet's lineage traces back to Isma'il, peace be upon him. His mother Aminah bint Wahb belongs to Quraysh – and Wahb was one of the nobles of the Arabs.

The Beginning Of Revelation To The Messenger Of Allâh ﷺ

The Messenger of Allâh ﷺ used to perform worship in the cave of Hira' (a mountain in Makkah), when, one day, Jibril, peace be upon him, came to him and said, "Read."

"I am not one who can read," he ﷺ said. So Jibril, peace be upon him, embraced the Prophet ﷺ three times, saying, "Read." And each time, the Prophet ﷺ said, "I am not one who can read." And so Allâh Almighty revealed:

$$\textarabic{﴿ٱقۡرَأۡ بِٱسۡمِ رَبِّكَ ٱلَّذِى خَلَقَ﴾}$$

Read! In the Name of your Lord, Who has created (all that exists).[2]

---

[1] From *Daleelul-Muslim*, pp. 1-11.
[2] (*Al-'Alaq* 96:1)

This is the first verse revealed from the Qur'ân.

His Invitation To A Purely Monotheistic Religion

After the first revelation, the Prophet ﷺ stayed in Makkah for three years, inviting specific people to devote their worship to Allâh Almighty alone. Then, in the next stage, he announced his message to all: that they should worship Allâh alone, without worshipping others or associating partners with Him in worship. He continued calling them for ten years, and then the five prayers were prescribed. After praying in Makkah for three years, he was ordered to migrate to Al-Madinah, where he was commanded with the rest of the Islamic legislation – there he ﷺ died, yet his religion remains. There is no matter that is good except that he ﷺ invited his nation to it, and no evil except that he ﷺ warned his nation from it.

The Prophet's Character And Manners[1]

I can summarize for you his noble and grand manners in one phrase: The Prophet ﷺ adorned himself with all of the exalted and grand manners that are mentioned in the Noble Qur'ân. He is a complete example for mankind, yet only those who are superior in character and manners follow him ﷺ.

Perhaps you already know that the Qur'ân pointed out and encouraged us to adorn ourselves with every exalted and noble characteristic or manner.

Patience, forbearance, generosity, bravery, justice, truthfulness, modesty, justice in fulfilling the promise, satisfaction with having only a little – when you read about any of these characteristics in a verse of the Qur'ân, be perfectly sure that this characteristic is found in the Prophet ﷺ to a greater degree than it is found in anyone who preceded him, or anyone who came after him ﷺ.

Seeking permission to enter another person's home; arguing with those of a contrary view with better and more honorable words; lowering one's voice, yet raising it when needed, such as when addressing a group of people; walking humbly on the earth – and when you read of these manners in a verse of the Qur'ân, know that

---

[1] From the book *Muhammad Rasoolullâh* ﷺ *wa Khaatamun-Nabiyyeen*, by the Shaikh of Al-Azhar, Muhammad Al-Khidhr Husain, with minor editing.

it is one of the Messenger of Allâh's manners and that he ﷺ would never be derelict regarding it.

I do not say all of this simply because he ﷺ was conveying the Qur'ân, and from the very nature of one who conveys the Qur'ân is that he applies its exalted and grand manners; rather, I base what I say both on the above and on how the Qur'ân describes him, such as in this verse:

$$﴿ وَإِنَّكَ لَعَلَىٰ خُلُقٍ عَظِيمٍ ﴾$$

And verily, you (O Muhammad ﷺ) are on an exalted standard of character.[1]

Then I base my conclusions on the books of authentic Sunnah, books that contain such of his noble and grand manners as will amaze you.

He ﷺ Faced Many Hardships

When reading the Prophet's biography, you will – if Allâh wills – see how he ﷺ faced hardships and calamities without weakening. He would bear hardships without shaking or deviating from his set course. Sufficient as an example of his forbearance is the harm that was inflicted upon him in Makkah, before he migrated to Al-Madinah. Then you can look further and see the hardships he ﷺ faced during many different battles. In the face of all of the above, his determination only strengthened and his patience increased.

The Prophet's Humbleness

The Prophet's humbleness was natural. His character when he and his followers were weak and when he was alone in calling to Allâh, having to deal with harm inflicted upon him by the foolish from among the inhabitants of Makkah, is the same character as he ﷺ had after migrating and after defeating his enemies and after people entered into Allâh's religion in multitudes.

Some Of The Well-Known Manners From His Biography

When entering a gathering, rather than seeking a location that signified importance or status, the Prophet ﷺ would sit beside the last man who entered, or in other words, in the first open space that

---

[1] (*Al-Qalam* 68:4)

would have been available for any newcomer.

He would give a share of his company to all those who were present at a gathering, so that no one would think that another Companion was more honored than he.

The Prophet ﷺ wouldn't cut anyone off in his speech; instead he waited until that person finished. Either the person would finish or the Prophet ﷺ would stand.

If a man welcomed him and shook his hand, the Prophet ﷺ would not remove his hand from the other man's hand, always waiting until the other man pulled back his hand first.

Nor would he ﷺ turn his face away from that man until he turned away his face first.

Anas bin Malik, may Allâh be pleased with him, said, "Among the people, the Messenger of Allâh ﷺ had the best character, (we would notice this) even though he would mix with us often. So much so that he said to my young brother,

«يَا أَبَا عُمَيْرٍ مَا فَعَلَ النُّغَيْرُ»

O Abu 'Umair what did An-Nughair do."[1]

His Lack Of Care For Material Possessions And Worldly Comfort

The Prophet ﷺ took care not to seek out the pleasures and treasures of this world, even though the world came running to him, especially after the conquest of Makkah. He didn't change at all in his ways – not in his eating habits, not in his clothing, and not in the furniture of his home.

'Aishah, may Allâh be pleased with her, said, "Since they came to Al-Madinah, the family of Muhammad ﷺ never filled themselves with food for three nights in a row, until he (the Prophet ﷺ) died."

She also said, "The family of Muhammad ﷺ never ate two meals in one day unless one of those meals was dates."

In *Jami' As-Sahih*, Imam Al-Bukhari related that 'Umar bin Al-

---

[1] Here the Prophet ﷺ was joking with a young boy and comforting him at the same time regarding the death of his bird; the words rhyme in Arabic and carry the said effects.

Khattab, may Allâh be pleased with him, once entered upon the Prophet ﷺ, who was lying down on a sandy mat, and there was no mattress between him and the mat. The effects of the mat left traces on his sides. 'Umar, may Allâh be pleased with him, said to him, "O Messenger of Allâh, invoke Allâh to give generously to your nation, for indeed the Persians and Romans have been given generously and have been given the world, yet they do not worship Allâh." Now sitting and no longer reclining, the Prophet ﷺ said:

«أَوَ فِي هَذَا أَنْتَ يَا ابْنَ الْخَطَّابِ! أَنَّ أُولَئِكَ قَوْمٌ قَدْ عَجِلُوا طَيِّبَاتِهِمْ فِي الْحَيَاةِ الدُّنْيَا»

What is this you are saying O son of Al-Khattab! Indeed they are a people who have hastened their pleasures in the life of this world.

His Mercy And Gentleness

The Prophet ﷺ had a very merciful heart, he loved generosity, and he had a cheerful face. It is known from his biography that he never once struck another with his hand; he ﷺ never struck a woman or a slave. The only occasion on which he physically inflicted harm upon others was when he was fighting in the way of Allâh.

One person who informed us of the Prophet's mercy was Malik bin Huwairith, may Allâh be pleased with him, who said, "We, a group of young men of about the same age, went to the Messenger of Allâh ﷺ. We stayed with him for twenty nights, after which he thought that we were missing our families, and so he asked us regarding the families we left behind, and we informed him about them. He was gentle and merciful and said,

«ارْجِعُوا إِلَى أَهْلِيكُمْ فَعَلِّمُوهُمْ وَمُرُوهُمْ وَصَلُّوا كَمَا رَأَيْتُمُونِي أُصَلِّي»

Return to your families; teach them and order them. And pray as you have seen me pray."

Malik, may Allâh be pleased with him, said he was "gentle and merciful," a statement that he could only have said about the Prophet ﷺ after having witnessed the Prophet's gentleness and mercy and after having witnessed those qualities on more than one occasion during their stay.

In *Shama'il-At-Tirmithi,* (no. 105) 'Abdullah bin Juz' said, "I have not seen anyone smile more than the Messenger of Allâh ﷺ."

Jarir bin 'Abdullah Al-Bajali, may Allâh be pleased with him, said, "The Messenger of Allâh ﷺ was never inaccessible to me from the day I accepted Islam, and he would never see me without smiling."[1]

His Forbearance And Forgiveness

The Prophet ﷺ had a natural disposition to the qualities of forbearance and forgiveness, qualities he showed even when he was able to exact retribution. The following saying is found in *Sahih Al-Bukhari* (10:524): "The Messenger of Allâh ﷺ never sought retribution for himself; but when Allâh's boundaries were transgressed, then he would seek retribution for Allâh."

The occasions in which the Prophet's noble quality of forgiveness comes to light are indeed many and are not paralleled in history; those instances are found in books of *Hadith* and of the Prophet's biography.

In a *Hadith* related by Muslim and others from among the eminent compilers of *Hadith,* eighty men from the inhabitants of Makkah descended upon the Prophet ﷺ and his Companions in full armor. They came from the direction of the Tan'im Mountain, and they wanted to take the Messenger of Allâh ﷺ off guard. Their plot was foiled, however, and they were taken as prisoners. But instead of punishing them, the Prophet ﷺ forgave them, and Allâh Almighty referred to this story in the following verse:

$$وَهُوَ ٱلَّذِى كَفَّ أَيْدِيَهُمْ عَنكُمْ وَأَيْدِيَكُمْ عَنْهُم بِبَطْنِ مَكَّةَ مِنۢ بَعْدِ أَنْ أَظْفَرَكُمْ عَلَيْهِمْ$$

And He it is Who has withheld their hands from you and your hands from them in the midst of Makkah, after He had made you victorious over them.[2]

It is also established in the Prophet's biography that he ﷺ would

---

[1] Recorded by Al-Bukhari, in the chapter, "The Good Traits of Jarir bin 'Abdullah Al-Bajali."

[2] (*Al-Fath* 48:24)

forbear the harshness of strangers. Anas, may Allâh be pleased with him, said, "I was walking with the Prophet ﷺ, who was wearing a Najrani garment, the hems of which were rough. A desert Arab accosted him, and violently pulled at his garment. I looked at the surface of the Prophet's shoulder and I saw that the hems of the garment harmed his skin from the severity of the man's pulling. Then the desert Arab said, 'O Muhammad, order for me from Allâh's wealth that is with you.' The Prophet ﷺ turned to him, laughed, and ordered for him to be given (a share of wealth)."[1]

His Generosity

In giving to good causes, the Prophet's hands were extended; he would spend the wealth Allâh Almighty gave to him in order to elevate Allâh's Word.

Ibn 'Abbas, may Allâh be pleased with them, said, "The Prophet ﷺ was the most generous from among the people, and he was most generous during Ramadhan, when Jibril, peace be upon him, would meet him. Jibril would meet him every night during Ramadhan and study the Qur'ân with him. The Messenger of Allâh ﷺ was more generous with good than the free wind."[2]

His Bravery

He ﷺ added bravery and composure to the quality of generosity; 'Ali, may Allâh be pleased with him, said, "When the fighting would become most violent and intense, we would shield ourselves with the Prophet ﷺ: there would be no one closer to the enemy than him ﷺ."[3]

The caller to truth, especially one commissioned with the task of conveying it, must be brave and composed in proportion to the level of stubbornness and harshness of those whom he calls, and in proportion to the greatness of the truth that he is calling to, and how it goes against the norms and desires of society and against their preconceived beliefs.

---

[1] Recorded by Al-Bukhari (in *Fath Al-Bari*: 10:75) and by Muslim (2:730), and narrated by Anas, may Allâh be pleased with him.

[2] Al-Bukhari

[3] Recorded by Ahmad in *Al-Musnad* (1:156) and Al-Baghawi in *Sharhus-Sunnah* (13:257), from a *Hadith* narrated by 'Ali, may Allâh be pleased with him.

Considering that Allâh Almighty granted bravery and serenity to the heart of Muhammad ﷺ in difficult times, one should not be surprised that the Prophet ﷺ had the greatest share of those qualities, for none were more obstinate in their ways than the Arabs, who were the first to be invited by the Prophet ﷺ. Islam signified an end to their false beliefs; moreover it disparaged their objects of worship. Islam also nullified much of their habits, habits that were contrary to Allâh's *Shari'ah*, for Islam took them away from their desires, so that they could follow the truth and apply it.

The Prophet's *Haya'* (Modesty)

Imam An-Nawawi relates that the scholars define *Haya'* as, "A manner that impels one to abandon that which is lewd and disgusting and prevents one from being negligent in the rights of others."[1]

The Prophet ﷺ was naturally inclined to modesty; the Prophet ﷺ informed us that it is from the manners of Islam, when he ﷺ said:

«لِكُلِّ دِينٍ خُلُقٌ، وَخُلُقُ الْإِسْلَام الْحَيَاءُ»

Every religion has a character, and the character of Islam is *Haya'* (modesty).[2]

In a *Hadith* related by 'Imran bin Husain, the Messenger of Allâh ﷺ said:

«الْحَيَاءُ لَا يَأْتِي إِلَّا بِخَيْرٍ»

Al-Haya' can only result in good.[3]

---

[1] *Riyadhus-Salihin*, Imam An-Nawawi; the chapter on "*Haya'*."

[2] Recorded by Malik in *Al-Muwatta'*: (2:905): from Zaid bin Talhah bin Rukanah from the Prophet ﷺ which is a *Mursal* chain (disconnected at the last chain). Ibn Majah related it in *As-Sunan* (2:1399) from Mu'awiyah bin Yahya, from Az-Zuhri, from Anas, from the Prophet ﷺ, with the wording, "Indeed to every religion is a character..." Yet the scholars of *Hadith* have said that Mu'awiyah bin Yahya As-Sudfi is weak. Ibn Majah related it from another route, from Muhammad bin Sa'id Al-Warraq, from Salih bin Hayan, from Muhammad bn Ka'b Al-Qurazi, from Ibn 'Abbas, from the Prophet ﷺ, with the same wording as in the narration of Anas, may Allâh be pleased with him. But Muhammad bin Sa'id Al-Warraq and Salih bin Hayyan are both weak. And Allâh Almighty knows best.

[3] Al-Bukhari and Muslim

One of the results of having this noble characteristic is that the Prophet ﷺ would not outright say something in the face of another that would cause him harm, so if someone deserved to be scolded, the Prophet ﷺ would advise everyone, without mentioning that person's name. He would generalize, for instance, saying:

«مَا بَالُ أَقْوَام يَشْتَرِطُونَ شُرُوطًا لَيْسَتْ فِي كِتَابِ اللهِ»

What is wrong with people who stipulate conditions that are not found in Allâh's Book![1]

Allâh Almighty Blessed Him With Dignity And Made The Hearts Of People Hold Him In Awe

In spite of the Prophet's humbleness, gentleness, mercy, forbearance, and modesty, he would fill the hearts of people with veneration and awe. With a description of his gathering, it has been related that when he ﷺ would speak, his listeners would bow down their heads (listening attentively and silently) as if there were birds perched on their heads.

Only when he ﷺ would finish his talk would they begin to speak.

Whenever he ﷺ would speak to them, they would remain quiet, listening to him until he finished:

﴿لَّقَدْ كَانَ لَكُمْ فِى رَسُولِ ٱللَّهِ أُسْوَةٌ حَسَنَةٌ﴾

Indeed in the Messenger of Allâh you have a good example to follow...[2]

This verse, although it consists of few words, yet it carries many deep, penetrating meanings. In this verse, you are being guided to follow the way of the Messenger of Allâh ﷺ. It also alludes to the fact that, from the creation, Muhammad ﷺ has the most upright character and way: from the creation, he is most noble in behavior, best in speech, and most superior in deeds.

What Sunnah To Follow In Terms Of His Actions

If we were to contemplate his noble qualities and praiseworthy

---

[1] Al-Bukhari and Muslim; the former related it in *Al-Manaqib* and the latter's narration can be found in (3:1142); the *Hadith* is related by 'Aishah.

[2] (*Al-Ahzab* 33:21)

actions, we would find that they are of two categories:

Regarding the first category, we are not ordered to follow him, either because it is a matter in which we have no choice because it is a blessing from the Creator, such as his handsome face, his noble lineage, his eloquent speech – or because it is from those matters that are specific to the Prophet ﷺ – for example, him being allowed to have nine wives at one time – or because it is a matter that has to do with habits and inclinations, matters in which we can perceive no order, command, or legislation – such as the way he sat or stood on certain occasions, his preference for certain kinds of foods, his dislike for other kinds of foods – for he refused to eat a lizard when it was presented to him, while he also said:

«لَيْسَ بِحَرَامٍ، وَلَكِنْ لَمْ يَكُنْ بِأَرْضِ قَوْمِي فَأَجِدُنِي أَعَافُهُ»

It is not forbidden, but it is not from the food of the land of my people, so I find myself repulsed by it.[1]

From the Prophet's actions that are from the above category, though following him in certain cases may be permissible, doing so is not prescribed, and does not fall under the general meaning of this verse:

﴿لَّقَدْ كَانَ لَكُمْ فِى رَسُولِ ٱللَّهِ أُسْوَةٌ حَسَنَةٌ﴾

Indeed in the Messenger of Allâh you have a good example to follow.[2]

This verse orders us to follow the Messenger of Allâh ﷺ in situations and actions that are related to choice, not in matters wherein habits are concerned. We also must follow the Prophet ﷺ in all other matters, unless there is a clear proof indicating that that matter is from those rulings that are specific for him ﷺ.

We must follow the Prophet ﷺ in those actions of worship that he ﷺ performed, seeking closeness to Allâh.

Therefore, this requires that we research those acts of worship that

---

[1] Al-Bukhari, the Book of Food, chapter nos. 10 and 14, and in the Book of Slaughtering, chapter no 33; Muslim (3:1543), in a *Hadith* related by Ibn 'Abbas, may Allâh be pleased with them.

[2] (*Al-Ahzab* 33:21)

he ﷺ would perform, seeking closeness to the Creator – acts such as the prayer, fasting, *Hajj*, remembrance, and we must also consider the way in which those acts were performed, their times, and the extent to which the Prophet ﷺ strived to perform them.

By searching out for those matters and actions, a Muslim protects himself from perpetrating acts of innovation, from performing acts of worship during times when they are not legislated, or from becoming extravagant in the religion.

Innovations only crept into the religion at the hands of those who did not study the biography and Sunnah of the Prophet ﷺ; or at least they did not study it in a way that allowed them to distinguish between false acts of worship and correct ones.

Examples Of When The Messenger of Allâh ﷺ Is To Be Followed

We must follow the Prophet's attitude and forbearance in dealing with the struggles of life; also, in the patience he displayed, patience that, without shaking itself, would shake firm mountains.

The upright believers from the early and later generations of Islam followed him regarding the above-mentioned qualities. When faced with calamity - such as loss of wealth or the death of one's child, they were examples of patience and resolution.

When the Prophet ﷺ called others to the truth, he ﷺ had to face resistance, stubbornness, and scorn, yet he ﷺ was patient, and so should we be when calling others to Islam.

Despite having such harms inflicted upon him by the polytheists of Makkah, the Prophet's determination did not diminish in the least.

A broken tooth, fracture, and injury on his lower lip – these were the Prophet's injuries during the Battle of Uhud; with his injuries, he prayed *Zuhr* in a seated position, and on the next day he called out when setting out to search for the enemies, saying:

«لَا يَخْرُجْ مَعَنَا إِلَّا أَحَدٌ حَضَرَ بِالْأَمْسِ»

No one may accompany us except he who attended (the battle) yesterday.

The study of these aspects of the Prophet's biography should serve to elevate the determination and resolution of religious scholars and callers to the truth, because they will then make Allâh's pleasure and the victory of truth and virtue to be the goals after which they strive in their lives.

We must follow the Prophet ﷺ in the way he dealt with individuals and groups, for he was gentle and generous when calling them to the truth, to the different paths of doing good, and to the ways that lead to happiness.

The study of these aspects of the Prophet's biography should open the way for the keen student, so that he learns how to conquer the hearts of people – regardless of whether they are in the higher or lower ranks of society, and regardless of where they are from.

Moreover, one learns how to govern and rectify souls that are prisoners of their desires, by returning them to a pure and virtuous life.

The keen observer will find that when one calls to the truth, one cannot be successful in spreading his message unless he follows the guidance of the Prophet ﷺ, for his dealings serve as a standard, even in his dealings with his opponents or enemies.

We must also follow the Prophet ﷺ in the way he ﷺ would reciprocate harm with forgiveness; he ﷺ would do so even though he was able to inflict harm in return.

Whoever studies this aspect of the Prophet's biography will be amazed at the number of times he ﷺ displayed the noble quality of forgiveness.

Add to the quality of forgiveness when individually harmed, the quality of firm resolution when one of Allâh's boundaries was transgressed. 'Aishah, may Allâh be pleased with her, said, "The Messenger of Allâh ﷺ never took revenge for himself; the only time he would seek retribution is when one of Allâh's inviolable boundaries was violated." And in a similar narration, "But when one of Allâh's forbidden boundaries was transgressed, he would seek retribution for Allâh."[1] This saying guides Muslims to

---

[1] Al-Bukhari, in the Book of *Al-Manaqib*, chapter no. 3, Manners, chapter no. 80, *Al-Hudood*, chapter no. 10. Also related by Muslim (4:1813). The *Hadith* is narrated by 'Aishah, may Allâh be pleased with her.

following the Prophet's way, the way of the best of creation. And this requires from us that we research his Sunnah and his biography, to learn his ways, and moreover, to apply them in our life. While making such a research, the Muslim appreciates the pinnacle of human excellence in the Prophet ﷺ, and by following him in performing good deeds, the Muslim achieves a good life in this world and in the Hereafter.

Islamic Manners And Characteristics

Good Manners

Thus does Allâh Almighty describe His Prophet, Muhammad ﷺ:

$$﴿ وَإِنَّكَ لَعَلَى خُلُقٍ عَظِيمٍ ﴾$$

And verily, you (O Muhammad ﷺ) are on an exalted standard of character.[1]

The Prophet ﷺ said:

«أَكْمَلُ الْمُؤْمِنِينَ إِيمَاناً، أَحْسَنُهُمْ خُلُقاً»

The believer with the most complete faith is he who has the best manners.[2]

He also said:

«إِنَّ الْمُؤْمِنَ لَيُدْرِكُ بِحُسْنِ خُلُقِهِ دَرَجَةَ الصَّائِمِ الْقَائِمِ»

Indeed, through his good manners, the believer reaches the ranking of the one who fasts and stands (in the night for prayer).[3]

Forbearance, Deliberateness, Gentleness, And Forgiveness

Allâh Almighty says:

$$﴿ وَالْكَاظِمِينَ الْغَيْظَ وَالْعَافِينَ عَنِ النَّاسِ ﴾$$

Those who repress anger and who pardon men.[4]

And:

$$﴿ خُذِ الْعَفْوَ وَأْمُرْ بِالْعُرْفِ وَأَعْرِضْ عَنِ الْجَاهِلِينَ ﴾$$

Show forgiveness, enjoin what is good, and turn away from the foolish.[5]

And:

---

[1] (*Al-Qalam* 68:4)

[2] At-Tirmithi, who said the *Hadith* is *Hasan Sahih*.

[3] Abu Dawud and Ibn Hibban who declared it to be authentic.

[4] (*Aal 'Imran* 3:134)

[5] (*Al-A'raf* 7:199)

﴿وَلْيَعْفُوا۟ وَلْيَصْفَحُوٓا۟ أَلَا تُحِبُّونَ أَن يَغْفِرَ ٱللَّهُ لَكُمْ﴾

Let them pardon and forgive. Do you not love that Allâh should forgive you? [1]

The Prophet ﷺ said to the head of the delegation of 'Abdul-Qais:

«إِنَّ فِيكَ خَصْلَتَيْنِ يُحِبُّهُمَا اللهُ: الْحِلْمُ وَالْأَنَاةُ»

Indeed, in you are two qualities that Allâh loves: forbearance and deliberateness.[2]

And in another *Hadith*, he ﷺ said:

«مَنْ يُحْرَم الرِّفْقَ، يُحْرَم الْخَيْرَ كُلَّهُ»

Whoever is deprived of gentleness is deprived of good in its entirety.[3]

Truthfulness

Allâh Almighty says:

﴿يَٰٓأَيُّهَا ٱلَّذِينَ ءَامَنُوا۟ ٱتَّقُوا۟ ٱللَّهَ وَكُونُوا۟ مَعَ ٱلصَّٰدِقِينَ﴾

O you who believe! Be afraid of Allâh, and be with those who are true (in words and deeds).[4]

And the Prophet ﷺ said:

«إِنَّ الصِّدْقَ يَهْدِي إِلَى الْبِرِّ، وَإِنَّ الْبِرَّ يَهْدِي إِلَى الْجَنَّةِ، وَإِنَّ الرَّجُلَ لَيَصْدُقُ حَتَّى يُكْتَبَ عِنْدَ اللهِ صِدِّيقاً . . . »

Indeed, truthfulness leads to righteousness, and righteousness leads to Paradise; and a man continues to speak the truth until he is written with Allâh as a truthful one...[5]

Trusts, Fulfilling Contracts And Treaties, And Being Just Among People

Allâh Almighty says:

---

[1] (*An-Nur* 24:22)
[2] Muslim
[3] Muslim
[4] (*At-Tawbah* 9:119)
[5] Agreed upon

﴿إِنَّ ٱللَّهَ يَأْمُرُكُمْ أَن تُؤَدُّواْ ٱلْأَمَٰنَٰتِ إِلَىٰٓ أَهْلِهَا وَإِذَا حَكَمْتُم بَيْنَ ٱلنَّاسِ أَن تَحْكُمُواْ بِٱلْعَدْلِ﴾

Verily! Allâh commands that you should render back the trusts to those to whom they are due; and that when you judge between men, you judge with justice.[1]

And Allâh Almighty says:

﴿وَلَا تَقْرَبُواْ مَالَ ٱلْيَتِيمِ إِلَّا بِٱلَّتِي هِيَ أَحْسَنُ حَتَّىٰ يَبْلُغَ أَشُدَّهُۥ وَأَوْفُواْ بِٱلْعَهْدِ إِنَّ ٱلْعَهْدَ كَانَ مَسْـُٔولًا ٣٤ وَأَوْفُواْ ٱلْكَيْلَ إِذَا كِلْتُمْ وَزِنُواْ بِٱلْقِسْطَاسِ ٱلْمُسْتَقِيمِ ذَٰلِكَ خَيْرٌ وَأَحْسَنُ تَأْوِيلًا﴾

And come not near to the orphan's property except to improve it, until he attains the age of full strength. And fulfil (every) covenant. Verily! the covenant, will be questioned about. And give full measure when you measure, and weigh with a balance that is straight. That is good (advantageous) and better in the end.[2]

Allâh Almighty praised the believers, saying:

﴿ٱلَّذِينَ يُوفُونَ بِعَهْدِ ٱللَّهِ وَلَا يَنقُضُونَ ٱلْمِيثَٰقَ﴾

Those who fulfill the Covenant of Allâh and break not the *Mithaq* (bond, treaty, covenant).[3]

Generosity And Spending One's Wealth For Good Causes

Allâh Almighty says:

﴿وَمَا تُنفِقُواْ مِنْ خَيْرٍ فَلِأَنفُسِكُمْ وَمَا تُنفِقُونَ إِلَّا ٱبْتِغَآءَ وَجْهِ ٱللَّهِ وَمَا تُنفِقُواْ مِنْ خَيْرٍ يُوَفَّ إِلَيْكُمْ وَأَنتُمْ لَا تُظْلَمُونَ﴾

And whatever you spend in good, it is for yourselves, when you spend not except seeking Allâh's Face. And whatever you spend in good, it will be repaid to you in full, and you shall not

---

[1] (*An-Nisa'* 4:58)
[2] (*Al-Isra'* 17:34,35)
[3] (*Ar-Ra'd* 13:20)

be wronged. [1]

And Allâh Almighty praised the believers, saying:

﴿وَيُطْعِمُونَ ٱلطَّعَامَ عَلَىٰ حُبِّهِ مِسْكِينًا وَيَتِيمًا وَأَسِيرًا﴾

And they give food, in spite of their love for it (or for the love of Him), to the *Miskin* (needy), the orphan, and the captive,[2]

The way of one who follows the Prophet ﷺ in his generosity is such that he spends any wealth he has remaining with him for a good cause. One of the Prophet's Companions, Jabir, may Allâh be pleased with him, said, "It never happened that the Prophet ﷺ was asked and his reply was 'no.'" The Prophet ﷺ especially encouraged us to honor and show generosity to our guest, when he ﷺ said:

«مَنْ كَانَ يُؤْمِنُ بِاللهِ وَالْيَوْم الآخِرِ فَلْيُكْرِمْ ضَيْفَهُ»

Whoever believes in Allâh and the Last Day, then let him honor his guest.[3]

Patience

Allâh Almighty says:

﴿وَبَشِّرِ ٱلصَّـٰبِرِينَ﴾

And give glad tidings to *As-Sabirin* (the patient ones, etc.).[4]

And:

﴿إِنَّمَا يُوَفَّى ٱلصَّـٰبِرُونَ أَجْرَهُم بِغَيْرِ حِسَابٍ﴾

Only those who are patient shall receive their rewards in full, without reckoning.[5]

The Prophet ﷺ said:

«الصَّبْرُ ضِيَاءٌ»

Patience is illumination.[6]

---

[1] (*Al-Baqarah* 2:272)
[2] (*Al-Insan* 76:8)
[3] Al-Bukhari (5:205)
[4] (*Al-Baqarah* 2:155)
[5] (*Az-Zumar* 39:10)
[6] Muslim

And he ﷺ said,

«وَمَنْ يَتَصَبَّرْ يُصَبِّرْهُ اللّٰهُ، وَمَا أُعْطِيَ أَحَدٌ عَطَاءً خَيْرًا وَأَوْسَعَ مِنَ الصَّبْرِ»

Whoever strives to be patient, Allâh makes him become patient, and no one was granted a better and more spacious favor than patience.[1]

Allâh Almighty says:

﴿ وَٱخْفِضْ جَنَاحَكَ لِلْمُؤْمِنِينَ ﴾

And lower your wings for the believers (be courteous to the fellow-believers).[2]

In another *Hadith*, the Prophet ﷺ said:

«إِنَّ اللهَ أَوْحَى إِلَيَّ أَنْ تَوَاضَعُوا حَتَّى لَا يَفْخَرَ أَحَدٌ عَلَى أَحَدٍ، وَلَا يَبْغِي أَحَدٌ عَلَى أَحَدٍ»

Indeed, Allâh has inspired me that you should be humble toward one another until not one of you is proud over another, and not one of you wrongs another.[3]

In yet another *Hadith*, the Prophet ﷺ said:

«وَمَا تَوَاضَعَ أَحَدٌ لله إِلَّا رَفَعَهُ»

No one behaves humbly for Allâh except that He raises him.[4]

The Trust

Allâh Almighty says:

﴿ إِنَّ ٱللَّهَ يَأْمُرُكُمْ أَن تُؤَدُّوا۟ ٱلْأَمَٰنَٰتِ إِلَىٰٓ أَهْلِهَا وَإِذَا حَكَمْتُم بَيْنَ ٱلنَّاسِ أَن تَحْكُمُوا۟ بِٱلْعَدْلِ ﴾

Verily! Allâh commands that you should render back the trusts to those to whom they are due; and that when you judge

---

[1] Al-Bukhari and Muslim
[2] (*Al-Hijr* 15:88)
[3] Recorded by Muslim.
[4] Muslim

between men, you judge with justice.[1]

The Prophet ﷺ said:

«آيَةُ الْمُنَافِقِ ثَلَاثٌ: إِذَا حَدَّثَ كَذَبَ، وَإِذَا وَعَدَ أَخْلَفَ، وَإِذَا اؤْتُمِنَ خَانَ»

The signs of the hypocrite are three: when he speaks, he lies; when he promises, he breaks his promise; and when he is trusted, he betrays.[2]

Al-Haya' (Modesty)

The Messenger of Allâh ﷺ said:

«الْحَيَاءُ لَا يَأْتِي إِلَّا بِخَيْرٍ»

Al-Haya' brings good only.[3]

In another *Hadith*, he ﷺ said:

«وَالْحَيَاءُ شُعْبَةٌ مِنَ الْإِيمَانِ»

Al-Haya' is one of the branches of faith.[4]

Good Speech And A Smiling Face

Allâh Almighty says:

﴿وَلَوْ كُنتَ فَظًّا غَلِيظَ ٱلْقَلْبِ لَٱنفَضُّوا۟ مِنْ حَوْلِكَ﴾

And had you been severe and harsh hearted, they would have broken away from about you.[5]

The Prophet ﷺ said:

«اتَّقُوا النَّارَ وَلَوْ بِشِقِّ تَمْرَةٍ، فَمَنْ لَمْ يَجِدْ فَبِكَلِمَةٍ طَيِّبَةٍ»

Protect yourselves from the Fire, even if it is with part of a date. And whosoever cannot find (even that), then with a good word.[6]

---

[1] (*An-Nisa'* 4:58)
[2] Agreed upon
[3] Agreed upon
[4] Agreed upon
[5] (*Aal 'Imran* 3:159)
[6] Agreed upon

He ﷺ also said:

«وَالْكَلِمَةُ الطَّيِّبَةُ صَدَقَةٌ»

The good word is charity.[1]

Dutifulness To Parents And Joining Ties With Relations

Allâh Almighty says:

﴿وَقَضَىٰ رَبُّكَ أَلَّا تَعْبُدُوٓا۟ إِلَّآ إِيَّاهُ وَبِٱلْوَٰلِدَيْنِ إِحْسَٰنًا إِمَّا يَبْلُغَنَّ عِندَكَ ٱلْكِبَرَ أَحَدُهُمَآ أَوْ كِلَاهُمَا فَلَا تَقُل لَّهُمَآ أُفٍّ وَلَا تَنْهَرْهُمَا وَقُل لَّهُمَا قَوْلًا كَرِيمًا ۝ وَٱخْفِضْ لَهُمَا جَنَاحَ ٱلذُّلِّ مِنَ ٱلرَّحْمَةِ وَقُل رَّبِّ ٱرْحَمْهُمَا كَمَا رَبَّيَانِى صَغِيرًا﴾

And your Lord has decreed that you worship none but Him. And that you be dutiful to your parents. If one of them or both of them attain old age in your life, say not to them a word of disrespect, nor shout at them but address them in terms of honor. And lower unto them the wing of submission and humility through mercy, and say: "My Lord! Bestow on them Your Mercy as they did bring me up when I was small."[2]

Ibn Mas'ud, said, "I asked the Prophet ﷺ, which deed is most beloved to Allâh Almighty? He ﷺ said:

«الصَّلَاةُ عَلَى وَقْتِهَا»

'Prayer in its time.'

I asked, 'Then what?' He said:

«بِرُّ الْوَالِدَيْنِ»

'Being dutiful to one's parents....' "[3]

The Prophet ﷺ also said:

«مَنْ أَحَبَّ أَنْ يُبْسَطَ لَهُ فِي رِزْقِهِ، وَيُنْسَأَ لَهُ فِي أَثَرِهِ، فَلْيَصِلْ رَحِمَهُ»

Whoever loves that his sustenance should be made abundant

---

[1] Agreed upon

[2] (*Al-Isra'* 17:23,24)

[3] Agreed upon

and that his life should be prolonged, then let him join ties with his relations.[1]

Honoring the sacredness of Muslims, showing mercy and compassion to them, mutually advising one another to what is good and right, cooperating in piety and righteousness, forgiving others, spending generously for good causes, turning away from the ignorant ones, forbearing hardship, avoiding what may be permissible from the fear that it might lead to the unlawful, leaving doubtful matters, attending to the rights of one's neighbors, fulfilling the needs of Muslims, making peace between people, being gentle and kind to orphans and to the weak, overlooking the faults of other Muslims, being dignified and calm, being virtuous, fulfilling the trust and promise, showing leniency when buying and selling, preferring others over one's own self. These are only some of the many noble and good qualities of the believer, qualities that Allâh Almighty praised, qualities that the Prophet ﷺ is described with, and qualities which he ﷺ came to complete.

Ihsan: Doing Deeds In A Good Manner[2]

The religion of Islam orders us to do things well, in all of our deeds: those apparent and those hidden. The Arabic word that corresponds to the meaning of doing things well is *Ihsan*. *Ihsan* in worship means that we should purify all of our worship, making it pure for Allâh, and purifying it from *Shirk*, which nullifies worship. We are also ordered to perform *Ihsan* to orphans, the poor, and the needy, which means that we should console them, show compassion to them, bring happiness to them, and perform our duty to them by giving wealth to them as much as we are able. *Ihsan* toward mankind in general means to work to further their state of well-being, both when it relates to this world and the next. *Ihsan* to animals means that we should be gentle with them, not making them carry more than they can bear; it also means that we should generously maintain those animals that are under our care. In general terms, *Ihsan* toward other Muslims means that we should love for good things to happen to them in all circumstances; to strive so that good things happen to Muslims indeed leads to a high rank and status in Islam –

---

[1] Agreed upon
[2] From the book *Daleelul-Muslim*.

it indicates that one has reached a very high level of manners.

Enjoining Good And Forbidding Evil

Enjoining good and forbidding evil is one of the greatest symbols and the strongest of foundations in Islam. Upon it stands the society and the individual. Allâh Almighty says:

﴿كُنتُمْ خَيْرَ أُمَّةٍ أُخْرِجَتْ لِلنَّاسِ تَأْمُرُونَ بِالْمَعْرُوفِ وَتَنْهَوْنَ عَنِ الْمُنكَرِ وَتُؤْمِنُونَ بِاللَّهِ وَلَوْ ءَامَنَ أَهْلُ الْكِتَبِ لَكَانَ خَيْرًا لَّهُمْ مِّنْهُمُ الْمُؤْمِنُونَ وَأَكْثَرُهُمُ الْفَسِقُونَ﴾

You are the best of peoples ever raised up for mankind; you enjoin *Al-Ma'ruf* (i.e., Islamic Monotheism and all that Islam has ordained) and forbid *Al-Munkar* (polytheism, disbelief and all that Islam has forbidden), and you believe in Allâh. And had the People of the Scripture (Jews and Christians) believed, it would have been better for them; among them are some who have faith, but most of them are *Al-Fasiqun* (disobedient to Allâh – and rebellious against Allâh's Command).[1]

Allâh Almighty describes the Muslims thus – as the highest and most advanced society, because of the noble characteristics and high manners that they are adorned with, not to mention their truthful fervor to safeguard and honor the truth. The righteous and guided society is that society whose individuals work together to promote the truth, combining their efforts to ward off evil, to banish the wicked, to hold the foolish one accountable for his deeds. Allâh Almighty says:

﴿وَلْتَكُن مِّنكُمْ أُمَّةٌ يَدْعُونَ إِلَى الْخَيْرِ وَيَأْمُرُونَ بِالْمَعْرُوفِ وَيَنْهَوْنَ عَنِ الْمُنكَرِ وَأُوْلَئِكَ هُمُ الْمُفْلِحُونَ﴾

Let there arise out of you a group of people inviting to all that is good (Islam), enjoining *Al-Ma'ruf* (i.e., Islamic Monotheism and all that Islam orders one to do) and forbidding *Al-Munkar* (polytheism and disbelief and all that Islam has forbidden). And it is they who are the successful.[2]

---

[1] (*Aal 'Imran* 3:110)
[2] (*Aal 'Imran* 3:104)

Meanwhile, Allâh Almighty reproached the society in which evil is rampant, in which wicked deeds are the norm – a society that boasts the most ridiculous of customs. Their zeal to protect the true religion is dead; of them, Allâh Almighty says:

﴿لُعِنَ ٱلَّذِينَ كَفَرُواْ مِنۢ بَنِىٓ إِسۡرَٰٓءِيلَ عَلَىٰ لِسَانِ دَاوُۥدَ وَعِيسَى ٱبۡنِ مَرۡيَمَۚ ذَٰلِكَ بِمَا عَصَواْ وَّكَانُواْ يَعۡتَدُونَ ﴿٧٨﴾ كَانُواْ لَا يَتَنَاهَوۡنَ عَن مُّنكَرٍ فَعَلُوهُۚ لَبِئۡسَ مَا كَانُواْ يَفۡعَلُونَ﴾

Those among the Children of Israel who disbelieved were cursed by the tongue of Dawud and 'Iesa son of Maryam. That was because they disobeyed and were ever transgressing beyond bounds. They used not to forbid one another from the *Munkar* (wrong, evildoing, sins, polytheism, disbelief, etc.) which they committed. Vile indeed was what they used to do.[1]

---

[1] (*Al-Ma'idah* 5:78,79)

The Lawful

To make sure that your supplications are answered, eat and drink from only that which is lawful.

The Rights Of Brotherhood

Abu Hurairah, may Allâh be pleased with him, related the following saying of the Messenger of Allâh ﷺ:

«إِيَّاكُمْ وَالظَّنَّ، فَإِنَّ الظَّنَّ أَكْذَبُ الْحَدِيثِ، وَلَا تَحَسَّسُوا، وَلَا تَجَسَّسُوا، وَلَا تَنَافَسُوا، وَلَا تَحَاسَدُوا، وَلَا تَدَابَرُوا، وَكُونُوا عِبَادَ اللهِ إِخْوَانًا كَمَا أَمَرَكُمْ.. الْمُسْلِمُ أَخُو الْمُسْلِمِ: لَا يَظْلِمُهُ، وَلَا يَخْذُلُهُ، وَلَا يَحْقِرُهُ، التَّقْوَى هَهُنَا، التَّقْوَى هَهُنَا»، وَيُشِيرُ إِلَى صَدْرِهِ، «بِحَسْبِ امْرِىءٍ مِنَ الشَّرِّ أَنْ يَحْقِرَ أَخَاهُ الْمُسْلِمَ، كُلُّ الْمُسْلِمِ عَلَى الْمُسْلِمِ حَرَامٌ: دَمُهُ، وَعِرْضُهُ، وَمَالُهُ، إِنَّ اللهَ لَا يَنْظُرُ إِلَى أَجْسَادِكُمْ، وَلَا صُوَرِكُمْ، وَلَكِنْ يَنْظُرُ إِلَى قُلُوبِكُمْ وَأَعْمَالِكُمْ»

Guard against assumptions, for verily assumptions are the greatest forms of lying in speech. Do not try to seek information about the faults of others; do not spy on others to seek out their faults; do not compete with one another (in boasting worldly achievements); do not be jealous of one another; do not plot against one another; and be Allâh's worshippers, brothers unto one another as He ordered you. The Muslim is the brother of a Muslim: he does not wrong him, forsake him, or look down upon him. *At-Taqwa* (piety and righteousness) is indeed here; *At-Taqwa* is indeed here (As he said this, he pointed to his chest). It is sufficient evil for one to look down upon his brother Muslim. All of the Muslim is sacred to the Muslim: his blood, honor, and wealth. Indeed, Allâh does not look at your bodies or your appearances; rather, He looks at your hearts and deeds.

In another narration:

«لَا تَحَاسَدُوا، وَلَا تَبَاغَضُوا، وَلَا تَجَسَّسُوا، وَلَا تَحَسَّسُوا، وَلَا

تَنَاجَشُوا، وَكُونُوا عِبَادَ اللهِ إِخْوَانًا»

Do not be jealous of one another; do not hate one another; do not spy on one another, do not seek to find out the faults of one another; do not deceitfully outbid one another; and be Allâh's worshippers and brothers unto one another.

In another narration:

«لَا تَقَاطَعُوا، وَلَا تَدَابَرُوا، وَلَا تَبَاغَضُوا، وَلَا تَحَاسَدُوا، وَكُونُوا عِبَادَ اللهِ إِخْوَاناً»

Do not cut off ties with one another, do not plot against one another, do not hate one another, do not be jealous of one another, and be Allâh's worshippers and brothers unto one another.

And in yet another narration:

«وَلَا تُهَاجِرُوا، وَلَا يَبِعْ بَعْضُكُمْ عَلَى بَيعِ بَعْضٍ»

Do not desert one another and let not one of you sell over the sale of another.[1]

---

[1] Muslim related all of the above narrations; Al-Bukhari related most of them.

The Youth And Islamic Manners

Manners for Dealing With Others:[1]

1) Use expressions that portray good manners when talking to others, expressions such as the following:
   - *"Athaabakallâh* (May Allâh reward you)."
   - *"Baarakallâhu Feek* (May Allâh bless you)."
   - *"Hafidhakallâh* (May Allâh protect you)."
   - *"Jazaakallâhu Khairan* (May Allâh reward you well)."
   - *"'Afwan* (Pardon)."

2) Address your elders, showing reverence; for example, saying, "O my uncle,"

3) If someone is of a similar age to yours, address him respectfully, saying, "My brother," or using any other name that is most pleasing to him.

4) When dealing with others and especially upon meeting them, share your smiling face with them.

5) Train yourself to be patient, forgiving, and to abandon the pursuit of revenge, especially when you are able to exact revenge.

6) Respect those who practice a trade and those whose jobs are generally looked down upon as being menial.

7) If you deal with servants or other employees, treat them in a dignified and good way.

8) On Islamic holidays, congratulate others, supplicating for the Muslims to see that holiday again the next year.

9) Make it a habit of yours to be organized and disciplined, especially when making promises to others; and show others your good manners.

10) Do not keep company with those who are wicked.

11) Help your elders and those who need help, and show mercy to the young.

---

[1] *As-Sulook* for the second primary level in the Kingdom of Saudi Arabia.

The Islamic Greeting (*"As-Salaam"*: Greetings Of Peace)

Islamic manners regarding greetings are as follows:

1) The *"Salaam"* should precede all other speech; say, *"As-Salaamu 'Alaikum wa Rahmatullâhi wa Barakaatuhu* (May the peace, mercy, and blessings of Allâh be upon you)."

2) Answer this greeting, for answering the *Salaam* of one who initiates the greeting is compulsory, saying, *"Wa 'Alaikumus-Salaam wa Rahmatullâhi wa Barakaatuhu* (And upon you the peace, mercy, and blessings of Allâh)."

3) Greet all Muslims in the said manner, regardless of whether you know them or not.

4) When you wish to leave the company of an individual or of a group, say, *"As-Salaamu 'Alaikum."*

5) The younger one should initiate the greeting with his elder; the one who is riding should initiate the greeting with the one who is walking; and the one who is walking should initiate the greeting with one who is standing.

6) Greet every Muslim you meet at work, at school, or in the street with the said Islamic greeting, for that is the greeting of the Muslims.

The Rights Of Parents

How I become dutiful to my parents:

1) I initiate the Islamic greeting with them, so if I enter a room that they are in, I say, *"As-Salaamu 'Alaikum wa Rahmatullâhi wa Barakaatuhu."*

2) Before entering a room whose door is shut, I seek their permission first by knocking, saying, *"As-Salaamu 'Alaikum;* may I enter?"

3   Before leaving the home, I first seek their permission. I don't leave unless I have permission to leave.

4) I address my parents in a gentle manner, and I never raise my voice when speaking to them.

5) Whenever I come home with my parents, I let them enter first. And whenever I leave with them, I let them exit the house first.

6) I obey my mother and father's orders, and I listen attentively to them when they speak to me.

7) I do not call them by their names; rather, I say, "My father," or "My mother."

8) I do not begin to eat or drink before they do.

Some Of The Favors That Your Parents Have Done For You

Their favors are many, but here are a few:

1) Your mother carried you in her abdomen for nine months, after which she experienced great pain to give birth to you.

2) Your mother fed you from her milk; she would wash you and clean away your urine and feces.

3) Your father spent his money to raise you, giving you what you wanted in terms of food, drink, clothing, and toys.

4) Both your mother and father strove to keep you in good health.

5) Your mother stayed up nights when you were sick.

6) Your father and mother sent you to a school so that you could learn, so that you could become a righteous individual – one who worships Allâh Almighty based upon sound knowledge – and so that you can become able to earn sustenance in Islamically legislated ways.

Manners When Dealing With One's Neighbors

1) Make it a habit to deal in a good way with your neighbor's children; seek friendship with those of your neighbor's children who are righteous, and avoid wronging them, whether it is with speech or deed.

2) Never damage or harm any of your neighbor's possessions – for example, his car or lights.

3) Do not disturb them with screaming, with a loud voice, with a radio or tape-recorder.

4) Do not play with a ball in the house (or apartment) if doing so disturbs your neighbors or results in the destruction of furniture.

5) Don't place garbage in front of your neighbor's house.

6) Visit your neighbors and participate with them in both festive and sad occasions.

7) Visit your neighbors when they are sick: comfort them and supplicate for them.

8) Do not spy, seeking to find out your neighbor's secrets; even if you happen to find out one of their secrets, reveal them to no one.

9) Do not look into your neighbor's house or the house of anyone nearby by standing on the roof or by looking through your windows.

Manners Related To Looking After Specific And General Property

By specific property, I mean possessions such as your car, books, your family's wealth, as well as the property of others, such as your neighbor's car or one of your friend's possessions.

By general property, I refer to parks, streets, schools, streetlight poles, payphones, *Masjids*, and so on.

Manners Related To Looking After Specific Property:

1) Do not tear, destroy, or mutilate your books.

2) Do not be negligent in the upkeep of your books. When reading a book, do not bend it.

3) Take special care to maintain those books that contain the remembrance of Allâh Almighty, and in no way whatsoever should you debase such books.

4) Take care of your toys; don't break them and don't deal with them in such a way as may cause them to break or to become ruined; nor should you lend them to one who is likely to break them.

5) Take care of your clothes; don't tear them or make them dirty, nor should you play with your clothes in a manner that may cause damage to them. Do not write on them, and do not sit on dirty places.

Manners Related To Looking After General Property:

1) Do not write on walls – not in your home, in school, in class, in the *Masjid*, in a park, or on the side of a road.

2) Do not harm trees in your garden, in the street, or in the park.

3) Help maintain trees by watering them, or by trimming them, making them look beautiful.

4) Always return lost property to the rightful owner.

5) Help maintain public possessions, such as the payphone and the streetlight post.

6) Be gentle with animals and birds; do not harm them or their homes in any way, and do not take their young ones from them. Furthermore, do not hunt animals unless you do so for food.

7) Help maintain a decent level of cleanliness in public places, such as schools, streets, parks, and *Masjids*.

8) Always throw your garbage in garbage cans or the like, and not onto the road, sidewalk, or grass.

Manners Regarding Food And Drink

1) Say, *"Bismillâh* (In the Name of Allâh)" before eating and drinking.

2) Sit in an upright position when eating.

3) Eat that which is closest to you.

4) Say, *"Al-Hamdulillâh* (All praise and thanks are for Allâh)," after finishing a meal.

5) Treat food in a dignified way and do not find fault with food that is served to you.

6) Stay away from harmful foods.

7) Preserve food in clean places.

8) While others are eating, do not stare at them.

9) Do not make any movements that might cause others to become disgusted, such as speaking with your mouth full with food.

10) Share your food with a companion who has no food with him.

11) Do not completely fill yourselves: one-third for breathing, one-third for drinking, and one-third for eating.

12) Do not drink from the mouth of large containers, faucets, or coolers.

13) Do not take paper that has writing on it and then use it as a tablecloth, for it may contain honored writing, such as the

remembrance of Allâh Almighty, verses of the Qur'ân, or sayings of the Prophet ﷺ.

14) When drinking from a container, do not breathe into it.

15) Take small morsels when eating.

16) Wash your hands before eating.

17) Eat with your right hand.

18) With water and soap, wash your hands and mouth after eating.

Manners That Relate To Cleanliness

1) Take showers, especially on Fridays before the *Jumu'ah* prayer.

2) Wash your hands and mouth both before and after partaking of a meal.

3) Use *Siwak* and use a toothbrush.

4) Clip your nails on a regular basis.

5) Cut your hair and wash it frequently.

6) Maintain your clothes and wash them.

7) Take care of your dress clothing, taking it off at home, instead wearing something casual.

8) Do not take a shower in a flood, a dirty pond, or in a swamp.

9) Do not use other people's toothbrushes or towels.

10) When you are sneezing or if you have a cold, use a tissue or something similar, and place your hand over your mouth when you yawn.

11) Avoid blowing your noise or spitting in front of others.

12) Use washrooms properly, helping to keep them clean.

13) Do not write on the wall, on a chair, on a table, or on your body.

14) Do not waste water or electricity.

15) Always throw garbage into the place allotted for it.

16) Do not urinate in a standing position.

17) Do not play with your mouth or nose in front of others.

18) Use water and tissues to clean your mouth and nose.

Manners Related To Relieving Yourself

1) When you enter the washroom, let your left leg proceed,

because it is a filthy place (and because the right side is honored in Islam).

2) Before entering a place to relieve yourself, say, "In the Name of Allâh. O Allâh, I take refuge with You from all evil and evildoers."

3) As you are relieving yourself, do not speak and make sure that no one can see your private parts.

4) After you have finished urinating or defecating, purify yourself with water.

5) When you leave the washroom, let your right leg precede, saying, "I ask You (O Allâh) for forgiveness."

6) After purifying yourself from waste matter, wash your hands using soap.

Manners Related To Joking

1) Do not go to the extreme of joking too often.

2) Avoid using gestures or speech in an insulting or obscene manner.

3) Avoid joking with someone who doesn't appreciate your jokes, or merely doesn't want to participate in them.

4) While you are joking, do not utter a lie.

5) Just to get a laugh, do not make fun of others, mentioning their faults.

6) Avoid joking in the classroom, in the *Masjid*, or with your elders.

7) Abstain from joking if that is demanded of you.

8) In joking, follow the guidance of the Prophet ﷺ.

9) Be wary of what results from insulting jokes – for example, hatred, rancor, and enmity.

Manners Related To Participating In A Gathering

1) Both when entering and when leaving a gathering, you should give the Islamic greeting (i.e., *Salaam*).

2) Make space for others, and do not be the cause of another sitting uncomfortably.

3) Smile in the faces of those who are present.

4) Do not raise your voice in a manner that may annoy or harm

others.

5) Sit in a respectful manner, and do not sit in places that are either explicitly or implicitly reserved for elders.

6) Abstain from cutting others off while they are talking; rather, wait until they complete their speech.

7) Do not allow for your gathering to be void of the remembrance of Allâh Almighty and blessings upon the Prophet ﷺ.

8) Sit in beneficial and good gatherings, avoiding evil ones.

9) In a gathering, avoid making those movements that may annoy others or disgust them.

10) If the gathering is in a private home, for instance, do not go through the private possessions of the owner, unless he first gives you permission.

11) As a gathering breaks up, make the supplication for expiation of sins.

Manners Of The Tongue

1) Always speak the truth and abstain from lying.

2) Always speak good, honorable, and permissible words, avoiding obscene and lewd speech.

3) Use your tongue to frequently remember Allâh Almighty.

4) Do not speak of the faults of others.

5) Abstain from backbiting and spreading rumors from one person to another with the intention of sowing dissension among them.

6) Do not use your tongue to disparage or mock others.

Manners That Relate To Clothing

1) Wear clean clothes and always maintain their cleanliness.

2) First, avoid wearing strange attire, attire that no one else wears, and attire that makes you stand out. Second, if you are a man, avoid wearing clothing that is specific to women, and vice versa.

3) Be careful not to copy non-Muslims in their attire.

4) Do not overburden your father by demanding expensive clothing.

5)   Do not be extravagant when buying clothes; after you have bought what is necessary at a reasonable price, give what remains to charity.

6)   Take care of your clothes; do not allow for rips or tears to occur.

7)   On all occasions – but especially when playing sports, when swimming, or when changing your clothes – make sure that all of your body parts that must be covered Islamically are indeed covered.

8)   When putting on attire or shoes, make the appropriate supplication and always begin with your right side; when removing attire or shoes, always begin with your left side.

9)   Avoid clothing that contains pictures (pictures of animals or humans) or lewd, inappropriate, and forbidden phrases.

10) Avoid tight, transparent, or short clothing, especially concerning the areas of your body that must be covered Islamically.

11) For males specifically: do not allow for your clothing to fall down below the level of your ankles.

Daily Life For The Muslim

1)   Wake up early.

2)   As you are exiting from a state of sleep, make the appropriate supplications for waking up.

3)   Make an effort to observe the *Fajr* prayer and all other obligatory prayers with the congregation in the *Masjid*.

4)   Always adhere to those phrases of remembrance that, based on the Sunnah, you should say in the morning and evening.

5)   Make an effort to recite the Qur'ân daily.

6)   Try to eat breakfast early, and then head to school or work early.

7)   Memorize the Qur'ân and perform all obligatory deeds.

8)   Spend time with your family, especially during meal times.

9)   Help your parents whenever they need help.

10) As long as it is not demanded of you that you disobey Allâh, obey your parents and execute their commands.

11) When playing sports, avoid harming others.

12) Accompany your family whenever they visit relatives.

13) Avoid bad company.

14) Sleep early.

15) Never waste time; rather, find means of spending it productively – for example, fill any free time you may have by reading.

16) Regarding your individual pursuits and goals, first depend upon Allâh, then upon yourself, and not upon others – for instance, for organizing and cleaning your room.

Certain Forbidden Deeds[1]

1. *Shirk*

One who prostrates to other than Allâh Almighty, who supplicates to other than Allâh, who seeks to have a need fulfilled from other than Allâh, who sacrifices a slaughter for other than Allâh, who performs any kind of worship to other than Allâh – one who is guilty of any of the preceding sins has indeed perpetrated *Shirk*, and it makes no difference whether the object of worship is dead or alive, whether it is a grave, a statue, a rock, a tree, an angel, a prophet, a righteous man, an animal, or anything else. Allâh Almighty does not forgive His worshipper for having perpetrated *Shirk* unless he repents and re-enters Islam anew. Allâh Almighty says:

$$﴿إِنَّ ٱللَّهَ لَا يَغْفِرُ أَن يُشْرَكَ بِهِۦ وَيَغْفِرُ مَا دُونَ ذَٰلِكَ لِمَن يَشَآءُ وَمَن يُشْرِكْ بِٱللَّهِ فَقَدِ ٱفْتَرَىٰٓ إِثْمًا عَظِيمًا﴾$$

Verily, Allâh forgives not that partners should be set up with Him in worship, but He forgives except that (anything else) to whom He pleases, and whoever sets up partners with Allâh in worship, he has indeed invented a tremendous sin.[2]

Therefore the Muslim worships Allâh alone, supplicates to Allâh alone, and submits to Allâh alone.

$$﴿قُلْ إِنَّ صَلَاتِى وَنُسُكِى وَمَحْيَاىَ وَمَمَاتِى لِلَّهِ رَبِّ ٱلْعَٰلَمِينَ ۝ لَا شَرِيكَ لَهُۥ وَبِذَٰلِكَ أُمِرْتُ وَأَنَا۠ أَوَّلُ ٱلْمُسْلِمِينَ﴾$$

Say: "Verily, my *Salat* (prayer), my sacrifice, my living, and my dying are for Allâh, the Lord of the *'Alamin* (mankind, jinn and all that exists). He has no partner. And of this I have been commanded, and I am the first of the Muslims."[3]

Another form of *Shirk* is to believe that Allâh has a wife or child - far, far above is Allâh from any of that, for indeed Allâh Almighty says:

---

[1] From *Kitab Deenul-Islam*
[2] (*An-Nisa'* 4:48)
[3] (*Al-An'am* 6:162,163)

﴿قُلْ هُوَ ٱللَّهُ أَحَدٌ ۞ ٱللَّهُ ٱلصَّمَدُ ۞ لَمْ يَلِدْ وَلَمْ يُولَدْ ۞ وَلَمْ يَكُن لَّهُ كُفُوًا أَحَدُۢ﴾

Say: "He is Allâh, (the) One. *Allâhus-Samad* (Allah – the Self-Sufficient Master, Whom all creatures need, He neither eats nor drinks). He begets not, nor was He begotten. And there is none coequal or comparable unto Him."[1]

2. Going to Magicians, Soothsayers And Those Who Claim To Know The Unseen

Both fortune-telling and magic are acts of *Kufr* (disbelief), and a magician can only truly be a magician when he has ties with the devils and when he worships them instead of Allâh. Therefore the Muslim is not permitted to go to magicians or to ask them for anything, nor is it permitted for the Muslim to believe magicians or fortune-tellers who claim to know the unseen, for example, that such and such incident will occur in the future, regardless of whether they read palms or crystal balls or anything else. Allâh Almighty says:

﴿قُل لَّا يَعْلَمُ مَن فِي ٱلسَّمَٰوَٰتِ وَٱلْأَرْضِ ٱلْغَيْبَ إِلَّا ٱللَّهُ﴾

Say: "None in the heavens and the earth knows the *Ghaib* (Unseen) except Allâh."[2]

And:

﴿عَٰلِمُ ٱلْغَيْبِ فَلَا يُظْهِرُ عَلَىٰ غَيْبِهِۦ أَحَدًا ۞ إِلَّا مَنِ ٱرْتَضَىٰ مِن رَّسُولٍ فَإِنَّهُۥ يَسْلُكُ مِنۢ بَيْنِ يَدَيْهِ وَمِنْ خَلْفِهِۦ رَصَدًا﴾

(He Alone) the All-Knower of the *Ghaib* (Unseen), and He reveals to none His *Ghaib* (Unseen). Except to a Messenger (from mankind) whom He has chosen (He informs him of Unseen as much as He likes), and then He makes a band of watching guards (angels) to march before him and behind him.[3]

---

[1] (*Al-Ikhlas* 112:1-4)

[2] (*An-Naml* 27:65)

[3] (*Al-Jinn* 72:26,27)

3. Oppression And Wrongdoing

Oppression, injustice, wrongdoing – there are many deeds that fall under this category. To wrong oneself falls under this category, and so does wronging others and wronging society. Even wronging one's enemies falls under this category. Allâh Almighty informed us that He does not like the oppressors (or transgressors). The Messenger of Allâh ﷺ related that Allâh Almighty said:

«قُلْ يَا عِبَادِي إِنِّي حَرَّمْتُ الظُّلْمَ عَلَى نَفْسِي وَجَعَلْتُهُ بَيْنَكُمْ مُحَرَّماً فَلَا تَظَالَمُوا»

...O my worshippers, indeed I have forbidden oppression upon myself and I have made it forbidden among you, so do not oppress (or wrong) one another.[1]

And the Prophet ﷺ said:

«انْصُرْ أَخَاكَ ظَالِمًا أَوْ مَظْلُومًا»

"Aid your brother, be he the wrongdoer or the wronged."

A man asked, "O Messenger of Allâh, I help him when he is wronged, but if he is a wrongdoer, how can I help him?" He ﷺ said:

«تَحْجُرُهُ أَوْ تَمْنَعُهُ مِنَ الظُّلْمِ فَإِنَّ ذَلِكَ نَصْرُهُ»

"You prevent or stop him from wrongdoing, and that is indeed (what is meant by) helping him."[2]

4. Taking a Life, An Act That Allâh Forbade, Except When There Is An Islamic Right

This is one of the greatest of sins; Allâh Almighty promised the one who commits it a severe torment, not to mention a most severe punishment in this world: the murderer is executed, unless the guardians of the murdered forgive him. Allâh Almighty says:

﴿مِنْ أَجْلِ ذَلِكَ كَتَبْنَا عَلَى بَنِي إِسْرَءِيلَ أَنَّهُ مَن قَتَلَ نَفْسًا بِغَيْرِ نَفْسٍ أَوْ فَسَادٍ فِي ٱلْأَرْضِ فَكَأَنَّمَا قَتَلَ ٱلنَّاسَ جَمِيعًا وَمَنْ أَحْيَاهَا فَكَأَنَّمَا

---
[1] Muslim, along with its explanation (16:132)
[2] Al-Bukhari (3:168)

أَحْيَا ٱلنَّاسَ جَمِيعًا وَلَقَدْ جَآءَتْهُمْ رُسُلُنَا بِٱلْبَيِّنَتِ ثُمَّ إِنَّ كَثِيرًا مِّنْهُم بَعْدَ ذَلِكَ فِى ٱلْأَرْضِ لَمُسْرِفُونَ ۝

Because of that We ordained for the Children of Israel that if anyone killed a person not in retaliation of murder, or (and) to spread mischief in the land – it would be as if he killed all mankind, and if anyone saved a life, it would be as if he saved the life of all mankind. And indeed, there came to them Our Messengers with clear proofs, evidences, and signs, even then after that many of them continued to exceed the limits (e.g., by doing oppression unjustly and exceeding beyond the limits set by Allâh by committing the major sins) in the land![1]

And:

﴿وَمَن يَقْتُلْ مُؤْمِنًا مُّتَعَمِّدًا فَجَزَآؤُهُۥ جَهَنَّمُ خَلِدًا فِيهَا وَغَضِبَ ٱللَّهُ عَلَيْهِ وَلَعَنَهُۥ وَأَعَدَّ لَهُۥ عَذَابًا عَظِيمًا﴾

And whoever kills a believer intentionally, his recompense is Hell to abide therein, and the wrath and the curse of Allâh are upon him, and a great punishment is prepared for him.[2]

5. Transgressing Against Others By Wrongfully Taking Their Wealth

Theft, bribery, usurpation, trickery – regardless of which of the preceding methods one uses to wrongfully take the wealth of others, one is committing a great sin, for Allâh Almighty says:

﴿وَٱلسَّارِقُ وَٱلسَّارِقَةُ فَٱقْطَعُوٓا أَيْدِيَهُمَا جَزَآءً بِمَا كَسَبَا نَكَلًا مِّنَ ٱللَّهِ وَٱللَّهُ عَزِيزٌ حَكِيمٌ﴾

Cut off (from the wrist joint) the (right) hand of the thief, male or female, as a recompense for that which they committed, a punishment by way of example from Allâh. And Allâh is All-Powerful, All-Wise.[3]

And Allâh Almighty says:

[1] (*Al-Ma'idah* 5:32)
[2] (*An-Nisa'* 4:93)
[3] (*Al-Ma'idah* 5:38)

$$\lll وَلَا تَأْكُلُوٓا أَمْوَٰلَكُم بَيْنَكُم بِٱلْبَٰطِلِ \ggg$$

And eat up not one another's property unjustly (in any illegal way, e.g., stealing, robbing, deceiving, etc.).[1]

And:

$$\lll إِنَّ ٱلَّذِينَ يَأْكُلُونَ أَمْوَٰلَ ٱلْيَتَٰمَىٰ ظُلْمًا إِنَّمَا يَأْكُلُونَ فِى بُطُونِهِمْ نَارًا وَسَيَصْلَوْنَ سَعِيرًا \ggg$$

Verily, those who unjustly eat up the property of orphans, they eat up only a fire into their bellies, and they will be burnt in the blazing Fire![2]

Islam wages a fierce war against those who wrongfully take the wealth of others, exacting a severe punishment upon those who transgress Allâh's set limits in this regard, those who attack the very foundations of peace and safety in an Islamic society.

6. Cheating, Betrayal, And Treachery

All of the above are forbidden, forbidden in all forms of dealings: in buying, selling, making contracts, and so on. They are base qualities that Islam has categorically forbidden, for Allâh Almighty says:

$$\lll وَيْلٌ لِّلْمُطَفِّفِينَ ① ٱلَّذِينَ إِذَا ٱكْتَالُوا عَلَى ٱلنَّاسِ يَسْتَوْفُونَ ② وَإِذَا كَالُوهُمْ أَو وَّزَنُوهُمْ يُخْسِرُونَ ③ أَلَا يَظُنُّ أُوْلَٰٓئِكَ أَنَّهُم مَّبْعُوثُونَ ④ لِيَوْمٍ عَظِيمٍ ⑤ يَوْمَ يَقُومُ ٱلنَّاسُ لِرَبِّ ٱلْعَٰلَمِينَ \ggg$$

Woe to *Al-Mutaffifin* [those who give less in measure and weight (decrease the rights of others)]. Those who, when they have to receive by measure from men, demand full measure, And when they have to give by measure or weight to men, give less than due. Think they not that they will be resurrected (for reckoning). On a Great Day. The Day when (all) mankind will stand before the Lord of the *'Alamin* (mankind, jinn and all that exists)?[3]

---

[1] (*Al-Baqarah* 2:188)

[2] (*An-Nisa'* 4:10)

[3] (*Al-Mutaffifin* 83:1-6)

The Prophet ﷺ said:

«مَنْ غَشَّنَا فَلَيْسَ مِنَّا»

Whoever cheats us, then he is not from us.

And Allâh Almighty says:

﴿إِنَّ ٱللَّهَ لَا يُحِبُّ مَن كَانَ خَوَّانًا أَثِيمًا﴾

Verily, Allâh does not like anyone who is a betrayer of his trust, and indulges in crime.[1]

7. Wrongfully Attacking The Honor Of Others

It is strictly forbidden in Islam to attack the honor and dignity of others by cursing them, by backbiting them, by spreading rumors about them, by spying on them, by mocking them, and by any other means.

Islam strives to establish a pure and clean society, a society that is built upon love, brotherhood, and cooperation, which is why it fights so fiercely against those social ills that lead to a breakdown in society and that lead to hatred, enmity, and selfishness. Allâh Almighty says:

﴿يَٰٓأَيُّهَا ٱلَّذِينَ ءَامَنُوا۟ لَا يَسْخَرْ قَوْمٌ مِّن قَوْمٍ عَسَىٰٓ أَن يَكُونُوا۟ خَيْرًا مِّنْهُمْ وَلَا نِسَآءٌ مِّن نِّسَآءٍ عَسَىٰٓ أَن يَكُنَّ خَيْرًا مِّنْهُنَّ وَلَا تَلْمِزُوٓا۟ أَنفُسَكُمْ وَلَا تَنَابَزُوا۟ بِٱلْأَلْقَٰبِ بِئْسَ ٱلِٱسْمُ ٱلْفُسُوقُ بَعْدَ ٱلْإِيمَٰنِ وَمَن لَّمْ يَتُبْ فَأُو۟لَٰٓئِكَ هُمُ ٱلظَّٰلِمُونَ ⟨١١⟩ يَٰٓأَيُّهَا ٱلَّذِينَ ءَامَنُوا۟ ٱجْتَنِبُوا۟ كَثِيرًا مِّنَ ٱلظَّنِّ إِنَّ بَعْضَ ٱلظَّنِّ إِثْمٌ وَلَا تَجَسَّسُوا۟ وَلَا يَغْتَب بَّعْضُكُم بَعْضًا أَيُحِبُّ أَحَدُكُمْ أَن يَأْكُلَ لَحْمَ أَخِيهِ مَيْتًا فَكَرِهْتُمُوهُ وَٱتَّقُوا۟ ٱللَّهَ إِنَّ ٱللَّهَ تَوَّابٌ رَّحِيمٌ﴾

O you who believe! Let not a group scoff at another group, it may be that the latter are better than the former; nor let (some) women scoff at other women, it may be that the latter are better than the former, nor defame one another, nor insult one another by nicknames. How bad is it, to insult one's brother after having faith [i.e., to call your Muslim brother (a faithful believer) as: "O sinner", or "O wicked", etc.]. And

---

[1] (*An-Nisa'* 4:107)

whosoever does not repent, then such are indeed wrong-doers. O you who believe! Avoid much suspicions, indeed some suspicions are sins. And spy not, neither backbite one another. Would one of you like to eat the flesh of his dead brother? You would hate it (so hate backbiting). And fear Allâh. Verily, Allâh is the One Who accepts repentance, Most Merciful.[1]

Likewise, Islam wages war against division that is based upon racism or class distinctions: everyone in Islam is equal. The Arab is not superior to the non-Arab and the white man is not superior to the black man, unless one of them is stronger in his religion and piety, and because of these true standards, all compete with one another to perform good deeds. Allâh Almighty says:

$$﴿يَٰٓأَيُّهَا ٱلنَّاسُ إِنَّا خَلَقْنَٰكُم مِّن ذَكَرٍ وَأُنثَىٰ وَجَعَلْنَٰكُمْ شُعُوبًا وَقَبَآئِلَ لِتَعَارَفُوٓاْ إِنَّ أَكْرَمَكُمْ عِندَ ٱللَّهِ أَتْقَىٰكُمْ إِنَّ ٱللَّهَ عَلِيمٌ خَبِيرٌ﴾$$

O mankind! We have created you from a male and a female, and made you into nations and tribes, that you may know one another. Verily, the most honorable of you with Allâh is that (believer) who has *At-Taqwa* [i.e., one of the *Muttaqun* (pious). Verily, Allâh is All-Knowing, All-Aware.[2]

8. Gambling, Drinking Alcohol, And Taking Drugs

Allâh Almighty says:

$$﴿يَٰٓأَيُّهَا ٱلَّذِينَ ءَامَنُوٓاْ إِنَّمَا ٱلْخَمْرُ وَٱلْمَيْسِرُ وَٱلْأَنصَابُ وَٱلْأَزْلَٰمُ رِجْسٌ مِّنْ عَمَلِ ٱلشَّيْطَٰنِ فَٱجْتَنِبُوهُ لَعَلَّكُمْ تُفْلِحُونَ ٩٠ إِنَّمَا يُرِيدُ ٱلشَّيْطَٰنُ أَن يُوقِعَ بَيْنَكُمُ ٱلْعَدَٰوَةَ وَٱلْبَغْضَآءَ فِي ٱلْخَمْرِ وَٱلْمَيْسِرِ وَيَصُدَّكُمْ عَن ذِكْرِ ٱللَّهِ وَعَنِ ٱلصَّلَوٰةِ فَهَلْ أَنتُم مُّنتَهُونَ﴾$$

O you who believe! Intoxicants (all kinds of alcoholic drinks), gambling, *Al-Ansab*, and *Al-Azlam* (arrows for seeking luck or decision) are an abomination of *Shaitan*'s (Satan) handiwork. So avoid (strictly all) that (abomination) in order that you may be successful. *Shaitan* (Satan) wants only to excite enmity and hatred between you with intoxicants (alcoholic drinks) and

---

[1] (*Al-Hujurat* 49:11,12)
[2] (*Al-Hujurat* 49:13)

gambling, and hinder you from the remembrance of Allâh and
from *As-Salat* (the prayer). So, will you not then abstain?[1]

9. Eating Dead Flesh (unslaughtered animals), Blood, Pork, And All Filthy Things That Are Harmful To Man; Also, Eating From That Slaughtering That Was Performed For Other Than Allâh

Allâh Almighty says:

﴿يَـٰٓأَيُّهَا ٱلَّذِينَ ءَامَنُوا۟ كُلُوا۟ مِن طَيِّبَـٰتِ مَا رَزَقْنَـٰكُمْ وَٱشْكُرُوا۟ لِلَّهِ إِن كُنتُمْ
إِيَّاهُ تَعْبُدُونَ ۝ إِنَّمَا حَرَّمَ عَلَيْكُمُ ٱلْمَيْتَةَ وَٱلدَّمَ وَلَحْمَ ٱلْخِنزِيرِ وَمَا أُهِلَّ بِهِۦ
لِغَيْرِ ٱللَّهِ فَمَنِ ٱضْطُرَّ غَيْرَ بَاغٍ وَلَا عَادٍ فَلَآ إِثْمَ عَلَيْهِ إِنَّ ٱللَّهَ غَفُورٌ رَّحِيمٌ﴾

O you who believe! Eat of the lawful things that We have
provided you with, and be grateful to Allâh, if it is indeed He
Whom you worship. He has forbidden you only the *Maytah*
(dead animals), and blood, and the flesh of swine, and that
which is slaughtered as a sacrifice for others than Allâh. But if
one is forced by necessity without wilful disobedience nor
transgressing due limits, then there is no sin on him. Truly,
Allâh is Oft-Forgiving, Most Merciful.[2]

10. Perpetrating Fornication Or Adultery

Fornication is not only forbidden, but it is also from the greatest of
sins; it is a wicked sin that has harmful effects on the character of
society as a whole. Because of this sin, families are lost, one's lineage
is confused and distorted, and the children who are the result of
fornication feel the bitterness of the sin most acutely because of
society's scorn for them when their background is revealed. Allâh
Almighty says:

﴿وَلَا تَقْرَبُوا۟ ٱلزِّنَىٰٓ إِنَّهُۥ كَانَ فَـٰحِشَةً وَسَآءَ سَبِيلًا﴾

And come not near to the unlawful sexual intercourse. Verily,
it is a *Fahishah* [i.e., anything that transgresses its limits (a
great sin)], and an evil way (that leads one to Hell unless Allâh
forgives him).[3]

---

[1] (*Al-Ma'idah* 5:90,91)
[2] (*Al-Baqarah* 2:172,173)
[3] (*Al-Isra'* 17:32)

Fornication causes the spread of destructive sexual diseases as well, diseases that destroy the very roots of society. The Messenger of Allâh ﷺ said:

«مَا انْتَشَرَتِ الْفَاحِشَةُ فِي قَوْم قَطْ حَتَّى يُعْلِنُوا بِهَا إِلَّا فَشَا فِيهِمُ الطَّاعُونُ وَالْأَمْرَاضُ الَّتِي لَمْ تَكُنْ فِي أَسْلَافِهِمْ»

Whenever a most wicked deed spreads among a people until they announce it (or perform it openly), plague and disease spread among them, (plagues and diseases) that were non-existent in the times of those who came before them.[1]

That is why Islam ordered that all routes that lead to fornication must be blocked. Muslims are ordered to lower their gazes, for the forbidden look is the beginning of the road that leads to fornication. Women must cover themselves and wear *Hijab*, so that society is protected from the ill effects of wicked deeds. On the other hand, Islam orders its adherents to marry at an early age; indeed, it promises a great reward for doing that, so that honorable and virtuous families flourish, families that raise the children of today, moulding them so that they become the righteous men of tomorrow.

11. Consuming *Riba* (Usury and Interest)

Riba is one of the greatest of sins: it destroys the economy and it takes wrongful advantage of those who are in need of money, regardless of whether it is the businessman for his business or the poor man for his basic needs.

Basically, usury occurs (at least in one of its forms) when one person lends money to another person for a set period, stipulating that when that period arrives, the person pays a specific amount more than what was originally loaned. Therefore the one making the loan and those like him take advantage of those who are in need of money, forcing them to live a life of debt. Taking advantage of businessmen, and without incurring any risks in case of losses, the usurer takes a percentage over and above profits received. When the business goes down and the businessman is drowned in debt, the usurer will squash him. But had they been partners, both sharing in

---

[1] Ibn Majah (2:1332), and its chain is authentic.

profit and loss, one striving with his wealth the other with his business abilities, the wheels of the economy would continue to turn, but this time, for the benefit of all. Allâh Almighty says:

﴿يَٰٓأَيُّهَا ٱلَّذِينَ ءَامَنُوا۟ ٱتَّقُوا۟ ٱللَّهَ وَذَرُوا۟ مَا بَقِيَ مِنَ ٱلرِّبَوٰٓا۟ إِن كُنتُم مُّؤْمِنِينَ ۝ فَإِن لَّمْ تَفْعَلُوا۟ فَأْذَنُوا۟ بِحَرْبٍ مِّنَ ٱللَّهِ وَرَسُولِهِۦ ۖ وَإِن تُبْتُمْ فَلَكُمْ رُءُوسُ أَمْوَٰلِكُمْ لَا تَظْلِمُونَ وَلَا تُظْلَمُونَ ۝ وَإِن كَانَ ذُو عُسْرَةٍ فَنَظِرَةٌ إِلَىٰ مَيْسَرَةٍ ۚ وَأَن تَصَدَّقُوا۟ خَيْرٌ لَّكُمْ ۖ إِن كُنتُمْ تَعْلَمُونَ﴾

O you who believe! Be afraid of Allâh and give up what remains (due to you) from *Riba* (usury and interest) (from now onward), if you are (really) believers. And if you do not do it, then take a notice of war from Allâh and His Messenger but if you repent, you shall have your capital sums. Deal not unjustly (by asking more than your capital sums), and you shall not be dealt with unjustly (by receiving less than your capital sums). And if the debtor is in a hard time (has no money), then grant him time till it is easy for him to repay, but if you remit it by way of charity, that is better for you if you did but know.[1]

12. Miserliness

This sin indicates the wrong kind of individualism: the extreme love of one's self. The miser hoards his wealth, refusing to give even the compulsory charity to the poor and needy, showing his disdain for society, declining to accept the principles of mutual cooperation and brotherhood, principles that both Allâh and His Messenger ﷺ have ordered us to adopt. Allâh Almighty says:

﴿وَلَا يَحْسَبَنَّ ٱلَّذِينَ يَبْخَلُونَ بِمَآ ءَاتَىٰهُمُ ٱللَّهُ مِن فَضْلِهِۦ هُوَ خَيْرًا لَّهُم ۖ بَلْ هُوَ شَرٌّ لَّهُمْ ۖ سَيُطَوَّقُونَ مَا بَخِلُوا۟ بِهِۦ يَوْمَ ٱلْقِيَٰمَةِ ۗ وَلِلَّهِ مِيرَٰثُ ٱلسَّمَٰوَٰتِ وَٱلْأَرْضِ ۗ وَٱللَّهُ بِمَا تَعْمَلُونَ خَبِيرٌ﴾

And let not those who covetously withhold of that which Allâh has bestowed on them of His bounty (wealth) think that it is good for them (and so they do not pay the obligatory *Zakat*). Nay, it will be worse for them; the things which they

---

[1] (*Al-Baqarah* 2:278-280)

covetously withheld shall be tied to their necks like a collar on the Day of Resurrection. And to Allâh belongs the heritage of the heavens and the earth; and Allâh is Well-Acquainted with all that you do.[1]

13. Lying And Giving False Testimony

The Prophet ﷺ said:

«إِنَّ الْكَذِبَ يَهْدِي إِلَى الْفُجُورِ وَإِنَّ الْفُجُورَ يَهْدِي إِلَى النَّارِ وَلَا يَزَالُ الرَّجُلُ يَكْذِبُ وَيَتَحَرَّى الْكَذِبَ حَتَّى يُكْتَبَ عِنْدَ اللهِ كَذَّاباً»

Indeed, lying leads to wickedness, and indeed wickedness leads to the Fire. And a man continues to lie and search out for opportunities to lie until he is written with Allâh as a liar.[2]

One of the most wicked forms of lying is to give false testimony; the Prophet ﷺ emphasized its evil, warning against its results: He raised his voice, saying to his Companions:

«أَلَا أُنَبِّئُكُمْ بِأَكْبَرِ الْكَبَائِرِ، الشِّرْكُ بِاللهِ وَعُقُوقُ الْوَالِدَيْنِ.»

Shall I not inform you of the greatest of great sins – associating partners with Allâh and being undutiful to one's parents.

He was reclining, and then he sat up and said:

«أَلَا وَقُوْلُ الزُّورِ أَلَا وَشَهَادَةُ الزُّورِ»

Verily, and false speech; verily, and false testimony.[3]

He continued to repeat it in order to warn his nation not to perpetrate it.

14. Haughtiness, Pride, Arrogance, And Vanity

These are all offensive and hated qualities in the religion of Islam. Allâh informed us that he doesn't love the arrogant ones, and in terms of their end in the Hereafter, Allâh Almighty says:

﴿أَلَيْسَ فِي جَهَنَّمَ مَثْوًى لِلْمُتَكَبِّرِينَ﴾

---

[1] (*Aal 'Imran* 3:180)
[2] Al-Bukhari and Muslim (4:2013), in a *Hadith* narrated by Ibn Mas'ud.
[3] Al-Bukhari (3:225)

Is there not in Hell an abode for the arrogant ones?[1]
The arrogant one is hated by Allâh and hated by His creation.

Repentance From Forbidden Deeds

Because you will be held accountable for all of your deeds on the Day of Judgement – being rewarded for good and punished for evil – you should stay away from the grave sins and from all other sins. But if you do perpetrate any sin, you should be quick to repent to Allâh Almighty, asking Him for forgiveness and asking for protection from again falling into evil deeds. True repentance requires you to do the following:

1) To desist from the sin that you are repenting from.
2) To feel remorse for having perpetrated that sin.
3) To make a firm resolve not to return to it.

And there is a fourth condition if the sin you perpetrated involves the rights of others:

4) To return that which you wrongfully took to its owner or to seek forgiveness from the one you wronged.

These are the conditions of a true repentance: if they are met, Allâh will forgive you and not punish you for them. The one who repents from a sin is like he who has no sin. Thereafter, you should continue to ask Allâh for forgiveness; indeed, every Muslim should continually ask for forgiveness, for the grave sins he commits and for the small ones. Allâh Almighty says:

$$﴿فَقُلْتُ ٱسْتَغْفِرُوا۟ رَبَّكُمْ إِنَّهُ كَانَ غَفَّارًا﴾$$

"I said (to them): 'Ask forgiveness from your Lord; Verily, He is Oft-Forgiving'"[2]

When one repents often, he shows one of the characteristics of the true believer; Allâh Almighty says:

$$﴿قُلْ يَٰعِبَادِىَ ٱلَّذِينَ أَسْرَفُوا۟ عَلَىٰٓ أَنفُسِهِمْ لَا تَقْنَطُوا۟ مِن رَّحْمَةِ ٱللَّهِ إِنَّ ٱللَّهَ يَغْفِرُ$$
$$ٱلذُّنُوبَ جَمِيعًا إِنَّهُ هُوَ ٱلْغَفُورُ ٱلرَّحِيمُ ۝ وَأَنِيبُوٓا۟ إِلَىٰ رَبِّكُمْ وَأَسْلِمُوا۟ لَهُ مِن$$
$$قَبْلِ أَن يَأْتِيَكُمُ ٱلْعَذَابُ ثُمَّ لَا تُنصَرُونَ﴾$$

---

[1] (*Az-Zumar* 39:60)
[2] (*Nuh* 71:10)

Say: "O My worshippers who have transgressed against themselves (by committing evil deeds and sins)! Despair not of the mercy of Allâh, verily Allâh forgives all sins. Truly, He is Oft-Forgiving, Most Merciful." And turn in repentance and in obedience with true faith to your Lord and submit to Him, (in Islam), before the torment comes upon you, then you will not be helped.[1]

Some of the More Prevalent Sins that Many People Take Lightly

- To deem lawful that which Allâh has forbidden, or to deem forbidden that which Allâh has made permissible.

- To believe that the stars and planets have some kind of effect on the lives of people.

- To believe that certain things benefit, when in fact the Creator did not make them so.

- To believe in evil omens – because you hear or see something, for example, to believe that evil will befall you; that is a form of *Shirk*.

- Sitting with hypocrites or wicked people, seeking closeness to them or finding comfort in their company.

- Praying without tranquility.

- To make a lot of frivolous, extraneous movements during prayer

- For the follower to precede the *Imam* on purpose during any stage of the prayer.

- To come to the *Masjid* after having eaten onion or garlic or anything else that has a foul odor.

- Without having just cause, for a woman to refuse her husband's desire to have sexual relations.

- For a woman to request divorce from her husband without a valid Islamic reason.

- A practice known in Arabic as *Ath-Thihar*, i.e., for a man to say to his wife, "You are to me like my mother," when he intends to make her forbidden for him: this practice is forbidden based on the Qur'ân, the Sunnah, and *Ijma'* (consensus).

- To have intercourse with one's wife during her monthly period

---

[1] (*Az-Zumar* 39:53,54)

- To have anal sex.
- For you to be unjust with your wives, treating some better than others.
- To be alone with a strange woman, in other words, a woman who is not a *Mahram* (someone who you can never marry, who is also someone you can be alone with) for you.
- For a man to shake hands with a strange woman (i.e. one who is not a *Mahram*).
- As she leaves her home, for a woman to wear perfume, knowing that she will pass by men.
- For a woman to travel without a *Mahram*.
- For a man to look at a strange woman on purpose.
- For one to feel it is okay when one of his relatives (wives or children) fornicates.
- For one to lie about who his parents really are, or for a man to refuse to acknowledge his true son.
- When one is selling a product, to hide its defects.
- For one to bid on a product, intending to raise its price, but not intending to actually purchase it.
- After the second call to Friday prayer is made, to engage in trade
- To give or take bribes.
- To wrongfully usurp property.
- For you to accept a gift when intercession is required from you.
- To receive full services from an employee without paying him his due.
- To give to some of one's children more than to the others.
- Without actually being in need, to ask others for money.
- To seek a loan without intending to pay it back.
- To eat or drink that which is forbidden.
- To use gold and silver utensils or dishes and to eat using them.
- To give false testimony.
- To listen to musical instruments.
- Backbiting, which is to say about your brother that which he dislikes.

- To spread false rumors among people, intending to create dissension between them.
- To look inside the homes of others without their permission.
- When three are present, for two to speak to the exclusion of the third.
- For men to wear gold, regardless of how they wear it.
- For men to let their garments fall down below the level of their ankles.
- For a woman to wear thin, short, tight, or transparent clothing.
- For a man or a woman to attach false hair to the end of their natural hair, regardless whether that false hair is human or otherwise.
- For men to imitate women or vice versa.
- To dye one's hair black.
- To draw that which has a spirit (man or animal); this includes prints on clothes, painting on walls, drawing on paper, sculptures, and so on.
- To lie about one's dreams.
- Sitting or walking on a grave.
- To relieve yourself in a graveyard.
- When you are relieving yourself, for you to not take cover properly, allowing others to see you.
- To listen to other peoples' conversations when they dislike you to do that.
- To deal badly with your neighbor.
- To harm people on purpose in the writing of your will
- Playing dice, a game that relies on chance
- To curse a believer and to curse someone who doesn't deserve to be cursed
- To wail loudly when mourning (or to hire people to wail loudly when someone dies).
- To hit someone on the face; or to stamp someone's face (this includes branding the face of an animal).
- Without a valid Islamic reason, to stop talking to a Muslim for

more than three days.

What should one do immediately upon entering the fold of Islam?

When someone voiced his desire to enter the fold of Islam, the eminent Shaikh Muhammad bin Ibrahim, may Allâh have mercy on him, addressed him and later related what he said to the seeker of truth:

"When I heard what the man said I was very pleased and I congratulated him for this blessing – the blessing of accepting the truth. I praised and thanked Allâh Almighty for guiding him to Islam and I gave him glad tidings of what would result from him accepting Islam. I made him understand that his first obligation was to bear witness to the truth – that none has the right to be worshipped but Allâh, and that Muhammad is the Messenger of Allâh.[1] I told him that he had to absolve himself from every religion that was contrary to the religion of Islam, in terms of beliefs and acts of worship that are performed with speech or action. I continued to explain that he had to apply all obligatory aspects of Islam and that he had to believe that what is permissible is only that which the *Shari'ah* made permissible, and that which is forbidden is only that which the *Shari'ah* made forbidden. Then I explained to him the rest of the pillars of Islam, beginning with the prayer, its pillars, its compulsory elements, and its conditions, among which are the greater and minor state of purity; followed by *Zakat*, fasting, and *Hajj*. I informed him that circumcision is compulsory and that he had to take a shower upon accepting Islam.[2] Furthermore, I conveyed to him that he had to learn all that was obligatory to learn regarding the religion. After I informed him of everything mentioned above, he bore witness with his tongue to the phrase of *Tawhid* in front of me,

---

[1] Al-Imam Ibn Abi Al-'Izz, may Allâh have mercy on him, said in *Sharb Al-'Aqeedah At-Tahawiyyah* (1:23), "Therefore *Tawhid* is the first matter by which one enters Islam, and the last matter upon which one leaves this world."

[2] In *Zadul-Ma'ad*, Ibn Al-Qayyim said, "The most correct opinion in this issue is that it is compulsory for both the one who has been in a state of sexual impurity while he was a disbeliever and for the one who was never in a state of sexual impurity."

saying, 'I bear witness that none has the right to be worshipped but Allâh, and I bear witness that Muhammad is the Messenger of Allâh, whom Allâh sent to all of mankind.' The one who wishes to enter the fold of Islam must change his old name if that name carries implications that are contrary to the *Shari'ah*, such as a name designating him to be a slave to other than Allâh – for example, 'Abdul-Maseeh, or 'Abdul-Husain."[1]

If one wishes to enter the fold of Islam, one must also become circumcised because it is an Islamic obligation; however, one may delay in informing him of that obligation until Islam becomes more strong and stable in his heart.

The Permanent Committee for Scientific Researches and Religious Verdicts made the following ruling:

"Circumcision is compulsory upon men, and it is a noble quality in the case of women. But if one delays in informing someone who wishes to enter Islam about circumcision, waiting for Islam to become stable in his heart, then that is well, especially if he fears that by informing him about circumcision, he will be drawn away from Islam."[2]

As for the one who calls others to Islam, he should follow the guidance of the Prophet ﷺ, showing good manners and patience when dealing with others. The Prophet ﷺ said:

«فَوَاللهِ لَأَنْ يَهْدِيَ اللهُ بِكَ رَجُلًا وَاحِدًا خَيْرٌ لَكَ مِنْ أَنْ يَكُونَ لَكَ حُمْرُ النَّعَم»

By Allâh, for Allâh to guide through you one man is better for you than for you to own red camels.[3]

This book comprises of what one needs to know when entering the fold of Islam, as briefly outlined in Shaikh Muhammad bin Ibrahim's above-mentioned saying. And guidance lies with Allâh Almighty.

---

[1] See *Al-Muntaqa Min Fatawa Ash-Shaikh Al-Fawzan* (2:256)

[2] *Fatawaa Al-Lajnah Ad-Da'imah* (3:275)

[3] Al-Bukhari and Muslim, in a *Hadith* narrated by Sahl bin Sa'd, may Allâh be pleased with him. The references for this *Hadith* have been mentioned in the introduction of the book.

Marriage: Its Fruits And Benefits For The Short And Long Term

Dedication

To all fathers and mothers, sons and daughters, who want to follow the Sunnah of the Prophet ﷺ by lowering their gazes and guarding the purity of their private parts, so that they can become from those who will be displayed and honored on the Day of Judgement.

To all for whom we have dedicated this humble work, we hope that it finds ears that listen, hearts that are attentive, and minds that comprehend, so that Muslim families can be raised, families that are far from falling into the depths of ignominy.

Allâh's Book, His Messenger's Sunnah, and the books of the people of knowledge – from these sources I have drawn advice and guidance in regards to the topic of marriage, its fruits and benefits, both for the short and long term. It is a topic that requires special attention in these times of trial and tribulation, times wherein satellite dishes, television sets, the internet, and magazines pump poison into the minds of men and women in order to lead them astray.

Without a doubt, marriage – after Allâh's help – is an impenetrable fortress, helping one to lower his gaze, to guard the purity of his private parts, to stay away from deviant practices, especially for one who has a sincere intention that is pure for Allâh. Whoever seeks success and happiness through marriage with the intention of pleasing Allâh, then Allâh guides him and opens for him the doors of sustenance, safety, and peace. 'Umar bin Al-Khattab, may Allâh be pleased with him, said, "I am amazed at one who seeks richness, yet does not marry, for Allâh Almighty says:

$$﴿إِن يَكُونُوا فُقَرَآءَ يُغْنِهِمُ ٱللَّهُ مِن فَضْلِهِۦٓ﴾$$

If they be poor, Allâh will enrich them out of His bounty.[1]

I ask Allâh Almighty to grant us sincerity in speech and deed, and understanding as well as firmness upon the right way, for indeed He has the power to answer our supplications. Success lies with Allâh Almighty and it is He Who guides to the straight path.

---

[1] (*An-Nur* 24:32)

Some Factors That Contribute To The Growth Of The Muslim Family

Islam Honors Women

After being disparaged, divested of rights, and downright oppressed in the Days of Ignorance, women found their dignity and honor in Islam. Here are some of the ways in which Islam honors women:

Women are the Counterparts of Men

1. Islam established this when the Prophet ﷺ said:

«إِنَّمَا النِّسَاءُ شَقَائِقُ الرِّجَالِ»

Indeed women are only the counterparts of men.[1]

2. Just as Allâh Almighty gave the wife duties, He also gave her rights in what is reasonable:

﴿وَلَهُنَّ مِثْلُ ٱلَّذِى عَلَيْهِنَّ بِٱلْمَعْرُوفِ﴾

And they (women) have rights (over their husbands as regards living expenses, etc.) similar (to those of their husbands) over them (as regards to obedience and respect, etc.) to what is reasonable.[2]

3. Indeed, Islam bestowed dignity and honor upon the mother, sister, wife, and female relative, giving to each her right.

The Muslim woman wears *Hijab*, covers herself, and is forbidden from imitating men

1. Indeed, Islam ordered believing women to cover themselves and to not show anything from their beauty.

2. The opinion that calls for women to cover their faces is supported by stronger proofs (than the opposing view's proofs) and helps keep people further away from temptation; further-more, it is an opinion that is more in line with the reasoning behind the legislation of *Hijab*, for those who have a sickness in their hearts, first set their gaze on the face of a woman.

---

[1] Abu Dawud
[2] (*Al-Baqarah* 2:228)

3. Islam has strictly forbidden women from imitating men, and men from imitating women.

The Islamic Link Between Men and Women

Marriage is the only Islamic way to building a Muslim family; to establish sexual ties outside of this realm is to perpetrate a great sin indeed, a sin that angers Allâh and His Messenger ﷺ. Islam has effective rulings that not only help prevent one from falling into this sin, but also help prevent one from falling into those matters that lead to it, for indeed, Islam forbids fornication and forbids all sayings or deeds that lead to it. Therefore being alone with a stranger (stranger here means being alone with someone who, Islamically, one is not permitted to be alone with) is forbidden; mixing with strangers from the opposite sex is not permitted, speaking (unnecessarily) to strangers from the opposite sex is not permitted, and for a woman to travel without a *Mahram* is forbidden. It is also forbidden for a fornicating woman to marry until she repents.

How Islam Wants A Woman To Be[1]

1) That she should be strong in her religion, and not swayed by deceptive appearances, appearances that cause weaker souls to stray, because she knows that this world is made up of short-lived pleasures.

2) That she be patient, pleased with Allâh's Decrees for her, always invoking Allâh Almighty for well-being and forgiveness.

3) That she frequently and consistently remember Allâh, obeying Him, reciting His Book, and applying its precepts.

4) That she, along with her husband, raises and trains her children; that she becomes a comfort for her husband, and that she avoids falling into that which Allâh has forbidden.

5) That she be her husband's ally, helping him and encouraging him in his work.

6) That she remains honorable and virtuous, looking only at her husband.

7) That she be educated and cultured; that she gains beneficial knowledge, which she applies and then spreads to her friends.

8) That she be truthful in her life: to her husband, to her self, and to her children.

9) That she be a sincere and true friend to others, cooperating with them in the promotion of truth and good.

---

[1] *Al-Mar'atul-Muslimah,* Wahbi Sulaiman Ghawji, with minor editing.

The Wisdom Behind Marriage And Its Benefits

Islam Encourages Marriage

On many occasions and in different ways Islam encourages its adherents to marry. On one occasion we are told that marriage is from the ways of the Messengers and that those who follow their ways in this world will be resurrected with them in the Hereafter. For the Messengers are the leaders whom we must follow and be guided by – Allâh Almighty says:

﴿وَلَقَدْ أَرْسَلْنَا رُسُلًا مِّن قَبْلِكَ وَجَعَلْنَا لَهُمْ أَزْوَجًا وَذُرِّيَّةً﴾

And indeed We sent Messengers before you, and made for them wives and offspring.[1]

In a *Hadith* related by Abu Ayyub, may Allâh be pleased with him, the Messenger of Allâh ﷺ said:

«أَرْبَعٌ مِنْ سُنَنِ الْمُرْسَلِينَ: الْحَيَاءُ، وَالتَّعَطُّرُ، وَالسِّوَاكُ، وَالنِّكَاحُ»

Four are from the ways (*Sunan*) of the Messengers: *Al-Haya'*, to use fragrant oils, to use the *Siwak*, and to marry.[2]

On another occasion, Allâh mentioned marriage in the sense of it being a blessing and favor:

﴿وَاللَّهُ جَعَلَ لَكُم مِّنْ أَنفُسِكُمْ أَزْوَجًا وَجَعَلَ لَكُم مِّنْ أَزْوَجِكُم بَنِينَ وَحَفَدَةً وَرَزَقَكُم مِّنَ الطَّيِّبَتِ﴾

And Allâh has made for you wives of your own kind, and has made for you, from your wives, sons and grandsons, and has bestowed on you good provision.[3]

The Wisdom And Benefits Related To Marriage Are Many – Here Are Some Of Them

1. By marrying, one obeys the order of Allâh and His Messenger ﷺ, and by obeying Allâh and His Messenger ﷺ, one achieves mercy and success in this world and in the Hereafter.

---

[1] (*Ar-Ra'd* 13:38)
[2] At-Tirmithi and Ahmad
[3] (*An-Nahl* 16:72)

2. Through marriage the Muslim population increases, and through that increase the Islamic nation strengthens. Hence it becomes feared and becomes self-sufficient - that is, if it uses its strength and harnesses it according to Islamic principles.

3. Through marriage the boasting of the Prophet ﷺ on the Day of Judgement is supported. He ﷺ said:

«تَزَوَّجُوا الْوَدُودَ الْوَلُودَ فَإِنِّي مُكَاثِرٌ بِكُمُ الْأُمَمَ»

Marry the loving and fertile, for indeed I shall boast of you before the nations.[1]

4. Through marriage the links and ties between Muslims become stronger, for just as there is relationship through blood there is relationship through marriage:

﴿وَهُوَ ٱلَّذِى خَلَقَ مِنَ ٱلْمَآءِ بَشَرًا فَجَعَلَهُ نَسَبًا وَصِهْرًا ۗ وَكَانَ رَبُّكَ قَدِيرًا﴾

And it is He Who has created man from water, and has appointed for him kindred by blood, and kindred by marriage. And your Lord is Ever All-Powerful to do what He wills.[2]

5. Through marriage one achieves reward if one fulfills the rights of his wife and children, for instance, when he spends on them. The Prophet ﷺ said:

«إِنَّكَ لَنْ تُنْفِقَ نَفَقَةً تَبْتَغِي بِهَا وَجْهَ اللهِ إِلَّا أُجِرْتَ عَلَيْهَا حَتَّى مَاتَجْعَلَ فِي فِي امْرَأَتِكَ»

Indeed, whenever you spend on an expenditure, seeking by it Allâh's Face, you will be rewarded for it – even for what you put in the mouth of your wife.[3]

6. Through marriage, human beings continue to be as a species, until Allâh ends the earth and those who are on it. The Qur'ân here refers to this wonderful wisdom:

﴿وَٱللَّهُ جَعَلَ لَكُم مِّنْ أَنفُسِكُمْ أَزْوَٰجًا وَجَعَلَ لَكُم مِّنْ أَزْوَٰجِكُم بَنِينَ

---

[1] Abu Dawud and An-Nasa'i
[2] (*Al-Furqan* 25:54)
[3] Agreed upon

$$﴿ وَحَفَدَةً وَرَزَقَكُم مِّنَ ٱلطَّيِّبَٰتِ ﴾$$

And Allâh Almighty has made for you wives of your own kind, and has made for you, from your wives, sons and grandsons, and has bestowed on you good provision.[1]

And that is Allâh's Sunnah (way), for which you can find no replacement.

7. Through marriage, one's lineage is preserved, for people are proud when they are ascribed to their fathers. The individual is honored by his parentage. In society, good dealings and cooperation are found to be most prevalent among relatives.

8. Through marriage, society is protected from decadence and decline, because married couples are able to fulfill their most natural desires, desires that they love to fulfill, whereas sexual relations outside of marriage leads not only to social ills, but also to dangerous physical ailments that are all too prevalent today.

9. The married couple finds inner peace that issues from the mutual love, mercy, and compassion between husband and wife. When a husband comes home from work and gathers with his family, he forgets the anxieties and toils of his day; similar is the case for the wife when she gathers with her partner in life. And indeed Allâh is Most Truthful, for in describing the relationship between man and wife, He says:

$$﴿ وَمِنْ ءَايَٰتِهِۦٓ أَنْ خَلَقَ لَكُم مِّنْ أَنفُسِكُمْ أَزْوَٰجًا لِّتَسْكُنُوٓاْ إِلَيْهَا وَجَعَلَ بَيْنَكُم مَّوَدَّةً وَرَحْمَةً إِنَّ فِى ذَٰلِكَ لَءَايَٰتٍ لِّقَوْمٍ يَتَفَكَّرُونَ ٢١ ﴾$$

And among His Signs is this, that He created for you wives from among yourselves, that you may find repose in them, and He has put between you affection and mercy. Verily, in that are indeed signs for a people who reflect.[2]

---

[1] (*An-Nahl* 16:72)
[2] (*Ar-Rum* 30:21)

The Wisdom Behind A Man Being Allowed To Have More Than One Wife In Islam

When Islam legislated that a man could marry more than one wife, it was without doubt for a lofty wisdom, for the general welfare – for the needs of the individual and society. We limit our discussion, then, to the following:

1) The social benefits.
2) The individual benefits.
3) The natural wisdom.

The Social Benefits

1) With women outnumbering men, as is the case in many countries, divorced and single women are in great numbers.

2) Usually as a result of war or disaster, widows become abundant in society.

3) Where great numbers of women are not able to find husbands and where having multiple wives is forbidden, prostitution, fornication, and betrayal in marriage become widespread.

Benefits To The Individual

1) When a woman is not able to give birth – due to age or other cause – a man naturally desires to have offspring, and so having another wife is more honorable for the woman than to be divorced by her husband, who will wish to remarry in order to have children.

2) If a woman is afflicted with a chronic sickness or contagious or repelling disease that prevents her from having sexual relations with her husband, then while continuing to keep her under his care, the husband can marry another. And that is not only more honorable for the first wife, but more of a guarantee that they remain happy together.

3) When, because of the nature of his work, a man has to continually travel, sometimes remaining months away from home, he may find it difficult, or perhaps impossible, to take his wife and children with him. No doubt, in such a situation, a second marriage has benefits that are religious and social; but

moreover, benefits that prevent him from falling into dissolution and disgrace, which on a greater scale, can only have ill-effects on society.

4) With some men their sexual drive is so strong that one wife is not enough to satisfy their wants; therefore Islam legislated for such a man to marry another wife, so that he doesn't have to fulfill his lusts in forbidden liaisons.

5) Some men have a strong and resolute desire to have many children, which helps realize the honor of the Prophet ﷺ – when his, the largest of nations, will be displayed before the nations on the Day of Judgement.

6) A woman naturally experiences menstruation and post-natal bleeding; some women are physically weak or are cold, not desiring sexual relations, so that days may pass without her husband being able to approach her. By having another wife, a man protects himself from sexual deviation, for that kind of deviation is a great trial and tribulation.

7) There may be other factors – such as a woman being aged, unsightly, or afflicted with a physical defect – factors that make her undesirable as a wife to her husband, unless he has another wife.

The Natural Wisdom Behind The Legislation Of Multiple Wives

In order to preserve its morals, a nation made up of a greater number of women than men must allow men to have multiple wives. This will prevent single women who are not able to find a husband from wandering in this world without a family, and sometimes from wandering into degeneracy. To benefit society, to protect the honor of women, to protect society from prostitution and moral degeneracy – for these benefits, and more, polygamy and the spreading of Islamic relationships are needed.

The Dangers Of Turning Away From Marriage: On The Individual And On Society

When young men and women turn away from marriage, which Allâh legislated, and when their guardian or society places obstacles in the way to prevent them from getting married, dangerous sicknesses will prevail, shaking the individual as well as the structure of society.

The Most Dangerous Of Those Sicknesses

1) **The religious danger and the danger having to do with the Hereafter:** The one who is submerged in fulfilling his lust and desires in a non-lawful manner becomes afflicted with total aversion to the religion; thus he becomes miserable both in this life and the next.

2) **The health danger:** When members of a society turn away from marriage, venereal diseases become rampant.

3) **The psychological and mental danger:** Sexual deviation that results from not marrying leads to many kinds of mental disorders.

4) **The social danger:** Many dangers associated with dissolution and moral degeneracy become realities; moreover, families become destroyed, children are born to single mothers, misery becomes widespread, and family becomes no more.

5) **The economic danger:** One who feels no responsibility to his wife and children squanders his wealth and is unproductive in his work.

Why Young Men And Women
Turn Away From Marriage

There are economic as well as social factors, which by themselves or combined together, prevent the spread of marriage in society, marriage being the ship of virtue, purity, psychological, as well as physical well-being. We must all strive to remove any factor that stands in the way of marriage – in the way of a healthy society comprised of healthy individuals.

The Most Important Of Those Factors

1) Steep dowries (*Mahr*) and competing in who can pay the highest dowry and in who receives the highest dowry. Many people, shifting their gazes on this financial aspect, neglect other more important things to look for in a husband or wife - such as piety and manners. The guardians of young girls end up asking not about a man's piety, but about his wealth and properties, a morbid situation that the Prophet ﷺ warned us about when he ﷺ said:

«إِذَا أَتَاكُمْ مَنْ تَرْضَوْنَ دِينَهُ وَخُلُقَهُ فَزَوِّجُوهُ إِلَّا تَفْعَلُوا تَكُنْ فِتْنَةٌ فِي الْأَرْضِ وَفَسَادٌ عَرِيضٌ»

If you are pleased with the religion and character of one who comes to you (seeking marriage), then marry him (to the female of whom you are guardian), for if you do not do so, then there will be trials and vast corruption in the land.[1]

2) The great costs associated with the marriage ceremony and banquet is in reality a second dowry that is given to the wife. Extravagant marriages, though spurned on by customs and traditions, have no basis in Islam. How much wealth is spent on the banquet hall? On extravagant gifts, which are now given from the day the marriage is agreed upon (engagement) to the day of the actual marriage? On the many parties? On food and gifts for relatives? Before even considering such expenditures, a groom must have many misgivings as he is making all of the calculations.

---

[1] Recorded by At-Tirmithi and Ibn Majah

3) Studying barrier – an excuse for not getting married by members of both sexes, when in reality, marriage helps one in his studies.

4) Many are too shy to breach the topic of marriage to one's parents or guardians.

5) Profanity and lewdness are so rampant in certain societies, that the young man or woman satisfies his or her lusts and desires outside of lawful marriage.

6) Widespread unemployment, low wages, high costs of living, and the claim that one is saving to guarantee a decent standard of living – these are some factors that prevent one from marrying.

7) Sometimes it is not wise to allow women to interfere, for it is often the case that a mother prevents her son or daughter from marrying, either because of her foolish demands or because of her prying into affairs that are outside of the realm of her business. Such actions on her part may make getting married become a difficult affair indeed for her son (or daughter).

8) Some people are so weak in their religious beliefs that marriage doesn't even cross their mind; rather, they are satisfied with the life of sin and lust that they lead, which is especially the case in these times of ours, when the doors of evil are left wide open. Young men travel specifically to those countries that are known for lewdness so that they can fulfill their wicked desires – and we ask Allâh for safety and well-being.

9) Poverty – Allâh Almighty says:

﴿ وَأَنكِحُوا۟ ٱلۡأَيَـٰمَىٰ مِنكُمۡ وَٱلصَّـٰلِحِينَ مِنۡ عِبَادِكُمۡ وَإِمَآئِكُمۡ إِن يَكُونُوا۟ فُقَرَآءَ يُغۡنِهِمُ ٱللَّهُ مِن فَضۡلِهِۦ وَٱللَّهُ وَٰسِعٌ عَلِيمٌ ﴾

And marry those among you who are single and (also marry) the righteous of your (male) slaves and female slaves. If they be poor, Allâh will enrich them out of His bounty. And Allâh is All-Sufficient for His creatures needs, All-Knowing (about the state of the people).[1]

In this verse, Allâh orders guardians to marry off those under their care – men who have no wives and women who have no husbands,

---

[1] (*An-Nur* 24:32).

for sustenance and provision are in Allâh's Hand, and He has guaranteed to enrich them if they choose the path to virtue, purity, and modesty. Furthermore, this verse refutes those guardians who don't marry off their sons, making the excuse that their sons are poor and marriage will only serve to increase them in poverty.

The purely materialistic point of view, which results from weak reliance upon Allâh, is further refuted by reality, for how many poor men have achieved blessings and peace after marriage. The Prophet ﷺ said:

«ثَلَاثَةٌ حَقٌّ عَلَى اللهِ عَوْنُهُمْ»

It is a right upon Allâh to help three...

among them he ﷺ mentioned:

«النَّاكِحُ يُرِيدُ الْعَفَافَ»

The one who is getting married, seeking virtue thereby.[1]

Abu Bakr, may Allâh be pleased with him, said, "Obey what Allâh commanded you regarding marriage, and He will execute what he promised you in terms of richness."

Ibn 'Abbas, may Allâh be pleased them, said, "Allâh encouraged you to get married and promised you richness for it, for He said:

﴿إِن يَكُونُوا فُقَرَاءَ يُغْنِهِمُ ٱللَّهُ مِن فَضْلِهِۦ﴾

If they be poor, Allâh will enrich them out of His bounty."[2]

---

[1] At-Tirmithi, An-Nasa'i, Ibn Majah, and Ahmad
[2] (*An-Nur* 24:32)

Guidance And Advice

To My Brother Guardian And My Muslim Sister

It is obligatory upon you both to choose a righteous husband, one who has religion and good manners, and you must not take into consideration wealth and status, for indeed the Messenger of Allâh ﷺ said:

«إِذَا أَتَاكُمْ مَنْ تَرْضَوْنَ دِينَهُ وَخُلُقَهُ فَزَوِّجُوهُ إِنْ لَمْ تَفْعَلُوا تَكُنْ فِتْنَةٌ فِي الْأَرْضِ وَفَسَادٌ عَرِيضٌ»

If one comes to you and you are pleased with his religion and character, then marry him (to the one under your care), for if you do not do so, there will be trial and vast corruption in the land.[1]

To My Brother Guardian, Here Are Two Important Matters

1) You must not coerce an adult female to marry someone she is not pleased with, for Islam forbade you from doing so.

2) If a truthful and sincere man comes to you seeking marriage, and if you are pleased with his religion, then you must not prevent him from seeing the girl he wishes to marry; however, do not allow them to be alone. It is Sunnah in Islam for one to look at the person one wishes to marry. Al-Mughirah bin Shu'bah, may Allâh be pleased with him, asked to marry a woman and the Messenger of Allâh ﷺ said:

«انْظُرْ إِلَيْهَا فَإِنَّهُ أَحْرَى أَنْ يُؤْدَمَ بَيْنَكُمَا»

Look at her, for that is more likely to keep you remaining with one another.[2]

Meaning, it will cause agreement between you.

My Brother Guardian

Beware of asking for a high dowry, for that is a reprehensible act of greed; if it is known how much you ask for (even though the dowry is not for you, and is for the female under your care), then many

---

[1] At-Tirmithi and Ibn Majah
[2] Recorded by At-Tirmithi, An-Nasa'i, and others

eligible men may be prevented from asking to be married to your daughter or your sister...and because of that, you will have greatly wronged her by having prevented her from marriage, which is the right and hope of every young woman.

Every marriage that takes place based on a small dowry and small expenditure is blessed, for Allâh blesses the marriage and causes harmony between the husband and wife. Allâh does not bless the marriage that is extravagant – extravagant in the dowry or in the expenditures related to the marriage – nor the marriage that begins with music or other forbidden amusements (during the marriage parties and banquets); in fact, as happens so frequently, such a marriage leads to failure. May Allâh Almighty protect us all from the slippery paths of wrongdoing.

Advice That Should Be Read

From The Manners Of The First Night

The husband should try to make the wife feel as comfortable as possible, for instance, by talking to her nicely and proffering her a glass of juice or water.

Then he should hold her forelocks and say:

«اللَّهُمَّ إِنِّي أَسْأَلُكَ مِنْ خَيْرِهَا وَخَيْرِ مَا جُبِلَتْ عَلَيْهِ وَأَعُوذُ بِكَ مِنْ شَرِّهَا وَشَرِّ مَا جُبِلَتْ عَلَيْهِ»

Allâhumma Innee As'aluka min Khairiha wa Khairi Ma Jubilat 'Alaihi wa A'oothu Bika Min Sharriha wa Sharri Ma Jubilat 'Alaihi.

O Allâh, I ask You for the goodness within her and the goodness that you have made her inclined towards, and I take refuge with You from the evil within her and the evil that you have made her inclined towards.[1]

It is then recommended for them to pray two units of prayer together.

He should also say the following when he approaches her:

«اللَّهُمَّ جَنِّبْنَا الشَّيْطَانَ وَجَنِّبِ الشَّيْطَانَ مَا رَزَقْتَنَا»

Allâhumma Jannibnash-Shaitaana, wa Jannibish-Shaitana Ma Razaqtana.

In the Name of Allâh. O Allâh, keep the devil away from us and keep the devil away from what you have blessed us with.[2]

Also, it is not permissible for a man to miss prayer in the *Masjid* on the first day or on the first few days of marriage; rather, he is no exception and must therefore perform all of his prayers in the *Masjid*.

---

[1] Recorded by Abu Dawud and Ibn Majah
[2] Agreed upon

Certain Marital Rights

In the realm of human cooperation, Islam has legislated many partnerships, through which efforts and wealth are gathered and the welfare of all is sought. Islam has legislated the partnership of marriage to build the beginnings of society – the family – and to help achieve success and happiness for children. Allâh Almighty says:

﴿وَٱللَّهُ جَعَلَ لَكُم مِّنْ أَنفُسِكُمْ أَزْوَٰجًا وَجَعَلَ لَكُم مِّنْ أَزْوَٰجِكُم بَنِينَ وَحَفَدَةً﴾

And Allâh has made for you wives of your own kind, and has made for you, from your wives, sons and grandsons.[1]

In regards to this blessed partnership that Allâh has legislated, it is the responsibility of both partners to fulfill the rights of the other; each should work sincerely and honestly towards that end, without neglecting one's share of duties and responsibilities.

Some Of The Rights A Husband Has Over His Wife

1) She must obey him in all that is good and lawful, for the Messenger of Allâh ﷺ said:

«إِذَا صَلَّتِ الْمَرْأَةُ خَمْسَهَا وَصَامَتْ شَهْرَهَا وَحَفِظَتْ فَرْجَهَا وَأَطَاعَتْ زَوْجَهَا قِيلَ لَهَا ادْخُلِي الْجَنَّةَ مِنْ أَيِّ أَبْوَابِ الْجَنَّةِ شِئْتِ»

If a woman prays her five (prayers), fasts her month (i.e., Ramadhan), safeguards her private parts (from wrongdoing), and obeys her husband, it will be said to her: "Enter Paradise from any door of Paradise that you wish."[2]

A woman's obedience to her husband reaps benefits for both her own self and for her husband; however, she must not obey him if he orders her to sin, because there is no obedience to the creation in something that involves disobedience to Allâh.

2) The wife must take care of her home, protect her husband's wealth, and provide him with comfort and peace.

---

[1] (*An-Nahl* 16:72)
[2] Recorded by Ahmad

3) She must take his feelings into consideration, not hurting him with her tongue, deeds, or manners.

4) She is forbidden from leaving the house without his permission, and she has no right to bring anyone into the home without her husband's permission and satisfaction.

Some Of The Rights A Woman Has Over Her Husband

1) He must spend on her in a fair and good way according to the norms of society; he should not then be neglectful in providing her food, drink, and clothing. Furthermore, he must guide her in learning what she needs to know from Islam and from worldly matters.

2) He must be vigilant in protecting her from doubtful matters; hence he doesn't allow her to beautify herself for others, nor does he allow her to mix with strange men.

3) He must have good manners with her, speaking to her gently and looking past trifling matters. He should advice her in a gentle way, showing compassion and mercy.

4) He should be patient when she displeases him or when she shows bad manners, and he should try his best to rectify her, not resorting to divorce except as an extreme necessity. The Prophet ﷺ said:

«لَا يَفْرُكْ مُؤْمِنٌ مُؤْمِنَةً إِنْ كَرِهَ مِنْهَا خُلُقاً رَضِيَ مِنْهَا آخَرَ»

Let not a believing man despise a believing woman, if he dislikes a trait in her, he will be pleased with another.[1]

5) To my sensible sister in Islam: Know – and may Allâh guide us both to that which is good – that stubbornness and persistence in opposing the husband is from the greatest causes of a miserable life and of separation. You must obey him in that which is good and lawful. And remember: obedience to him, abstaining from disagreement with him, gentleness in your dealings with him – these are from the greatest causes of harmony and happiness.

Important Note

To my prudent and sensible brother: Divorce has many detrimental

---

[1] Muslim and Ahmad

effects, so trifling matters or matters that can be rectified or cured – such as a temporary discontentment with your spouse, lust for someone else, greed for money or status – should not be the cause of divorce. And each person will suffer the consequences of his own deeds.

When Islam placed divorce in the hands of the man, it did allow him to wield that prerogative in an evil way; there are boundaries: if one observes them, the divorce is permissible; if not, then one is sinning.

Here Are Those Limits And Boundaries

1) There is a reason that calls for the divorce, such as the wife having a bad character. If the man initiates the divorce without cause, he is sinning, yet the divorce he effectuated is valid and binding in the *Shari'ah*.

2) The husband must initiate the divorce after a menstrual period and before he engages in sexual intercourse with her (during that period of purity). If he divorces her while she is menstruating, then he is sinning and his divorce is contrary to what is legislated; similar is the case when he divorces her after she is purified from the menstruation and after he has engaged in sexual intercourse with her, because he does not know if she is pregnant or not.

3) When divorcing her, he must not do so more than once; if he divorces her after she is purified from her menstrual period and without having intercourse with her during that period of purity, then the divorce is valid, and there is no sin upon him because his action is in accordance with the *Shari'ah*. But if he divorces her three times in one phrase or in many different phrases, then his divorce is contrary to what is legislated, and he must seek a legal ruling from a *Fatwa* council if he wishes to take back the wife he divorced.

Finally, A Call To Early Marriage

The importance of marriage and its effects on protecting young men and woman from fornication and sexual deviation is a matter that is well known to people of knowledge, wisdom, and foresight. The Prophet ﷺ said:

«يَا مَعْشَرَ الشَّبَابِ مَنِ اسْتَطَاعَ مِنْكُمُ الْبَاءَةَ فَلْيَتَزَوَّجْ فَإِنَّهُ أَحْصَنُ لِلْفَرْجِ وَأَغَضُّ لِلْبَصَرِ، وَمَنْ لَمْ يَسْتَطِعْ فَعَلَيْهِ بِالصَّوْمِ فَإِنَّهُ لَهُ وِجَاءٌ»

O group of youth: Whoever from you is able to pay the dowry, then let him marry, for that will better help you protect your private parts (from evil) and will better help you lower your gazes. And whoever is not able (to pay the dowry), then upon him is fasting, for it decreases his sexual drive.[1]

Indeed a noble cause it is for scholars, parents, writers, and those who are respected in society to work together, finding practical ways to help realize early marriage for individuals in our Muslim societies, a cause that can be furthered by mutual counsel, cooperation, and theoretical as well as practical studies. Such efforts will – if Allâh wills – benefit society and protect it from the evil effects of late marriage.

---

[1] Agreed upon

Certain Rulings Related To Menstruation And Postnatal Bleeding

Menstruation

In accordance with woman's nature and without any other cause, menstruation is the blood that discharges from women at known intervals or times.

The Age Of Menstruation

There is no set age for when menstruation begins. Whenever an amount of blood discharges at any time, one must refer to that occurrence as menstruation. Therefore whenever a woman sees the blood of menstruation, she is menstruating, regardless of whether she is older or younger than nine years, and regardless of whether she is older than fifty years, because the *Shari'ah* established the rulings of menstruation based upon the presence of that blood.

The Period Of Menstruation

As it is natural blood, it differs according to the situation of the female, her environment, and the climate she lives in. Because of the clear difference between women, there is no lower or upper limit as to the number of days for menstruation. What is important is whether there is blood or not, because based on whether there is blood or not the *Shari'ah* established rulings. Nonetheless, six or seven days are most prevalent among women, though this number may increase or decrease, as we have already stated. Regarding the period of purity that separates between two menstrual periods, again, there is no limit in terms of number of days.

The Normal Period

When a woman experiences her first menstruation, she waits until she is purified, and the number of days that she was in her period becomes what is known as her "normal period." There is no harm, however, for the woman who is just beginning to menstruate to test for three months in a row to establish how many days her normal period are. If the number is stable, then that is her normal period. But if, in one of the later tests, her menstruation is cut short of the normal period or prolongs longer than the normal period, she is still considered to be menstruating, and she takes no heed of her previous normal period; rather, she has a new normal period. What is important is that the rulings of menstruation are related to the presence of menstrual blood.

Al-Istihadhah

The flow of blood outside of the regular time period, blood that is caused by sickness or blood that is rotten and is coming out of a vein. The *Mustahadhah* woman is one who sees blood that is neither menstrual blood nor the blood that comes out after giving birth. There are three situations for the *Mustahadhah*:

1) She knows her normal period before the sickness of *Istihadhah*. Because she knows the time-span and days of her period from every month, she depends on her normal period to know how many days she was menstruating. After that, she is considered to be *Mustahadhah* for all additional days.

2) She is a beginner, meaning that she has no normal period or she has forgotten the number of days for her normal period, yet she is able to distinguish between menstrual blood and *Istihadhah* blood – because of thickness and thinness of blood, color, or smell. Thick, dark, and a bad odor – these all take the ruling of menstruation; otherwise the blood is that of *Istihadhah*.

3) She has a normal period but is not able to distinguish between the two kinds of blood. She calculates that, for instance, her period is normally six or seven day, and so those days take the ruling of menstruation, while the rest of the days are that of *Istihadhah*.

An-Nifas (Postnatal Bleeding)

Blood that comes out of the womb while giving birth or during its early stages, blood that comes with pain and for the most part, continues to flow for forty days. The days before the delivery or the days in which signs of delivery were noticed are not considered.

The Period For *Nifas*: For the most part, forty days, yet there is no lower limit.

The Purity Of The Menstruation Woman And The Woman Experiencing Postnatal Bleeding

When a menstruating woman sees that she is purified and when the woman experiencing postnatal bleeding sees that the flow of blood has ceased, she must perform *Ghusl* to purify her body. The minimum requirement for this *Ghusl* is for water to reach every area of the body, including what is below the hair. But it is best and more complete to perform this *Ghusl* in the manner that is described in a *Hadith* related by Muslim.[1] When performing this *Ghusl*, a woman does not have to undo her braids unless they are tightly and very compactly tied and it is feared that water will not reach the roots.

The Purity Of The *Mustahadhah*

The *Mustahadhah* need not perform *Ghusl* but she must perform ablution (*Wudhu'*) for every prayer. When she performs ablution, she must first wash the bloodstains and tie something around the area from which the blood is flowing, so as to prevent the blood from spilling.

---

[1] *Sahih Muslim* (1:179)

Important Points

Five Obligatory Things Related to Menstruation

1) *Ghusl* or *Tayammum* if one is unable to use water or find it.

2) The woman who menstruates and has just been divorced must wait for three menstrual cycles to pass for marriage.

3) Islamically, when a woman first menstruates, she becomes an adult.

4) When one has had sex with his wife while she was menstruating, his atonement is to give a Dinar or half a Dinar in charity.

5) When a woman has waited for three menstrual cycles, it becomes established that the man who divorced her is not the father for any future pregnancy.

During A Menstrual Cycle, Ten Things Are Forbidden

1) Sexual intercourse.

2) Prayer.

3) Divorce.

4) Reciting the Qur'ân,[1] unless the menstruating woman fears that she will forget or unless she is forced to recite, for instance because she is a teacher or student during periods of examination.

5) Touching the Qur'ân – based on what has preceded.

6) Making *Tawaf* around the Ka'bah.

7) Staying in the *Masjid*.

8) Passing through the *Masjid* if she fears that some blood may spoil it.

9) Fasting.

---

[1] The second opinion in this issue is that a menstruating woman may recite, but not touch the Qur'ân – although she can hold it from behind a barrier. The sexually impure is categorically forbidden from reciting the Qur'ân until he is purified from the greater state of purity, and that is because the period of his impurity is short, as opposed to the menstruating woman. This opinion is held by the noble and eminent Shaikh 'Abdul-'Aziz bin Baz, may Allâh have mercy on him.

10) Counting (for the divorced woman) by the months because a woman counts by her menstrual cycle only.

If the menstruating woman or the one experiencing postnatal bleeding becomes purified during the time of a prayer, she must hurry to perform *Ghusl*, so that she can perform that prayer on time. If she cannot perform *Ghusl* because of travelling or because she couldn't find water, she may perform *Tayammum*, and then, when she is able, she can perform *Ghusl*. Some women fall into great error when they delay performing *Ghusl*, making the excuse of not being able to take the complete *Ghusl*. Rather, she must perform *Ghusl*, even if she performs only the obligatory elements of the *Ghusl*, so that she can pray on time. Then if there is more time later, she can perform the complete *Ghusl*.

If there is yellowness or cloudiness in the blood during the normal period time, then it is menstruation.

If menstruating blood stops but then starts again during her normal period days, then it is menstruation for sure.

Conclusion: A Call To Guiding People To The Truth

Every Muslim bears the responsibility of conveying the message of Islam to the people and every Muslim must be sincerely desirous of doing so. The Muslim should not distinguish between people, wishing to call to Islam only a certain race or only people of a certain color, or only people from a certain region. Allâh says:

$$﴿ٱدۡعُ إِلَىٰ سَبِيلِ رَبِّكَ بِٱلۡحِكۡمَةِ وَٱلۡمَوۡعِظَةِ ٱلۡحَسَنَةِ وَجَٰدِلۡهُم بِٱلَّتِي هِيَ أَحۡسَنُ﴾$$

Invite to the way of your Lord with wisdom and fair preaching, and argue with them in a way that is better[1]

"Wisdom" is the clear proof to the truth that wipes out all doubt. "Fair preaching" refers to beneficial admonition and convincing speech. The former (wisdom) is for the elite of the people and the latter (fair preaching) is for the general population. If there is a need to argue with others, the caller to truth does so with gentleness and compassion in order to calm their disquiet. When Allâh Almighty sent Musa and Harun, peace be upon them, to Fir'awn, He said:

$$﴿فَقُولَا لَهُۥ قَوۡلٗا لَّيِّنٗا لَّعَلَّهُۥ يَتَذَكَّرُ أَوۡ يَخۡشَىٰ﴾$$

"And speak to him mildly, perhaps he may accept admonition or fear Allâh."[2]

Allâh Almighty says:

$$﴿قُلۡ هَٰذِهِۦ سَبِيلِيٓ أَدۡعُوٓاْ إِلَى ٱللَّهِ عَلَىٰ بَصِيرَةٍ أَنَا۠ وَمَنِ ٱتَّبَعَنِي﴾$$

Say: "This is my way; I invite unto Allâh with sure knowledge, I and whosoever follows me (also must invite others to Allâh) with sure knowledge.[3]

Allâh ordered the Prophet ﷺ to inform people that calling to Allâh is based on knowledge and surety and proof – that is the Prophet's way

---

[1] (An-Nahl 16:125)

[2] (Ta Ha 20:44)

[3] (Yusuf 12:108)

and the way of those who follow him.

The Prophet ﷺ indeed expended all of his energies in guiding the people, and he was very sad when they turned away from the truth that he ﷺ came with – Allâh says:

﴿فَلَعَلَّكَ بَاخِعٌ نَفْسَكَ عَلَىٰ ءَاثَارِهِمْ إِن لَّمْ يُؤْمِنُوا بِهَٰذَا ٱلْحَدِيثِ أَسَفًا﴾

Perhaps, you, would kill yourself in grief, over their footsteps (for their turning away from you), because they believe not in their narration (the Qur'ân).[1]

And Allâh Almighty says:

﴿لَعَلَّكَ بَاخِعٌ نَفْسَكَ أَلَّا يَكُونُوا مُؤْمِنِينَ﴾

It may be that you are going to kill yourself with grief, that they do not become believers.[2]

Here Allâh consoles him and orders him not to allow for himself to perish because of his grief over them.

The Prophet ﷺ said to 'Ali bin Abi Talib, may Allâh be pleased with him:

«فَلَأَنْ يَهْدِيَ اللهُ بِكَ رَجُلًا وَاحِدًا خَيْرٌ لَكَ مِنْ حُمْرِ النَّعَمِ»

For Allâh to guide one man through you is better for you than red camels.[3]

Abu Hurairah, may Allâh be pleased with him, related that the Messenger of Allâh ﷺ said:

«مَنْ دَعَا إِلَى هُدًى كَانَ لَهُ مِنَ الْأَجْرِ مِثْلُ أُجُورِ مَنْ تَبِعَهُ لَا يَنْقُصُ ذَلِكَ مِنْ أُجُورِهِمْ شَيْئًا، وَمَنْ دَعَا إِلَى ضَلَالَةٍ كَانَ عَلَيْهِ مِنَ الْإِثْمِ مِثْلُ آثَامِ مَنْ تَبِعَهُ لَا يَنْقُصُ ذَلِكَ مِنْ آثَامِهِمْ شَيْئًا».

Whoever calls to guidance, he will have rewards similar to the rewards of those who follow him, without them being decreased in their rewards in the very least. And whoever

---

[1] (*Kahf* 18:6)
[2] (*Ash-Shu'ara'* 26:3)
[3] Al-Bukhari

calls to misguidance, then upon him is the sin similar to the sins of those who follow him, without their sins being decreased in the very least.[1]

*****

---

[1] Muslim